# Beyond Belief

*Colm O'Gorman*

HODDER

First published in Great Britain in 2009 by Hodder & Stoughton
An Hachette UK company

First published in paperback in 2010

2

Copyright © Colm O'Gorman 2009

The right of Colm O'Gorman to be identified as the Author of the Work has been
asserted by him in accordance with the Copyright, Designs and Patents Act 1988.

A CIP catalogue record for this title is available from the British Library

ISBN 978 0 340 92528 7

Typeset in Sabon by Hewer Text UK Ltd, Edinburgh
Printed and bound in the UK by CPI Mackays, Chatham ME5 8TD

Hodder & Stoughton policy is to use papers that are natural, renewable
and recyclable products and made from wood grown in sustainable
forests. The logging and manufacturing processes are expected to
conform to the environmental regulations of the country of origin.

Hodder & Stoughton Ltd
338 Euston Road
London NW1 3BH

www.hodder.co.uk

For my father Sean,
with love

# Acknowledgements

There are a few people I must thank for their support and guidance throughout the writing of this book; my agent Caroline Wood who convinced me to write it, Rowena Webb and Helen Coyle at Hodder and my editor David Moloney. Also Martina Deasy and Bernadette Morris who read draft after draft and gave invaluable feedback, my partner Paul for putting up with me as I wrote and the rest of my family, then and now, for their love and support.

In my work I have been privileged to meet many women and men over these past years who have travelled a journey similar to my own. Those people who came before me made it possible for me to speak out so publicly. The courage and resilience of all those I have met sustained my conviction that I could not be silent in the presence of such great injustice.

But telling the story of one's own life is a daunting thing to attempt. Not least because in telling one's own life story, one must also tell the stories of others.

I hope that the telling, and indeed the retelling, of this story does not cause distress to any of the people involved. I hope and pray that they will see the value of it. There are many victims of the events described in the pages that follow; and not all of them are obvious ones. There are families that have been scarred in a great many ways by what happened many years ago and for whom those scars remain raw. It is not my intention to cause them any further pain; I hope that I will not.

I spent years working to reclaim my lost life, to reclaim the history I had banished in order to survive. I used to feel like my life was a series of books that I'd once read. My connection to the truth of my life was so tenuous, so detached, that I didn't relate to it in any felt way, or even in an intellectual way. I knew for instance that I had lived on a farm until I was eleven years old. I knew where and when, I knew who with and some of the things that would have been part of the day-to-day of that life, but I didn't relate it to myself in any real way. I knew it to be true, to be fact, but had no real connection to it. And so it was across most of the first thirty years of my life. It broke down into a series of chunks of time, of living, that were each like books I had read. From the farm to rural small town life, to runaway and life on the streets to a final halting engagement with adulthood ... each a separate volume and not interconnected.

Over this past decade I have worked to reclaim my ownership of that history, so that now finally, my life is known to me and fits together. Ironic then that it has now become a series of chapters, but it is at last one volume, one connected, reclaimed life. And it is my own.

# Contents

# I

# Wexford, October 2001

'I really don't want to be here,' I said to Sarah as we stood on the main street of my hometown on a cold and grey afternoon.

'I just want to get out of here and never come back.'

Sarah put her arm across my shoulder and gave me a gentle hug. She was from New Zealand, and not Catholic. Over the past few days her outraged reaction to what she was filming offered me a more objective and reasoned insight into the story we were trying to tell. My story.

I felt pathetic standing there. I was so hurt. And I hated that. I felt like I might cry, and stuck my hands down into the bottom of my coat pockets, pulling my neck down inside my collar. It was cold, I stamped my feet, not so much to warm up but because it let out the frustration I felt. I needed not to feel like this.

Sarah looked at me; she'd become a good friend. I trusted her. That helped.

'Come on, time for a coffee,' she said.

We'd come back to Wexford only four days earlier. Sarah, myself and a cameraman, to make a film for the BBC about my battle to hold the Roman Catholic Church to account for the rape and abuse I experienced at the hands of a priest when I was a teenager. It had been a really difficult few days, confronting and documenting a past that still haunted me, and a battle that dominated much of my life.

We spoke to other men who had been abused by the same priest, also in the 1980s. I took Sarah and the camera back to the place where the abuse happened, the cold and stark house next to the church where the priest had served in a place called Poulfur, a tiny 'half-parish' in rural South-East Ireland.

One of the most difficult interviews was with a mother, Monica Fitzpatrick, whose son Peter had shot himself to death at the age of twenty-three. We discovered that it was likely he'd also been abused by the priest when he was a teenager. Monica broke my heart. I'd called her to ask if she would speak to us, I was horrified by the thought that I could be forcing open a trauma she might not even be aware of. But Monica and her husband John already knew. They had never said the words out loud, but seized on my call as an opportunity to say all the things they'd never allowed themselves to say about their son, his death and the pain that led him to take his own life.

As Sarah ended her interview with Monica we all wept. Peter's death and his parents' grief seemed so horrific, and the events that caused it all, obscene.

The next day we were back in Poulfur. We needed more background information and found ourselves at the home of a local businessman and his wife. They talked freely about the priest, how divisive he'd been and the trouble he caused. Before long we got on to discuss how he had sexually abused boys.

'He was always odd. He fought with anyone who defied him,' said the woman of the house.

'Did people have any idea what was happening, what he might be doing to the boys he had to stay?' I asked.

'Oh God, yeah,' came the reply. 'Everyone knew what he was like. They used to joke about it. They'd say, don't bend down in front of that fella in the churchyard.'

When she said it I felt like I'd been punched in the stomach. She knew why I was in her house; surely she knew that the priest had abused me? How could she joke about it? And how could people have joked about it back then?

Over the days that followed others confirmed that there was widespread suspicion that Sean Fortune had been abusing young boys.

I wanted to know just how explicitly people might have discussed it.

'Well, people would tell you without really telling you, if you know what I mean', said one man, 'but we kept our fellas away from him. We didn't want to risk it'.

What he meant was that people talked in whispers, taking care never to fully name what they knew, reducing their well-informed suspicions to gossip and innuendo. They shared enough for the thrill of the gossip and to warn their own of the danger, but never so explicitly that they would have to take responsibility for what they knew and be forced to act.

Years earlier I sat in the front pew of the church. I watched Fortune hold aloft the host at communion time, pronouncing it the body of Christ, and I wondered how his parishioners, those men and women all about me with their heads bowed, might react if they knew what he'd done to me less than an hour earlier.

And now it appeared that some of them had known all along. They had joked about it, dismissed it, protected their own and left me to it.

# 2

# *Adamstown, 1972*

It was a scorching hot summer's day. Back then summers seemed to last forever, each one felt like a lifetime all its own, days felt like weeks and weeks like years. School and the short cold days of winter seemed a world away. I was out in the fields, running around playing at working and watching the men bring in the harvest. I was only six; there wasn't much I could do, though I really wanted to help, to be one of the men.

Harvest was one of the few times when I got to spend time in the fields with my Dad and the workmen. I loved being with those men, good men who were focused on their work, men with purpose. The very picture of the man I wanted to become.

The huge green and yellow combine harvester snarled its way up and down the field. Its blades turning the waving sea of wheat into fresh shaved earth, the stubble of the straw sharp and rough under my feet. As the harvester swept along it left behind lines of fresh straw, which dried in the sun before being baled to use as bedding for cattle in the winter to come.

I stood next to a big round container made of sackcloth and chicken wire and watched as the combine harvester poured in a torrent of dusty, fragrant seed. The container was about four or five feet tall and maybe fifteen feet wide. One of the workmen grabbed me up and threw me laughing into an ocean of seed where I swam around in the warm sun seeking out jewels: iridescent beetles with bodies as black as the night reflecting bright greens and blues, ladybirds that crawled up my finger before they opened their backs, like some kind of machine to unfurl the most unlikely wings I'd ever seen and trundled off across the surface of the freshly shaven fields.

I jumped out when I saw my mother's car coming, her little green Hillman Hunter making its way across the field, bringing lunch to the workmen. As her car approached the combine harvester fell quiet and the work stopped, the men walking over to where she parked next to my Dad's tractor.

I sat down beside my Dad and leaned up against the big tractor wheel next to him as Mam shared out the food.

'Are you hungry?' he asked me with a grin. He knew I was, I was always hungry on a day like that.

'Yeah, of course I am.'

'Is there enough food for everyone? The men have to eat first. Maybe Mam didn't bring enough.'

He was teasing me now, and I knew it. I could see the smile in his eyes.

'Here you go,' he said and handed me a huge doorstep of a sandwich that was nearly as big as my own head.

Next came hot, sweet tea in bottles, golden and milky, and slices of fresh apple tart served off the plates they'd just been baked on. It was great; everything seemed to be great on days like this. Bliss.

Harvest was one of the few times I got to be with my father, or at least to be around him in the day-to-day of life. Working with him ... feeling useful and wanted, connected to him.

Most of the time he was too busy to spend time with me. There always seemed to be something he needed to do that was more important.

I lived on a farm in the village of Adamstown. I was the son of the son of a farmer, the second son and the third born, one of six. The farm and our home was a busy place. As there were six of us, my three sisters, my two brothers and me, there was always something happening, someone doing something, someone making noise and someone needing quiet. But it's not through the shared moments that I can look back and get a sense of myself then but rather through the memory of being out on the land, or playing with animals, or heading off alone to Mass, all moments of solitude. I think these were the moments when I felt most able to be myself, just free to be me.

The farmyard was older than the house. My grandfather had also farmed this land. Before Dad built our house in the 1960s there was just the barn and farmyard with an old stone house known as 'Kevin's House', a cottage that had been home to farm workers years before. A lane lined with huge beech trees led past the cottage down to the farmyard. Those trees were ancient and their bark was scored with graffiti that was decades old. Love notes and messages from those who had trooped down the lane fifty and sixty years earlier, to dances held in my grandfather's barn. I loved reading those love tokens and messages etched deep into the grey bark of the huge trees. There were even pictures,

like hieroglyphics, carved into them. Mystery everywhere
and my fertile imagination turned it all into fantastic fables
and romantic tales. Fantasy often became my escape when
I needed it, when the idyllic became much darker.

The remnants of a garden remained in the farmyard in
shrubs and plants that had gone wild and survived across
generations. Fuscia with its little scarlet flowers thrived
on the edges of the yard. We used to pluck the flowers in
summer and suck the honey-sweet nectar from the base
of the exotically shaped blossom. There were also elegant
crocosmia with long, vivid green leaves and flowers like
orange plumes of flame. Their bulbs spread and clumped in
groups, flowering in summer like flashes of fire. I love both
plants still. Where I live now they grow wild in hedgerows.
The sight of them on a summer's day can take me back to
the farmyard in an instant.

Beyond the farmyard were open fields and worn paths,
full of so much life; the farm stock of cattle and sheep,
of pigs and at one point, even rabbits. There were other
animals too, the mice and rats in the haggard. At the end
of winter when the hay barn was being cleaned out and
prepared for that year's crop, there they were. Whole
families of baby rats, all pink and blind, curled up cosily
in their nests. But not for long. There was little room for
my brand of sentimentality on a busy working farm; they
were thrown out into the haggard, drowned in puddles,
killed with a shovel or pecked apart by the hens. Their
hapless parents were bludgeoned by shovels or stabbed
with pitchforks.

I had no stomach for this; I was soft, not a man, the
object of mirth to my father and the workers. I decided not

to watch. I couldn't stop what was happening but I didn't have to witness it. I could return when all was quiet and calm.

Feral cats roamed the farm. I'd turn a corner on a path and almost bump into one. We both stood stock still watching the other, the cat waiting for me to make a move so it could run and me barely breathing, wanting to meet. Eyes locked, careful, watching. It might take an hour but eventually that wild and gorgeous creature would be curling its back under my hand. I loved and still love animals. Besides the cats there were hamsters and budgies, tiny bantam hens and even eels captured from the stream at the end of the field in front of the house. I loved them without realising that my love might kill them. No one told me that eels could not live in buckets.

At the back of the farmyard was the barn, constructed from old stone that suggested earlier use, from a house maybe. It had two levels. Upstairs was a loft, used for occasional storage. It had an old threshing machine in one corner. I remember a photograph, black and white, of men using pitchforks to lift freshly cut wheat into the thresher where the wheat would be separated from the stalks; seed and straw divided out. It was redundant now and spent its retirement gathering dust beneath the flight and fluttering of the hundreds of pigeons that had taken ownership of the loft, its greying wooden body gradually becoming covered in feathers and droppings. All of which only served to make it seem more mysterious and magical to my boy's mind. It certainly had a faded glamour and intrigue very different to that of the combine harvester that thundered through the fields of wheat in its place.

Below the loft was the milking parlour with its own machinery ... modern and pristine, made of glass, rubber and steel.

Sex in its simple way was everywhere. The bull who sired the calves, the cows who gave birth and milk, the calves who suckled ... they were just beautiful, all legs and gangly. I remember feeding them and watching them grow, and my father caring for them, his worry if one was sickly and the effort that went into its care. Who said men couldn't nurture? It always seemed to me that farmers do, the good ones, the ones who care about their animals and not solely because they need them to thrive so they can make a profit. There is often much tenderness in the care a farmer gives his animals. It's unsentimental, at least in an obvious way, but it's there.

I, of course, was wholly sentimental. I remember the excitement of waking on a cold, wet spring morning to find a newborn lamb in the warming oven of the Stanley Stove in the kitchen. I would come down and see a tiny head peeping out of the door of the blanket-lined oven. It might be a lamb with splints for legs broken as it was born or perhaps one rejected by a mother too young to know what to do with this creature that had fallen out of her body.

God, it was joyous though, feeding those hungry lambs with warmed bottles. I can remember their height compared to mine. I was young enough to be unbalanced by their greedy, eager suckling. I laughed and giggled as I held onto that glass bottle with its rubber teat while they tugged and tugged; the rhythm of their suckling, that lovely, simple need that had to be satisfied. I laughed with delight as I fell on my bottom when they butted my stomach looking for the rich, warm, silky satisfaction of milk.

What a gift it was to grow up with life fulfilling itself all around you every day; conception, birth and death.

My father built our house. It was a good house, practical and spacious. At its centre was the kitchen with the stove that felt like the heart of the house, heating, cooking and keeping everything moving. The house sat at the top of a hill. The front garden was lined with cherry trees, which for a few short weeks each spring would shower the lawn with a confetti of pink blossom. At the foot of the hill there was a stream, with cold clear water we splashed about in during the summer heat and which in winter often flooded, turning the bottom of the field into a dirty brown lake.

Out the back of the house was a smaller garden with raised beds where I planted cabbages and lettuces. And beyond that garden was the grove.

The grove was like a forest to me. Huge evergreen trees towered to the sky. The ground beneath the trees was golden and musty with their discarded needles, spongy and soft with a layer of fallen spindly leaves that were not at all like leaves. It was a magical place, dark and hidden but full of promise and mystery. We played there, cowboys and Indians ... endless games of fantasy in a place that felt fantastic. We even had a swinging boat. It was made of chipboard, the mould for an arch in a house my father was building. In the grove, hung from sturdy branches, it became a ship, a swinging pirate ship that sailed through the air between the trees as we laughed and sang. The grove was a place of miracles, a children's place. Pine cones as big as a man's fist were hand grenades, or priceless treasure or just what they were, cones that curled open with age to reveal the seeds within.

The land our house was built on and the farm had been in my father's family for generations. My grandfather died when Dad was still a boy, suddenly and cruelly.

Granddad died young, at the age of 54. A heart attack I think. Dad never talked about that loss, but even as a boy, I knew that such silence spoke of a grief never released. We visited the grave on Pattern Sunday each year. The Pattern is an old Irish tradition which pre-dates Christianity. Its origin lies in medieval gatherings or assemblies where tributes and dues were paid to the king and livestock traded. Known as the festival of Samhain, it marked the end of the harvest. In Celtic folklore it was a time when the boundaries between the living and the dead became thinner; a time to remember the dead.

Like many other ancient Celtic festivals, it eventually became part of Catholic tradition too. In parts of the country it remains a day to remember and pray for the dead. A day for Mass in the air among the graves, for fresh flowers and best clothes as the priest said Mass and spoke the prayers for them over a tinny microphone ... and silence as we knelt at the grave of my long-dead grandfather who I'd never known.

A few years ago I saw a photo of my father as a boy. He must have been only six or seven. He had a huge smile on his face as he sat on the lawn in front of his father's house with a bantam hen and chicks clucking about him. I wonder did his father take that picture? When I look at it I see him and I see me; him as the boy smiling up at his father ... and me as the boy smiling up at him. That was a picture that might have been taken had his father not died and left him frozen in so many ways. My father had a heart the size of the world and when his father died some of that world froze over. It was an ice age I could never understand when I was little and hopeful for his love, for his approval. All I knew was the cold, the distance I couldn't understand and couldn't cross.

He didn't seem to understand me at all. I was mad about animals and loved taking care of them. I wanted to be a doctor when I grew up, or do something that was all about helping people. Once, my sisters and I made a play hospital in a room next to the garage. We set up rows of wooden boxes along the wall and put pillowcases on them as sheets. We had dolls in each bed, with heads or legs bandaged and red ink for bloodstains. We had little dolly mixture sweets in jars for pills and an operating theatre off to the side. I was delighted with our efforts and couldn't wait to show Dad.

He wasn't at all impressed.

I asked him to come look when he got home one afternoon as he parked his car outside the garage.

'What's all this about?' he asked me.

'It's our hospital,' I replied. 'Look, over there is the operating theatre and here are all the patients in bed.'

'What are you doing playing with dolls?' he asked me. 'Why aren't you off out with John kicking a ball or something? What's wrong with you?'

I was crushed.

I never felt good enough for him. He didn't have time for me and I didn't make him happy like I thought my older brother could. John had my father's name, and the name of my grandfather, John Joseph, though Dad was known by the Irish version, Sean. It seemed to me that John was the kind of son my father wanted. He could drive the tractor on the farm, play sports and use his hands. Nothing like me ... I could never penetrate the distance between Dad and me, never find the thing we might have in common that would bring us together.

I never felt my hand enveloped in his as we walked the fields together. I never viewed the world from his shoulders as he carried me home. I never heard him sing, or read me a story, or play a game, or tell me of his passions. I never slept on his lap, or against his chest where the deep rhythm of his heart might have lulled me to sleep. All those iconic images of fathers and sons were not real for my Dad and me. I missed that, even then. I know now it wasn't that he didn't want to be there or that he didn't love me enough; it's just that he didn't know how. It's strange to think that you might miss something you've never had, but I did. I needed my Dad, and he wasn't there. Boys need their fathers.

So Dad was absent. His role was limited to disciplinarian. If we made too much noise or misbehaved in any way we knew we would be for it when he got home.

If Mam sent John and me to bed early for some kind of mischief, we knew that the sound of Dad's car and then his footsteps on the stairs would bring not a hug and a hello but a telling off and a smack. There were six of us, so we were a handful; it seemed to me there were a lot of telling offs. I don't remember looking forward to Dad getting home often, and that seems very sad to me now, for both of us.

Mam was always there. My mother is a remarkable woman, still ahead of her time in so many ways. She was born in 1937, the daughter of a printer and a nurse and grew up in Wexford town. She went to the local convent school and then to train as a nurse herself before marrying my father. After that, she left nursing; she had little time for it once they had six children and a business, a farm and my Dad's political work as a councillor.

I know little of her childhood; she never told us stories about growing up in Wexford or about her family. She rarely talked about her past. I remember her father as a small man with a full head of grey hair who was quiet and kind. He died when I was about eight.

The funeral Mass was in Rowe Street Church in Wexford town. We travelled in with Dad, the six of us in his car. Mam wasn't with us. When we arrived at the church we sat near the front, but behind where Mam sat with her sister and brothers. I wanted to get to her; I knew her Dad had died and that she was sad.

At the end of the Mass the priest said prayers as he walked around the coffin shaking a silver pot on chains with smoke coming out if it. It smelled sweet and rich; frankincense, as I now know. Then men in dark suits stepped forward and the coffin was raised onto their shoulders. An altar boy dressed in black and white raised a brass cross high and led off, followed by the priest, then the coffin bearers and Mam and her family. She was dressed in black and looked so sad. We had to wait until it was our turn to step out of the pews and join the procession out of the church.

When we got outside I looked around.

'Where's Mam?' I asked my Dad.

He was herding us all together towards our car. I couldn't see Mam anywhere. Then I spotted her getting into a big black car parked just behind the long car that now held the coffin.

'Where is she going? Can I go too?'

'No. We have to go home.'

I didn't know why I wasn't allowed to go with Mam. It was strange to see her all alone and so sad. It felt wrong for us all to leave and go home as if nothing had happened.

My mother was beautiful and bright, but also warm, soft and fragile. There was a delicacy to her. It's hard to describe without doing her a disservice. She was and is a powerful and wise woman, but she also seemed to me so delicate that I watched to see if she would break. I can't describe it better than that, I knew she was vulnerable and I knew I was afraid of that. I loved her and wanted desperately to protect her from a world that she seemed to fear and distrust in some ways.

Mam was a nurturer. She put a lot of thought and effort into a healthy diet and good clothes. I remember once finding a tinned pie outside the local shop in the village and thinking it was dog food; we never had tinned food like that. Instead Mam would make sure as much of our food as possible was fresh, natural and home-cooked. We never had breakfast cereals either; Mr Kellogg was banned from our table. Mam was dismissive of claims that such cereals were nutritious, saying that there was more nutrition in the box the cereals came in. We were given porridge, fresh orange juice and vitamin supplements of cod liver or garlic oil in golden pearl-like capsules.

She had very strong and quite radical views about the environment and farming. I remember her saying that the farming methods of the time were storing up huge problems for the future. She was concerned about the use of drugs and medicines in the rearing of cattle and sheep and the impact of such drugs on people when the animals were slaughtered and entered the food chain.

I recall her once debating with Dad the kind of feed given to cattle. She'd discovered that cattle feed was being manufactured with protein from animal carcasses.

'It's not right Sean,' she said. 'Cows are vegetarian, they don't eat meat, it's not natural to them. You can't just change that and feed them animal protein, and rubbish at that, the waste, from meat processing. It's madness, we don't understand how it might affect them.'

Dad didn't really reply. Mam and Dad never really argued in front of us. He just listened and nodded. And the cows kept getting the feed.

As the BSE crisis of the 1990s would show, Mam was right.

Life on the farm as I remember it was rich and good. Of course, it's easy to remember the light, the sun and the beauty. Childhood is meant to be idyllic and in so many ways mine was. I was loved, that much I know now.

It's easier to remember the light; it's less frightening, less threatening. No one turns away from the good stuff, everyone smiles at beauty. I learned to deny the reality of anything really, really bad. I learned from all the adults around me that as long as you were good and acted happy and didn't bother anyone, then everything was OK ... even when it really wasn't. And all these years later, after all that's happened, that's still the truth of my childhood.

# 3

# The Sacred and the Shadow

I was an altar boy when I lived on the farm. I loved getting up on bright, freezing cold spring mornings, mounting my bike to ride to the church to serve first Mass and the way my breath froze into fog as I pedalled my way up the road. I loved those mornings, earthly silent, still, fresh and full of the promise of the warmth of the day to come.

Church was everywhere, in every part of my life. In school as I learned my catechism, at home as we knelt as a family to say the rosary and of course at church, whether serving Mass or dressed in my Sunday best. It was like a womb, safe and certain, a universe in which you could live in ignorant bliss, free of difficult choices and questions: just fit in and conform to the demands, and give blind faith and all was fine.

The priest would be waiting for me when I arrived at the church. 'Good morning Father', I would say as I walked in, bowing my head respectfully as I passed him before getting dressed in scarlet and white robes from a huge mahogany wardrobe in the sacristy.

Once dressed I would return to where Father Redmond waited. Then I helped him dress in his elaborate robes.

First was a crisp, white full-length robe placed over the solemn black of his everyday clothes.

With each layer Father Redmond prayed, preparing himself to celebrate the sacrament that was to come. It was a meditation, a silent and solemn ceremony, punctuated only by his prayers, spoken in reverent tones.

Next came a belt that tied tightly around the waist. Father Redmond prayed. 'Gird me, O Lord, with the girdle of purity, and extinguish in me all evil desires, that the virtue of chastity may abide in me.'

Then he kissed a long stole, a strip of purple silk like a scarf worn around his neck and hanging down over his chest. Last of all came a brightly-coloured cape, a chasuble, worn like a poncho over the white robes beneath.

Before Mass began I would place the water and the wine with their small silver tray on the altar which was covered with crisp, immaculate white linen.

Then we went to the altar with our heads bowed as the priest began to say those words that recalled a supper before the sacrifice that saved our souls. When the moment came, I struck the gong and the congregation bowed before the body and blood of Christ.

Adamstown was a small village, no more than a crossroads with a church, school, post office, shop, a parish hall and a pub. You could walk through it in five minutes. We lived at the top of the hill, and further up the road was the village proper. Then it seemed to my short legs that we lived miles away from the school I walked to or the shop my mother would send me to for messages, but really it was only a brief stroll away. Out of the gate to the right and along past the grove to the top of the farmyard lane, that's where the milk churns used to be left for collection before we got our own tank and the creamery started to send big tanker trucks to collect the milk directly from the parlour.

Up a little further, the first house was my infants' class schoolteacher's, and next to that Bradley's shop, run by two sisters who were kind and generous with their smiles. From there the village proper started, a row of a few houses and then the local secondary school.

I could write more about the geography ... about Booth's sweet shop opposite my primary school, where a big black labrador dog called Major lived; he once took a chunk out of my sister Barbara as she ran away from him. I could tell you about St Abban's Hall, which displaced my grandfather's barn as the local dance venue, about the tiny health clinic where I had my vaccinations, or the post office, the church, the pub ... there is a lot I could write about. But it would be a diversion on my part, an attempt to avoid telling about the darkness, or at least what little I can remember or now know of it.

There were two men living in our village who hurt children. They were sick, depraved men in a world where such things were not supposed to exist. We lived in Catholic Ireland. We were a holy, noble people who had fought to free ourselves of the mantle of colonialism. We had a duty to be the utopian nation our leaders told us we must be. The expectation to be perfect was everywhere. It was cultural and absolute; we heard it from the pulpit and from the politician. Having won our independence we were now free to fulfil our destiny, to once again become a land of saints and scholars and hardy, happy farmers who would feed the people and make us self-sufficient. No evil of the kind perpetrated by these two men could exist in such a land. But where its existence is denied, evil will thrive.

So the two men raped and abused. They hurt a great many children, some of whom have not lived to speak of that harm and many others who have somehow moved beyond it and locked it away in the dark recesses of their minds. What they did remains largely unspoken, but I can feel it when I go back to Adamstown. I can feel the deadness of the place like a ghost amid the houses and people. The beauty is still there too, the memories of the good things and the laughter, but on the edges of perception linger the dark spirit of that time and those men.

I was one of the children they hurt.

I have only a sense of it. I remember big hands and a silence broken only by my sobs and a man's rasping breath. I remember shame, his guilt and sickness abandoned unto me. What happened, even to my child's mind, was clearly wrong, unspeakably wrong; all hurt and pain and mess and smells. I remember my pants being removed and a burning in my rear. I remember hands on my head and pushing that made me gag and choke. It was secret and furtive and manipulative. I don't know the cold hard facts of it beyond those memories and feelings. I don't know how many times or how frequently or what was done, not in detail and not in a way that can be told with words that join together to make sense, to tell a story. I was only five or so. It was too much to know and too much to live with.

Years later I got letters from other people, some I'd shared my childhood with, and one broken-hearted mother. They told me how they too had been hurt. In their words I could see me, at five and six and seven, sore and soiled, bruised and broken.

I was back in that village recently, in the local pub having a drink with some friends. A man my father's age was talking to me. Small talk really, about everything and nothing. Then he leaned in and whispered, 'The men who hurt you are all dead now.'

It seems there are no secrets, only words unspoken, truth disowned.

I could never have used words to tell anyone about what was happening to me. Not just because I was afraid to or because in that world such things were not considered possible, but because I did not *have* the words. I simply did not know them. In my family, in my community, we never spoke about our bodies, about intimate things.

But children always do tell, if not with words then with how they are and what they do. Almost thirty years later, my mother told me of a day when she came into our front room to silence me and my noisy siblings as we ran and shouted and laughed. She came in and yelled at us to be quiet. She remembered me shooting up from behind an armchair, sheet-white and silent.

'It must have been when it first happened to you, you were so scared, so pale and shocked,' she said.

It stuck with her for all that time, and yet the reality facing her back then was just like mine: everything must be fine, nothing awful can be allowed to happen. She went back to the business and demands of her day without asking any questions. But the memory stayed with her and finally made sense three decades later.

I wet the bed. A lot. So much that when I was seven or eight I was sent to a children's hospital for four weeks to try and discover why. When I was there I only wet the bed once or twice compared to almost nightly at home. It was a good place in the main. The other children were good company and I learned to play Monopoly, which had just become a craze. I missed my mother and my brothers and sisters. I remember my brother John sending me a toy helicopter that had working rotors and flew in circles suspended on catgut. I loved it, and knew at some level it was a message of brotherly love, which made it all the more special. As one of six children within a family that wasn't especially demonstrative, that act of generosity hit my heart and warmed me as I struggled to get used to this strange new environment.

I slept in a ward with four or five children and the daily routine was necessarily regimented. We ate at the same time and within fifteen minutes after lunch were marched into a room to sit on pots until we went to the toilet. It was all very odd, sitting there in a circle with our trousers around our ankles as the nurses watched and waited until we performed as required.

One boy always strained and strained to try and get it done so he could get out of there. 'Stop that Oliver,' the nurse would snap. 'If you push like that your insides will come out.'

I was horrified by the thought of my insides coming out of my bottom – how would I get them back in again? I wanted to get out of there, but wouldn't be allowed until I'd gone to the toilet, but now I was scared my insides might come out. It all became very fraught.

Once we'd managed to go, the contents of the pot were examined and documented and we were allowed to leave. I felt sorry for the nurses. Imagine having to examine all that poo and write down what it looked like? I hated that routine; it felt so exposing and embarrassing.

Stranger yet was the nightly routine of being woken by a nurse, who would turn me on my side to administer a dose of some drug or other by pushing a suppository up my rear end. As you might imagine, given my experiences of abuse thus far, this was both unsettling and uncomfortable. I have no idea what the drug was aside from being told it was to help me sleep, which made little sense to me at the time considering they had to wake me up to give it to me!

One truly bright part of the whole hospital experience was one of the nurses who worked there. Her name was Mary Walsh, she was young and pretty and full of fun and she treated me like I mattered. We laughed and talked and got along brilliantly. I felt she saw something worthwhile in me. I remember her running into the ward one night when she was meant to be off-duty and giggling as she sat on my bed to say goodnight. She was a joy, and in hindsight I recognise just how important meeting her was to me at that time. She saw me for who I really was and she gave me her time and her affection without asking for or demanding anything in return. When I was with her I felt worth something, worth knowing. She gave me a great gift, which helped me immeasurably, and I've never forgotten her.

In the end I was sent home with a declaration that there was nothing physically wrong with me but that I was an 'anxious child'. No one asked why I was anxious though.

Instead, I went home equipped with an electric alarm to be fitted to my bed, which would wake me if I began to wet the bed, and a prescription for some kind of barbiturate. We used the alarm but, my mother, to her eternal credit, flushed the pills and binned the prescription. And that was that.

It's amazing how resilient children are in so many ways. I went home from hospital and just slotted back into the day-to-day. I went to school, back to life on the farm and with my family.

I found school to be a scary place. I was three years old when I started, younger than anyone else in my class. I thought our teacher was mean and corporal punishment was both extremely prevalent and legal at that time. She would lash the back of my calves with a bamboo cane; it was still a time when boys wore short trousers. I can remember wishing I were big enough to wear long ones.

More than once I wet myself because I couldn't wait and was not allowed to leave the class. I would sit there in a puddle that became cold and acrid, wet-through, distressed and embarrassed.

I learned lessons at school that had little to do with love or respect. I learned that if you were big and had a stick then you could do what you liked. I learned not to argue or talk back, not to say if I thought something was wrong. I learned to be quiet and not cause a nuisance. It was an education.

Several months after my return from the hospital, a teenage boy from the area offered to give me music lessons. I was delighted and my mother easily agreed. What she didn't know was that the offer was in fact a cover to get me alone. The first time he gave me a lesson he told me 'dirty' stories. I was thrilled. He was five or so years older than me, older even than my big brother, and he was treating me as if I was big like him.

Then he started to show me what the stories meant, how the man in the story would take off the knickers of the girl, but it was my underpants he was taking off and me he was touching. By now I knew what was to happen next. I knew the routine and how to perform. Those other men had shown me and I knew what I was meant to do.

This happened about half a dozen times. It happened in his house, in his bedroom, while his parents were in their living room watching television. It happened in my own house too, up in the bedroom I shared with my brother, as my mother went about her routine downstairs.

I don't remember ever feeling frightened when this boy abused me. Not like when the men did it. He talked to me. They didn't. He let me go if I said I had to go home. They didn't. And if he hurt me and I said so he would stop. And so I didn't fear him.

What I can see now is that my understanding of what was happening was entirely based on my experience of abuse at the hands of the older and crueller men. I'm shocked at the memory of how I'd become so accustomed to abuse, to the act of rape, that when this teenage boy did it to me I just accepted it as normal. And the tragic truth is, it was normal for me.

When I was eleven we left the village and moved to Wexford town. It was only about fifteen miles away but it was a huge change. I left my small, co-educational village school and finished my last year of primary education at the Christian Brothers National School in Wexford. In many ways this dramatic shift from rural to urban life was a chance for a whole new start and I embraced it. I left Adamstown, the farm and all those difficult memories behind. I closed the box in my mind assigned to that section of my life and started anew.

# 4

# *Town Life*

Wexford town was a big change for all of us. No more farm animals, no acres of open fields for me to roam. We moved because Dad had opened a business in the town. He had for years been both a farmer and a building contractor. He opened a joinery and builders' providers in Wexford town, and as that new business grew he gave up farming and we moved.

In time I forgot everything that had happened back in the village. It was the past and offered me nothing. I still continued to bed wet, was still in some ways anxious and desperate to please, but I started to come out of my shell. I made friends and began to fit in. I forgot the men who had hurt me. I forgot my neighbour and his music lessons. I became normal.

We moved to a white four-bedroomed bungalow in a suburb of the town. Mulgannon was about twenty minutes from my new school. The journey home took me up a really steep hill. Starting out from the bottom of that hill was a trial; it was a narrow, windy road all the way to the top, with very few houses along most of the way. I hated that walk, and quickly discovered other routes across empty, overgrown land that took me home more easily.

The house was rented. The plan was that Dad would build our new house once they had found a site. I wasn't the only one who missed the farm. It was obvious to me that Dad was struggling to come to terms with having sold it. The farm had been his father's and his father's before him, and land that was passed down like that was expected to stay in the family, from father to son across the generations. Land is important to the Irish. It's not about money especially, rather it's a reflection of years of colonialism, of generations left landless and destitute, an agricultural people without the fields to grow the food they needed to feed their families. The land was who we were, and once regained it was cherished as a source of security and identity.

Dad seemed stressed and at odds with himself for months afterwards and was very quick tempered.

Mam, however, was happy to be back in her hometown. Even though Adamstown was only fifteen miles from the place where she was born, she never felt like she belonged there. She seemed to me to be lighter and happier living in Wexford.

I think moving created some tension between my parents. The night the farm was sold at auction I heard them shouting, something that never happened. I remember being shocked, but the next morning everything seemed well enough and they were busily getting on with planning the move.

There were open fields to the back of our new house, but no farm to wander and get lost in. Instead I lost myself to reading. I would read anything. I started out with the *Famous Five*, but quickly moved on to *Alfred Hitchcock*

*and the Three Investigators.* My brother John was a fan of
the Hardy Boys, so I of course had to find a series of my
own. I even had a go at writing my own story a few times.
My heroes were known as the 'Fabulous Four', rather an
intriguing title for a team of ace detectives I thought at the
time. Before long I also started to read historical novels.
The political intrigue of royal courts and tales of rebellion
and revolution fascinated me.

My new school was entirely different to my old one. For
a start it was an all boys' school, and it was huge compared
to Adamstown National School. In my old school there
were only five classrooms with two years in each class. In
the Christian Brothers School there were two classes for
every year, so sixteen classrooms in all and hundreds of
kids. The absence of girls made it very different too. It was
harsher and rougher. The favourite playground game was
'Bulldog'. Many torn knees and skinned hands were the
result. But I loved it. We would never have been allowed to
play games like that at my old school.

My new teacher was a tall Kerry man with a thick
accent. He was a fiery character, prone to launching a
lump of chalk or a wooden duster at the head of any
boy he thought wasn't paying enough attention. In those
days, corporal punishment remained part of the system
of education.

The first time he did it to me I nearly had a heart attack.
'O'Gorman,' he roared, 'get up here.'

The next thing I knew the duster hit me a glancing
blow to the side of the head, luckily with the soft part,
and I was coughing on chalk-dust as I made my way to
his desk.

'I don't know what kind of carry on you got up to in your old school,' he said, 'but in my class you will listen and you will learn.'

'I was listening,' I protested.

'Enough! Hold out your hand.' He reached over his desk and picked up a metre-stick, a long wooden ruler. I held out my hand. 'Three on each,' he said, red-faced and fuming.

He gave me three almighty whacks on the palm of my right hand before I had to hold out my left for the same treatment. As he belted my left hand I clenched my burning right hand into a fist behind my back and squeezed my eyes shut to make sure I didn't cry.

I walked back to my desk getting sympathetic looks from the other boys. It was only my second day at the new school.

My new teacher didn't like me and I knew it pretty quickly. He seemed irritated by me. I didn't have to do much. All it took to send him off roaring was to look at him the 'wrong' way, whatever that was. I hadn't a clue what I was doing wrong and tried to work out what he wanted me to do.

I was pretty miserable. I'd left my friends behind and didn't have the farm to roam anymore. I was making new friends but it took time and I felt like a fish out of water at my new school. The other boys said I was a 'culchie', which meant from the country, which was true enough. But some of them made it sound like a bad thing, which I didn't understand.

One day I was in my room finishing my homework. Mam came in and found me panicking as I tried to get a particular maths problem right. She tried to help me but

I just got more and more anxious as I tried to wrack my brain to remember how my teacher had told me to do it.

'It's OK,' she said, 'you can do it like this. It's getting the right answer that matters.'

'No. I have to get it right. I have to do it the way he said to do it.' I was getting increasingly frantic.

'Colm, what in heaven's name is the matter with you? It's OK. Just do it this way. It will still be right and then you can ask your teacher to show you his way again tomorrow.'

'No. I can't. He'll get mad. He'll hit me again.'

'What did you say? He hit you, when?'

'All the time,' I blubbed, sobbing now. 'He hates me and I can't get anything right.'

'It will be fine,' Mam said as she gave me a hug. 'Let's just do our best.'

She helped me finish the problem. The next morning she gave me a note for my teacher and told me to give it to him as soon as I got into class.

I handed it to him as soon as I got there. 'What's this?' he asked gruffly. He opened the envelope and read it, his facing turning crimson as his eyes went down the page. I watched, certain I was really for it now. He finished reading, put the note back in its envelope and put it in the drawer of his desk. 'Sit down and get your books out.'

I breathed a sigh of relief and did as I was told.

Later on, after break I was making my way back across the playground. As I turned the corner I saw my mother walking towards me, out of the school doors. It was a sunny day, crisp and clear. She was going on to a business meeting with my Dad and was all dressed up, wearing a gorgeous green suit and her hair and make-up were immaculate. She looked beautiful and seeing her was so unexpected that she took my breath away.

She walked towards me, and gave me a hug. 'Everything OK?'

'Sure, why are you here?'

'Don't worry about that. Just enjoy yourself and work as hard as you can. Do your best, everything will be fine.'

She gave me a peck on the cheek and headed off. I was eleven at the time, old enough not to get kissed by my mother in the schoolyard. And old enough for the boys who were there to take the piss out of me for that kiss. But they didn't.

'Was that your Ma?' one of them asked.

'Yeah.'

'She's really gorgeous.'

'Yeah.'

'What the fuck happened to you then?' he yelled as he laughed and punched me playfully on the shoulder.

Everything was all right after that. My teacher didn't ever hit me again. He still roared at me, but less often. He still didn't like me but he did treat me better.

I made my confirmation that year. When I was born my parents and godparents stood for me as I was baptised into the Catholic Church. Now at almost twelve, I was to take the next step and affirm my membership of the faith myself.

It was a big deal. Everyone got all dressed up and the bishop himself led the ceremony. We had extra religious instruction for ages before the day itself. Confirmation, we were told, would 'render our bond with the Church more perfect.'

I hadn't a clue what it meant, but that didn't seem to matter. We were told what to think and what to believe, there was no discussion or process of guided discovery, we learned by rote. No questioning of dogma was tolerated.

All I knew was that it would be a big day for me and I would be made a bit of a fuss over. I had a new suit. It was a cream three-piece with a waistcoat and gorgeous burgundy silk lining. As this was 1978, it also had flared trousers that flapped around my ankles as I walked. It was the business. My first grown-up suit, and I loved it.

On the day of my confirmation my family all went down to Bride Street Church together. My godfather was my Uncle Noel, my father's youngest brother. He was supposed to walk with me to the altar, it was rather like his last function, handing me over as I made my own vow at last. But on the day he was late. I was convinced he wouldn't arrive at all and that I would have to go up on my own. He got there at the last minute though, and we walked up together. I stood at the altar with Uncle Noel behind me and his hand on my right shoulder as the bishop approached.

The bishop wore red robes. The red was to signify the fires of the Pentecost, the moment when the Holy Spirit came down to the apostles. This was because at confirmation, I too would receive and be confirmed with the Holy Spirit, I would become a soldier of Christ. Or so I was told. I was a bit lost to be honest and didn't really get it. But I was taken by the majesty and solemnity of it all, and I did feel it was a very special moment. I was growing up.

When you make your confirmation you take a new name, a confirmation name. I chose Anthony. He was my favourite saint, St Anthony of Padua, the saint of lost things. Whenever anything got lost in our house, his name was called and a prayer offered. And it worked; we usually found what we were looking for. I don't know whether it was his intervention or the calm the prayer brought to the panic of trying to remember where the lost thing had been last left, but it worked more often than not.

St Anthony was also a Franciscan friar. And I really loved St Francis of Assisi who founded the order. St Francis had a way with animals, he was said to have preached to them and to have understood them. I could relate to that since I almost preferred animals to people myself.

St Francis was also a champion of those living in poverty. I remember hearing about how he gave away everything he owned to a beggar, to the rage of his rich merchant father who then disowned him. He cared for lepers, for beggars, for those on the margins of his society. I loved his compassion, his love of life. His was one story I loved to hear, one I could relate to and be inspired by.

So Anthony it was for me that day. I was excited to have a new name. Colm Oliver Anthony. I had never much liked Oliver, my second given name, but I loved Anthony, not least because I had chosen it myself.

It was a great day. Dad was there with us all and we went for a family meal together at a hotel in the town to celebrate. Despite having moved to town to be closer to his business, he was still very absent from our day-to-day lives. As the third born of six, I didn't often get this much attention. It was lovely. I also made a bit of money. I was handed pound notes and fivers by uncles and aunts and had a great time spending it all over the next few months.

A week or so later I took the entrance exam required to get into secondary school. It was the first time I ever had to do a formal exam and I was petrified of it, but it went well enough and I got in without any problems.

The secondary school was next door to my primary school. It was also a Christian Brothers school but unlike the primary school where all of the teachers were lay teachers, the secondary school had several teachers who were religious brothers.

I was quite intimidated by the brothers who strode around the school in their long black robes imposing order as they went. They were strict and serious men. It was clear that many of them were very dedicated to their vocation as teachers, but their approach could hardly have been described as child-centred.

They had a reputation as strict disciplinarians, and were fond of using a leather strap to punish errant behaviour of any kind. But I never witnessed or experienced the kind of savage brutality that would be revealed to be endemic to their order in Ireland, Canada and Australia in the years ahead.

The Christian Brothers' Manual of School Government, published in 1832, laid great stress on the use of 'mildness, affection and kindness', describing 'blows' as 'a servile form of punishment' which 'degrade the soul ... They ordinarily harden rather than correct ... and blunt those fine feelings which render a rational creature sensible to shame.'

Tragically this enlightened ethos appears to have been entirely abandoned by the mid nineteenth century and the brothers became known for their harsh approach to discipline.

In the mid 1980s shocking details of the sexual and physical abuse of children by brothers at Mount Cashel Boys Home in Newfoundland, Canada would eventually lead to the bankruptcy of the order in Canada. By the mid 1990s more than one hundred Christian Brothers would also be accused of savage acts of abuse by many hundreds of former child residents of institutions in Australia. In 2001, the Australian Senate reported on its investigation into the Christian Brothers. The report described a culture of 'systemic criminal assault' perpetrated by 'a large number of brothers over a long period.'

Letters from the Australian Christian Brothers to their Irish counterparts dating from the 1940s revealed that the order was very much aware of the abuse of children being perpetrated by some of its members.

'Offences are becoming frequent among us,' said one letter back to Ireland. Another letter declared, 'the frequency is alarming.' Another a decade later said that, 'such shameful betrayals' were still 'on the increase.'

Back in 1978 as I started my first year at the Christian Brothers School in Wexford I was entirely unaware of the horrors yet to be revealed in Australia and Canada, and it would be 1999 before Mary Rafferty's ground-breaking documentary series *States of Fear* would result in the final exposure of the depth of abuse in Irish institutions.

When I started at the secondary school that September, John was already there and as is the gift of being an elder brother, he got to terrify me with tales of what awful initiations I would be subjected to. He teased me for weeks. That said, forewarned was forearmed and I made the most of the insider information.

There was an old bath sitting beneath a hedge on a path that ran from the yard of the secondary school down to the sports fields. The bath was full of rainwater and was rancid and green and covered with slime. On the first day of school each year, the older boys delighted in grabbing the first-years and dunking them head first into that stinking bath. I was determined I wouldn't get caught.

That first morning I waited as everyone else ran from our new classroom out into the yard and the waiting horde. When the older lads were busy chasing other hapless victims, my friend and myself ran up the steps back into our old primary schoolyard and headed into the toilets. We leaned over the sinks and gave our heads a good soaking, making sure our shirts looked good and drenched too, then headed off back to our new school.

Everyone thought someone else had grabbed us and so we were left alone. John was gutted when I told him later. It's not that he wanted to see me drowned or anything, but it was the initiation everyone was meant to endure; he'd had to and so should I. In the end though he laughed and promised not to give me away.

It was exciting moving into secondary school and I felt like I was growing up; becoming a teenager loomed large. Secondary school was a lot more demanding than primary of course, and with lots of new subjects. I had to do Latin for my first year but thankfully didn't have to keep it up in the second year. I really didn't like it much. It wasn't the language, which was rich and round and poetic, it was the way it was taught, the monotonous recitation of verbs and phrases.

We had a great maths teacher in the first year. His name was Colm Flynn and he was a real hippy with curly hair and dressed in colourful striped sweaters. I say he was a great maths teacher, but it was more that he was a great teacher who happened to teach maths. It was the other things he talked to us about that made him great for me.

He talked about the world and the things that were happening in it. He talked about politics in a way I'd never heard before; he didn't talk about political parties at all, but about political ideas, about justice and power. He told us about how people in some countries were not free to say or even allowed to believe, what they believed. How men and women in those countries were imprisoned for expressing their opinions and beliefs. He called them prisoners of conscience and told us about an organisation he was a member of called Amnesty International that campaigned to free them. I was gripped. When he spoke about human rights and explained what that meant the world made sense to me in new ways. The idea of a code of principles, a set of rights that each of us possessed by nature of being human, and his outrage at dreadful violations of those rights made sense of how I felt about the world.

Before long he had us all writing letters and getting fired up. We may not have done as much maths as we should have but he taught me many, many important lessons.

He also got me involved in a cause that would see me take action for the first time. At the time there were plans afoot to build a nuclear power plant in Ireland. The proposed location was Carnsore Point, a coastal site not far from the town.

I got very fired up about the damage such a plant could do to the environment. Mam had always been passionate about the environment as well; that and my own love of nature stirred me into action. Within weeks I went everywhere with my bag and coat covered in red and yellow 'Nuclear Power: No thanks' badges. I spent my Saturdays collecting signatures on a petition opposing the building of the plant. It was all very passionate stuff and I loved it. It gave me a great sense of purpose and of connection to others. I was gutted when I wasn't allowed to go to either of the two big concerts held at Carnsore Point to oppose the plans. In the end though, we won and the plans for the plant were abandoned.

Despite all of this I still struggled a bit to fit in at school. I was quite timid and didn't ever stand up for myself. That left me easy prey for any and every class bully. I remember one skinny boy nicknamed Badger. He picked on me mercilessly. I could hardly ever stand up to him even though I was bigger and stronger than he was. One day he slapped me across the ear and I snapped. I threw him on the ground and sat on him. I wanted to punch him silly, but I couldn't. I wasn't able to hit anyone; I didn't know why, I just couldn't do it. All I could do was sit on him to stop him from hitting me.

Things at home were fine though. Dad was around a little bit more, though I still didn't get to spend any time with him really; he always seemed to have something he had to do. After a year in the house in Mulgannon we moved again, this time for the summer to a chalet we had bought near the sea, on a beach called Carne, close to where the nuclear power station had been proposed. My parents had finally found a site for the house and were due to start building soon, but it wouldn't be ready before our lease on the bungalow was up and so we had to move.

We had a great summer at the chalet. One of our neighbours from Mulgannon had a mobile home in the same holiday park so we knew some other kids. The beach was minutes away and we got to go fishing out on boats rented from the quay at Carne.

I think Mam found it tough going though. She had the six of us to cope with in a little beachside chalet for three months. It must have been hellish. And Dad was as busy as ever with work and everything else, so she was pretty much alone with us. I could tell there was a tension between them during that summer. They had moved house three times in a year, and would move at least once more before we finally settled into our new home.

At the end of the summer we moved into another rented house, this time a few minutes walk from the site where our new house was being built. We all got to work on the house; John and I had regular summer jobs with Dad and we were delighted to be part of building our new home.

We moved in just before Christmas 1979. The house wasn't really ready. The walls in the hallway weren't even plastered and parts of it still looked like a building site, but we were in at last. This was home.

I was by now involved in lots of different clubs and activities. I was in the folk group at church and a youth group that met every Friday night. We met in a local convent called Bethany House, a huge old building with enormous rooms. It was a great place and the nuns who ran it were really lovely. They are long gone now and the convent has been turned into apartments, but back in the late 1970s and early 80s it was a place full of music and words and questions. It was a reflective space where we often discussed big themes, both spiritual and secular. It was a space of discovery and questioning. I loved it.

Church, then, was still everywhere, just as it had been in Adamstown: in my school, my youth group, the folk group at Mass on Sundays. Dances at school were organised and supervised by religious brothers and nuns; our lives were entirely wrapped up in the Church. At school our only experience of philosophical or social discussion was directed and informed by the teachings of the Church, which gave us our values, informed our thoughts and directed our dreams.

And it was often great, but not always.

# 5

# *The Priest*

I was fourteen when I first met Father Sean Fortune. He was in his late twenties then and tall and imposing. He wore glasses and dressed in clerical garb, the black suit and Roman collar. Sometimes he would wear the long, flowing Roman style black robes. Always one for the dramatic, he knew how to use costume to its fullest effect. And he was loud. Little was ever softly-spoken, but on the rare occasions when he talked in a low voice it was to threaten or intimidate. There was nothing subtle about him; he was all force and bluster. I later learned that in the seminary they'd called him 'Flapper'. He was like a whirlwind wherever he went: loud, destructive and unstoppable.

That first meeting took place at a youth group event. Fr Fortune wasn't my parish priest; he was there with some kids from his own parish. I was sat on the edge of a stage, watching what was happening in the room, happily taking it all in. Behind me were red velvet curtains, the kind you see in small community theatres everywhere. He appeared from behind the curtains.

'Who are you?' he asked me.

I told him my name. He asked me where I was from and which school I went to. I answered his questions, politely and respectfully. It was normal enough; after all, I spoke to priests every day. He seemed unremarkable, though friendly and familiar.

He came to my house two weeks later. He arrived, unannounced, with the absolute expectation of an open door; that he had the God-given authority to impose himself was never in question. His collar was his pass to every home, his key to our front door.

He explained to my mother that he'd met me at the church event and wanted to talk to me about the youth club in his own parish. Tea was made and he was granted the use of the family living room for his chat with me. We sat either side of the fire glowing in the big granite hearth in our living room. I sat to the left of the fire, he sat to the right, the door and the rest of my family behind us both.

He talked with careful and considered purpose, working his way past any barriers. He talked about me and what interested me, a careful and considered flattery, making me feel important and seeming to value my ideas and thoughts.

'I was impressed by you when we met a few weeks ago,' he told me. 'Tell me more about the folk group you're in. Tell me about the youth group. They're lucky to have you involved. You seem a bright boy.'

I talked about the folk group, telling him that I wasn't all that important in the group, that I didn't sing solos or anything and I wasn't that good.

'But you obviously give a lot,' he said. 'You have a real interest in it, and that shows.'

'And the girls must love you, you're such a good-looking boy. You must have lots of girlfriends.'

'No I don't, not lots.' I blushed.

'At your age you must be careful. Hormones going mad, your body changing and all kinds of temptations before you.' He hooked me in and then went further, talking about more personal things, testing my boundaries and no doubt finding to his enormous satisfaction that they were at best flimsy.

'Do you masturbate?' he asked, looking at me over his tea-cup.

I didn't answer, blushing furiously and staring at the fire.

'Don't worry,' he laughed. 'It's normal. You won't go blind or get hair on the palms of your hands. It's grand … you're grand.'

'So,' he said, placing his cup and saucer on the table beside his armchair. 'I wondered if you might be willing to come and help me out a bit in my parish. I'm only there a few weeks and I want to get a good folk group and youth group up and running. There's a bit of a youth group there but it needs a lot of work. I think you could help me a lot, you'd have some great ideas. You could come down and help me. What do you think?'

'I don't know,' I replied. 'I'd have to ask Mam.'

I was flattered. I felt important suddenly, like I had something valuable to contribute; I must have or he wouldn't have come to find me and ask me to help him. I agreed.

'That's it so,' he said. 'I'll talk to your mother, she'll be fine with it I'm sure.'

And so a week later he took me to his house for a weekend, to see his work and help him. Twenty-six years later it sounds insane that a grown man could arrive unannounced at a home and a week later take a fourteen-year-old son away, unquestioned. And it *was* insane. But back then we were all still ignorant and blind.

He collected me on a Friday evening in his cream-coloured car. We drove out of town and down the narrow roads that led to his home in a place called Poulfur, a few miles from Fethard-on-Sea, the nearby village that was a popular holiday destination at the time. It took about thirty minutes to get there, and on the way he stopped at a parishioner's house for tea. He brought me in and didn't bother to explain my presence, after all, who would question his actions or motives? And so we had tea with this family, who for all I know may well have been used to their local priest bringing teenage boys to their house.

It was dark when we arrived at his house, a big building with three floors and a basement. It was painted a sickly peach colour with a textured finish to its exterior. There was a front room that had once been a garage, now converted into a meeting room for one of the two youth groups that met at the house every week. The group was already there when we arrived. The lights were on and I could hear them laughing and joking. I thought we would go straight in there; after all this was why I'd been brought down for the weekend, to work with his youth group. I didn't get to meet them. Instead I was ushered through the hall and into a room that seemed to be both an office and a living room. There was a TV and a desk as well as a sofa and office equipment. I was left there alone as he went in to see the group and wind up the evening.

After a while I heard everyone leave, calling out and laughing and saying goodbye. I couldn't understand why I was left in the house on my own, but knew I had no right to question a priest. He came back in and brought me to the kitchen for more tea. I don't remember what we talked about. It was late and I was tired and a little confused. I kept trying to work out why I hadn't met his youth group, but I couldn't ask.

Eventually he said it was time to head for bed. He told me that there was only one bed in the house and that we would have to sleep in it together.

'I'm only here a few weeks and I haven't gotten the place furnished properly yet. But we'll be all right in the one bed won't we?' he said as he headed up the stairs without waiting for my answer.

I followed, feeling grateful that I had a new pair of pyjamas with me that my mother had bought me that week. I'd stopped wearing pyjamas a year or two earlier, preferring to sleep in my underwear, but that wouldn't have done at all. Not in a priest's house.

I took my pyjamas and toothbrush and got ready for bed in the downstairs bathroom before climbing the staircase up to the bedroom. His room was the first on the left with a big old wooden door painted a gloss white with an old-fashioned ceramic doorknob. There were two other doors off the same small landing, leading to rooms without beds I assumed.

I went into the room. There was a huge old wardrobe on the right-hand wall, as I came into the room, it was open and I could see his priestly robes and other clothes hanging there. Just beyond it was a corner-sink and on the opposite wall a dressing table with a mirror over it. To my left was the bed, big and made of old polished wood.

He was sitting up in the bed, on the left-hand side, applying hand-cream. I remember the smell of it clearly, sickly and sweet. As I walked in he looked at me with a half-smile on his face.

'In you get so.'

I got into the other side of the bed.

'Goodnight,' I said, turning my back to him and pulling the bed covers up over my shoulders.

'Goodnight.'

He turned the lights off and I started to drift off, feeling odd and uncomfortable at finding myself sleeping in a bed with a priest.

A little later I felt him move. He turned over and moved towards me. A few moments passed before I felt him move even closer and then drape his arm across my waist. I froze. I thought maybe he had just turned around as he slept, but then his hand began to stroke my stomach. He said nothing but I could hear his breathing become more laboured. I didn't know what to do. I wanted to get up and run out of the room but I couldn't. I froze completely. Then he moved his hand down ...

Words like abuse are easy to use. Words can't show what it was. Words can't describe the smell, the sounds, the taste of it all. Words can't tell you how it felt.

It was sordid and degrading and hateful. Hateful is an important word here ... it was full of hate. Full of his hatred of himself and of what I was to him. I believe he hated the boy, the boy he had been and the boy that I was before him now. He destroyed that boy. He seduced and sickened him. He defiled and destroyed him until he was no more.

And this time it was worse than when I was so much younger, or so it seemed. This time, I both knew and didn't know what was happening. I was still in so many ways an innocent. I'd never had any kind of sex education beyond schoolyard whispers and teenage jokes that were all huff and bluster, all pretend knowledge and sniggers.

And then this happened. This priest manipulated me into his bed and used my confusion and innocence against me. And once again the world as I knew it, as I was required to know it, as defined by every authority in my life, came crashing down.

I felt so betrayed by my own body, which reacted to what was happening. I was sickened that I could become aroused and experience sexual pleasure at the same time as feeling terrified and disgusted. At forty-one years of age and after years of coming to terms with it, I look back and see my fourteen-year-old body naked, responsive and charged and I don't feel sickened or ashamed, instead I feel grief and hurt for the boy I was and what that man did to me.

In my mind, I am back in that room now, standing beside that huge wardrobe, in the shadows, hidden from the man and the boy in that bed. I watch with a growing horror as I see him seduce the child I was, the youth that I had only begun to become. It's dark and silent. The room is oppressive; it reeks of his sordid intent. The boy lies there, frozen. The covers move as the priest moves over and brings his hand down. He starts to masturbate the boy, who lies there motionless. And then in moments it is over.

The confusion and urgency of the sexual charge that took me over and blurred all else has passed and there is only the shock and guilt of what has just happened. I am dizzy and frightened.

I can't do this ... and yet I can, and have. This can't be me ... and yet there I am, obscene, lost. I fight to regain control, to find a way to make it right. I flee the room. My mind is racing as I run down the stairs, through the old house and down a few more steps into the kitchen. It's an old kitchen, dated but practical. The sink is on the back wall to the left, beneath a window that looks out over trees and a stream below. It's dark and bleak outside. I put the kettle on. The table sits in the middle of the room, covered in a plastic cloth with a check pattern.

The ground is gone. It was there, solid and simple beneath my feet. A priest is good, always good, always right and never to be questioned. Always to be obeyed. He names the Truth and we follow his word. Sex is bad, never to be spoken of. This sex is worse than bad, it is evil. But he is a priest and cannot be evil, so *I* must be evil. The ground begins to form again, just enough for me to gather myself.

I take control, otherwise known as blame and masked as responsibility. I am too young to know the difference. I stand at the bottom of the stairs and then hesitate before calling him. What do I call him? 'Father' ... that can't be now, not right now. 'Sean' is my real father's name and I can't bring myself to use it for him ... I can't even say the name for fear it might somehow bring Dad into this. In the end I call him John. Not Father, not my father ... John. That makes this a bit more manageable.

A few minutes later I hear the stairs creak as he comes

down to the kitchen. He walks in, now in his pyjamas and dressing-gown. I make the tea. I fuss around, looking for cups, milk, sugar, keeping busy; anything to avoid thinking too much.

Finally, as I hand him a cup, I look at him.

'Father,' I say. 'That can never happen again. It's wrong.'

He nods his agreement but doesn't say anything. Instead he waits to hear what I will say next.

'It shouldn't have happened and I don't know what to do. It's so very wrong. I feel sick.'

He finally speaks just as I feel I'm about to burst apart with guilt and shame. 'You're right, of course you are right.'

'It was wrong and must never happen again. You must never do such a thing again.'

I leap at this offering and take his agreement as deference to my maturity and wisdom. I can feel safe and close the door on what has happened. Of course it was nothing of the sort. Today, all these years later, I wonder was he surprised at the readiness with which I made it all my responsibility?

In that moment his agreement offers me salvation, it offers me another option beyond the truth, beyond facing his manipulation and my powerlessness. If I can fix this, then I am not powerless. I can put the world to rights, he can be a priest again and I can just shut this all away. After all, I had done it before, and I could do it again.

The fact that he is a priest and agrees with me gives more power to my effort. If he says I am right, then I am right. I am saved.

I wasn't saved.

*       *       *

That Sunday evening we headed back to Wexford town and home. As we drove along the winding roads he chattered imperiously about nothing in particular and I sat there beside him focused on the road ahead. I could hear him talking but not the words he said. Instead, I thought about home, about getting there and resting, and letting go of the watchfulness and worry.

Before long we were close to home, just minutes away. He finally stopped speaking. It felt like the first silence in hours. Then he cleared his throat and said, 'I'm worried about you. You have a problem.'

I froze and said nothing, too scared to speak.

'I am a priest and I have a duty to do something about it.'

My mind raced, I didn't know what he meant by 'do something', I didn't have time to think it through, we were moments away from home, from my parents.

'I could talk to your father ... that might be best.'

I started to scream inside. Panic raced through me and the world started to spin. I wanted to escape, jump from the car, anything to get away from that awful moment. Anything to prevent what he said he might do. My father ... it would kill him to know what I'd done, what I was. He would die from shame.

'You need help and I am bound to help you,' he said with all the solemnity and authority of his priestly office.

I looked at him, struck dumb with fear and panic.

'Unless ...' he paused and looked at me. He looked me straight in the eye and I saw a shift, a change. The Priest steps back and the craven one stepped forward. 'Unless you come back to me and I will help you.'

He would 'help me'.

Never did those two words sound so malicious. Help me. I knew what the words meant, and I knew what *he* meant. Either I went back to him or he would tell what I was. There was no choice. I knew I could not stay alive in this world if everyone knew, especially if my father knew. I'd spent my first fourteen years as my father's son trying to find a way to his heart. I was so eager to win his love and admiration, so hungry to find myself reflected in him in some way. I had never been able to break through to him but I wanted to so desperately. And now the priest, that other father, threatened to take any hope of that from me.

As I sat there I felt I was losing my mind. I had to be, this couldn't be happening. All I could see was this man, this priest, this other father beside me, threatening to expose me to my real father as the foul thing I knew myself to be.

My voice screamed inside my head, 'There is no choice; the Father must know it all. All knowing Father, and when he knows it will kill him. I will have killed him, not on a cross but by the agony of my betrayal of his goodness.'

'The son will kill the father because of what he has done with the Father who twists the words of the Son of the Father. How can I stay sane? Who am I and where am I in this? What son am I and who is my Father? How do I live with my betrayal of the goodness of not one, but three Fathers, the Father of all, the Father who is mine and the Father whom I have defiled?'

I was lost in ways that defied any sense of place ... I couldn't know where I was because I couldn't live with who I knew myself to be. I was so lost I don't even know that there was such a thing as found.

So I went back with him. I had no other choice. He came to my home and took me away dozens of times. And he did not help me, he only hurt me.

# 6

# Drowning

The abuse continued for another two and a half years. As I became increasingly lost to it, I struggled to stay sane. I found myself splitting again, as I had in my earlier childhood. There was the hidden dark world of abuse and the 'real' world. In the real world I was like everyone else, normal, functional, healthy and outwardly happy. I could focus on other things, and that kept me alive.

Even when I was at the priest's house I would try and find ways to be normal. But he never let me join in when the youth group met, or hang around with any of the local kids. If I were away from the house for any period of time he would become angry and aggressive.

The housekeeper had a daughter close to my age, a pretty girl called Debbie who was full of fun. She helped out at the house at the weekends and during school holidays.

Fortune was careful not to let me spend too much time with her. She tried to warn me about him once, that he had tried to follow one of her friends into the toilet. I was breathless at the idea that someone else might know about him, but also scared that the truth might come out.

School became difficult at times. I felt isolated, like a freak because of what was happening to me. I hid it as well as I could, and made sure I found ways to escape and be myself. I still went to the youth group and sang at Mass. The youth group was great; I had good friends there and enjoyed it enormously, though I never so much as hinted at what was happening to me elsewhere. Unlike my school it wasn't an exclusively male environment, and the girls made it all a bit more peaceful and less hostile.

I went out with a few different girls at the youth group. I had no clue what it was all about, but everyone else was going out with someone and it was expected, so I did. We danced, walked along holding hands and kissed, but that was all. I had no inclination to go any further. Sexual arousal was a dangerous and unpleasant thing to me so I was happy to leave it unexplored in my peer relationships.

It was a relief and I never stopped to think that my lack of interest might mean something else. I'd never considered that I might be gay. To be honest, I didn't really know what it meant. It was just an insult boys at school used when slagging each other off. There was no sex education in school; our third year science teacher ignored the section on reproduction in our books, and references to sex were veiled in heavily disguised language and warnings of mortal sin. Homosexuality simply didn't exist in Ireland in 1981.

Even though I didn't make the connection at the time, there were also rumours of 'stuff' happening at St Peter's College, the other boys school in Wexford. As well as a boarding school, it was the seminary for the diocese and the subject of much sniggering and jokes about priests who were 'queering up' the boys there. I don't think anyone who repeated the gossip really understood what they were talking about, but if local kids were talking about it, then surely some adults must also have known of the rumours.

I was getting out and making friends, not just at the youth and folk groups but at school dances and out in the town. I became more and more interested in the things that were happening in the wider world, and was picked to be a member of our school debating team. My first debate related to the state of mental health institutions in Ireland. I argued that the poor standard of such facilities – all of them still sited in Victorian asylums – were a stain on our society and should either be upgraded or closed and relocated. Thirty years later in my work with Amnesty International Ireland we continue to argue for decent standards of services that respect the human rights and dignity of those experiencing mental health difficulties.

Life at home was changing too. Mam had discovered yoga and meditation, and we all got to experience some of it. There was a really lovely relaxation practice called Yoga Nidra, a guided meditation that we listened to at night on a tape playing in the hallway as we drifted off to sleep. As I listened to the soothing voice of a swami guiding me through the relaxation I felt all my worries melt away for a while.

This was exactly the kind of escape I needed so much. It is striking that many of the ways I found to escape the reality of the abuse involved spirituality in some form: singing or reading at church on Sundays, discussing ideas, philosophical songs and poems at youth group, and Mam opening me up to different ideas and concepts that spoke of love and peace.

But when I came back from that happy place, he was there. Dressed all in black, a shadow cast across the path I had wandered down. Whenever I tried to explore ideas of who I was in the world, of spiritual truths and possibilities, he would block my way, reminding me of my sin.

One day, Mam told us that some of the teachers from her yoga centre, an ashram in Belfast, were coming to give workshops in Wexford and would stay with us for a week. That weekend an old BMW pulled into the drive and a man and woman dressed in orange robes got out. Mam greeted them with her palms together, bowing slightly as she raised the tips of her fingers to touch her forehead and said, 'Hari Om, Swami Ji.'

Swami Ji was a sweet and gentle middle-aged man from Northern Ireland who wore his robe with such poise and grace you'd think he'd been born dressed from head to toe in homespun orange cotton. He was lovely, and despite the strangeness of it all, we were very happy to have him and Swami Om, his fellow swami, stay with us. All of us except Dad, who witnessed my mother's movement towards this new lifestyle with growing despair. As she moved towards it, she moved away from him. He would never be part of this life, this new and alien philosophy.

Over time they grew noticeably more distant from each other until eventually they began to live almost entirely separate lives. They had separate bedrooms, and only seemed to come together when they had to. Dad was out more, unable to relate to Mam, his frozen, silent hurt a constant presence when he was in the house. It was obvious that their marriage was coming to an end.

All this change meant that both my parents were less available to me than ever. Mam tried to navigate all this as best she could. As an adult I can only imagine how difficult it must have been for them both. He was distant and sullen as she grew further and further away from the life they had shared.

In the midst of this turmoil, Fortune, who had clearly picked up on the difficulties at my home, was still abusing me. I later found out that this was his pattern: he was expert at befriending wives in such circumstances, something that caused him to be despised by many husbands over the years.

I'd come home from school on a Friday evening and he'd be there, waiting. After he shared tea or supper with my mother and my brothers and sisters he would take me to his parish ... but with no more pretence of youth or folk groups. Instead, he started to abuse me as soon as we got past the last house on the road out of town. He would reach over and put his hand down my trousers and touch me. Often he made me perform oral sex on him as he drove along the narrow country road that led to his house.

My mind couldn't keep up with what was happening. When I got home he was there, the priest in all his grandiosity, lording it at my father's table, as if he blessed us with his very presence. Then within ten minutes of leaving the house he was pawing at me. And when that finished he would pull into the drive of a parishioner's house and, once more the priest, walk me in to more tea and pomposity.

I tried so hard to tell once. I was in my room. He arrived and Mam called out. 'Colm, Father Fortune is here. Are you ready to go?' I didn't answer, I just curled up on my bed praying that he would go away if I pretended I wasn't there.

I heard him tell her to go up and get me. She came into my room. 'Colm, what's the matter, didn't you hear me calling? Father Fortune is here, he wants to leave and get back in time for a youth group meeting. Are you packed?'

I shook my head. 'I don't want to go,' I said.

'Why not? Don't be silly, he's come all this way to collect you. You can't just decide you don't want to go now.'

'Please don't make me go with him. I really want to stay home this weekend. I don't want to go. Please.'

'Why not, what's wrong with you?'

I couldn't tell her. I wanted her to save me from him, from his eyes and his grabbing hands. I cried and asked to stay.

She went downstairs to him. He was in the kitchen, slurping tea as always. 'Why not?' he asked loudly. 'Why doesn't he want to go? Did he tell you why?'

'No, he just says he wants to stay home this weekend. Maybe he should stay, after all you shouldn't have to deal with him when he's like this.' I could hear Mam trying to find a way to defuse an awkward situation, to have me stay home but not offend him.

'That would be a bad idea I think. He's obviously made some arrangement with friends and is trying to skip out on the plans we made. It's very inappropriate and not a good idea to let him get away with that.'

Mam went up and down the stairs between us, telling him I didn't want to go, him saying in return that I must. I couldn't say why and she didn't know what to do. She didn't, couldn't understand.

Fortune was all-powerful in this. The power of that collar silenced me and blinded her; a strip of white with the might of an empire behind it.

He refused to leave without me, insisting that I must honour my prior commitment to him. And he won. I was told to go.

I remember the smirk of victory he gave me as I got into his car. He had me and he could get me as and when he wanted. There was no safe place, no one to protect me.

Until that moment I'd clung to the edge of what felt like a deep, dark pool. I clutched the sides, shivering, eyes shut tight as I was pulled and clawed and pawed. I clung limpet-like, for dear life, until life was dear no more.

When I had to get into that car under the triumphant sneer of his gaze, I let go. I let myself fall backwards, sinking into the depths of those greedy clutches that drained me of any sweetness and hope.

I gave myself over to whatever I could find down there that might relate to me – response, reaction, pleasure of whatever kind ... anything. Anything was better than nothing.

There was no escape. I was fourteen, fifteen and sixteen, living in a world where a priest who spoke the word of God used me for sex, and there was nothing I could do about it. There was no one to tell because the world where this horror happened didn't exist for anyone else.

In order to escape I would have to name the abuse and that couldn't happen because to do so would destroy the very fabric of the society I lived in. It's no exaggeration to say it would mean the end of the world ... or at least the end of the world as the Ireland of the early 1980s knew it.

A decade earlier, I had served a priest in my scarlet and white robes. I held my breath in awe of the sacred, watching him raise aloft the communion host as I knelt beside the altar. Now here I was, regularly forced to kneel yards from another altar watching another priest hold aloft the host.

But this time the man in robes defiled a sacred ceremony with the hands that less than an hour before had pawed at me. He had spewed out his lust and his need to dominate and humiliate, before donning robes and standing beneath a cross before a congregation determined not to see.

I didn't know who I was anymore. This wasn't just teenage angst and uncertainty, I despised myself for what I felt I was. I didn't have the words for it, but I hated it. I had become, in my mind, what he did to me.

I had become the act itself, the hateful, vile, corrupt act of his sexual abuse. Over the two and a half years I turned my anger and hate inwards. I came to despise myself as weak, pathetic and depraved. Worse still, I had become compliant. I no longer resisted, no longer tried to get away and no longer tried to tell anyone what was happening. I accepted it and played my part.

In the midst of all of this I still had to get on with 'normal' life, school and exams and all of the rest. I worked as hard as I could. My parents expected us all to go to university and for me to do well in my final exams. I decided to study hotel management since I was good at identifying and meeting the needs of others. I could be charming and put on a good show, and a job in the hospitality industry seemed perfect. Also, the course I wanted to do would mean I got a business degree which would keep my options open.

And so I coped. I was good at that. Life had taught me that I should make sure I was never a problem to anyone else, that to be good I must be compliant and cause no trouble. I did OK in my exams, though not as well as I should have and this added to my sense of failure. Elsewhere in my life I pleased everyone around me as best I could.

But the more I 'performed' for everyone, the more of myself I lost and the more I despised myself. I had no clue who I was and I didn't have anything to measure my life by.

My first sexual experiences were abusive. There was no awkward fumbling with someone my own age as we breathlessly began to explore our sexuality. Instead, there was coercion and bullying and rape. And that was all I had to relate to. I knew I wasn't healthy and good, I was sordid and bad.

Another impact of the abuse was that I lost any faith in my ability to stand up for myself. When I first went to the new primary school, I still had some self-confidence. I was quieter and more withdrawn than the other boys, but I remember standing up to a bully and pushing him back. But at fourteen my ability to defend myself was seriously tested. Fortune found me and I was unable to protect myself from him. He swept aside all my defences, and I was forced to tolerate and submit to his will.

I remember one occasion when I did try to stop him. He started to touch me again when I was in his house, in his bed. I don't know what was different this time, other than I'd reached a breaking point. I kept saying no and as usual he didn't listen, he just kept on pawing at me.

Before I knew what was happening I felt a flash of angry defiance. 'I said no!' I roared at him. 'Don't you understand that word at all? No, just leave me alone, I don't want to do this!'

I pushed him away and got out of the bed. I went to the room next door, which by then I discovered did have a bed in it, though I wasn't allowed to use it. I closed the door behind me and leaned against it, trembling as I waited to hear if he'd followed me. I couldn't believe I'd shouted at him, told him to stop and even pushed him off me. I was certain he wouldn't let me get away with such defiance.

But I heard nothing. The house was silent apart from the rattle of the window in the wind and the occasional creak of the old building. I got into the bed, alone. I was so happy I'd resisted him and got out of his bed and that room. I felt liberated. I fell asleep feeling like I'd finally found within myself the courage and strength to stand up to him and that this nightmare would now end.

I don't know how long I'd been asleep but I woke up to find myself forced over onto my stomach. I felt a searing pain as he forced himself inside me. His weight knocked the breath out of me and I couldn't speak. I was terrified. He didn't say a word to me. He treated me like an object, as though I wasn't human.

When he was finished he got off me, again without a word, and left the room. I lay there in shock, trying to pull myself together. I pulled my knees up to my chest and wrapped the sheet tight around me, sobbing in shock and pain. Eventually I fell asleep.

The next morning I came downstairs and found him in his dining room as usual. He bid me good morning and told me to sit down while Debbie served breakfast.

He acted as though there was nothing remarkable about that morning. He said nothing about the night before. He didn't have to. I got the message loud and clear: he could, and would, do whatever he wanted with me, whenever he wanted. What I wanted or didn't want was immaterial. I was nothing.

That annihilation of any remaining ability to defend myself was devastating. Not only did it mean I was now entirely at his mercy but it also led to my inability to defend myself in other situations. I became even more withdrawn and submissive, not a good thing for any teenage boy, and I suffered as a result. I was bullied and teased at school, and as I failed to defend myself, the bullying became worse and worse.

I was spat on, hit, pushed and ridiculed by a succession of boys who probably knew no better. I remember walking home from school one day, crying and telling myself to say it out loud, to tell my mother, to find a way not to have to go back to school again. I remember thinking that I didn't want to stay alive like this.

When I got home Fortune's car was parked in the drive. It was a school day, so at least I knew he couldn't take me away for the weekend. He often turned up unannounced for tea during the week. There he was, in my kitchen leering at me when my mother's back was turned to refill the teapot or rinse a cup, reminding me of who he was and who I was. Once again his presence silenced me. I said nothing about being bullied.

Over the two and a half years of the abuse certain things did change. I grew older and depressed. I put on a lot of weight, perhaps mirroring the way I felt in the way

I looked. Layers of fat were like layers of shame to me and had the perverse bonus of making me less attractive to him. Towards the end of those years I didn't have to see him as much.

I did my final school exams in June 1983, aged sixteen. I was functioning on autopilot, doing the things I had to do, getting through each day moment by moment.

Mam had decided to go to India and live in an ashram. She planned to take two of my sisters, Deirdre and Joy, and my youngest brother Eamon with her. She was going for a year but it was obvious that this departure marked the end of my parents' marriage. Dad was really struggling by this stage on every front. His marriage and family were breaking up and his business was failing. Everything was falling apart everywhere.

She left in September 1983. We all went to the airport to see the four of them off. It was awful. None of us said anything real, but went along with the notion that they were just heading off on a trip and would be back in no time. After we left them, Dad drove John and I back home to Wexford. Barbara was by now at university so there were only the three of us left at home. The heart and soul had gone from the house. There was no life, no noise or chatter, no messing or arguing, no cooking, no sounds or smells of normality.

Dad and John spent most of their time out of the house. I slept late in the mornings, too depressed to drag myself out of bed.

Fortune was still around, though I saw him very rarely. I remember the last time he abused me. He came to my house and stayed over. I ended up in his room, as ordered, while my father slept a few rooms away. That memory enrages me now. He was so dominant, so powerful that he could come into my father's house and abuse me. His obliteration of my father's authority in my life was complete. It made it even more sordid though the sexual act which happened that night was pretty minor. I think he'd lost interest in me at this point. I was now seventeen and grey, bloated and depressed.

The next day he told me he would give me money if I found him someone a bit younger than me who would have sex with him. I never saw him again after that. It was too much. I'd learned from him that I had no value. What he did to me he did because he could. I couldn't protect myself, but I couldn't countenance him using me to do this to someone else.

In the end I left. I couldn't exist in that place, so it was either leave or end my life. In January 1984, I packed a bag and hitch-hiked to Dublin. I ran away, from Fortune, from my family, from life.

# 7

# *Escape*

I was seventeen when I escaped. It was less than a month after Fortune asked me to find someone else to have sex with him. That was the last time I saw him for many years. That incident in my father's house turned out to be the last time I was used by him.

I had no idea what I was going to do but knew I had to get away, get out of Wexford and escape everything my life had become.

Life at home had become increasingly difficult. Dad's business was in grave trouble and money was very tight. Ireland was in the grip of a deepening recession, the economy in tatters with little hope of recovery. Emigration had been a constant reality for generations and it was getting worse not better. All the lads I went to school with were leaving, either to college or abroad to find work.

Mam was gone. Home wasn't home anymore; instead, it was a miserable reminder of everything that was wrong.

Dad was a man with a strongly-developed and personal sense of honour and duty to his family name. To find himself, aged forty-nine, separated and alone, facing the bankruptcy of the business in which he'd invested so much work and all his assets – including the proceeds of the sale of the land he inherited from his family – was devastating.

He was shattered. I left home with barely a nod from him. I remember going into the living room to say goodbye. He was sitting alone by the fire. Nearly all of us had left or were leaving; Mam, Deirdre, Joy and Eamon to India, Barbara at university, me about to walk out to nowhere. Only himself and John were left to face the disintegration of everything he'd worked for.

'I have to go to Dublin, Dad. I can't stay here. I need to try and get a job or something.'

He didn't say anything. He didn't ask me why I was going. He didn't tell me to take care of myself. He didn't ask me where I would stay or what I would do ... or even how I would get to where I was going. He didn't ask me if I needed anything or offer any advice. Nor did he wish me well for the road or tell me he loved me.

'You'll have to pay your own way now,' he said. 'If you don't, you'll have to come back here.'

From the vantage point of middle age I have some sense of what this period of Dad's life might have been like for him. At the time though it seemed to me that he was almost entirely uninterested that I was leaving home for the first time, and unconcerned about what might happen to me. I'm struck now by the memory of how numb to it all I was. It simply reinforced that I didn't matter to anyone. It was one more thing that forced me to run.

And so I left with a small brown suitcase containing some clothes and a few records that were of little use, given I had nowhere to live, never mind a stereo. I headed out of Wexford town and as soon as I reached the road to Dublin

I stuck out my thumb. I didn't have a penny on me and the only way I could get anywhere was by hitching a lift.

It was a grey January day. I was seriously depressed and alone with no idea of what was ahead of me. I was so alone and yet there was a release of sorts in that. At least I wouldn't have to hide how desperate and miserable I was and I wouldn't have to worry about being acceptable anymore.

When I got to Dublin I stayed with a friend for a week or so. She was at university and lived with a gang of other students in a house off-campus. Before long it became clear that her house-mates were not entirely happy about the idea of a long-term house guest, which was fair enough. I realised I would have to find work and a place to live. Apart from the fact I had no money to pay my way, I was finding living with students a constant reminder of the negative turn my life had taken. I was meant to be part of all this, and I wasn't.

So I left my case behind and headed off into Dublin to see if I could find work. Not such an easy proposition in 1984. Ireland was still in the grip of a decades-long recession and the only Celtic tiger to be found was in Dublin Zoo. Emigration and unemployment were the norm then, not iPods, perma-tans, SUVs and property investment. It was a time when churches were packed as we prayed for the intercession of the saints to help us find a house, a job, a spouse and a future. There were little or no opportunities, and we needed miracles to get by. It was a dismal time.

I couldn't find work because there was none to be found. I wandered the streets of Dublin, falling little by little out of step with normal society, further and further away from who I was meant to be and the life I was meant to live. I was looking for work at first, but in time it became just aimless walking. I would walk around at night, finding places to keep out of the cold and rain when I needed to, a doorway or an alleyway, somewhere quiet and hidden where no one would see how far I had fallen and how desperate I had become. I stayed away from other homeless people as I didn't see myself as one of them.

I had no contact with home at all. Dad's warning about finding work and paying my own way rang in my ears. I was scared that if he found out I hadn't got a job, I would be forced to go back, and I couldn't face that.

During the day I found places where I could sleep for a little while. The downstairs toilet of a Burger King restaurant on O'Connell Street was a good spot. I could go into a cubicle and lock the door, place the lid down on the seat, sit in the warmth and fall asleep for a while. I could wash my face and clean myself a little before I left, keeping up appearances, fitting in.

One day the toilets in Burger King weren't an option. One cubicle was out of order and when I locked myself in another to get some sleep it was only a matter of ten minutes before someone started knocking and asking me to hurry up. I left and went across the street to a public toilet hidden beneath the pavement in the centre of O'Connell Street. It was one of those old Victorian public toilets that have now all but vanished. I went down the stairs into the dark ceramic gloom and shut myself into a cubicle.

I needed to sleep so badly and this was the only place I might get some rest. The walls were covered in lurid graffiti advertising contacts from men seeking sex. The place smelled awful, a combination of stale urine, vomit and body odour. I was too exhausted to care and before long I slept.

When I woke up in the gloom and stink of the cubicle I could hear men talking outside. I waited until they were gone and then went out to wash and get myself together before heading back onto O'Connell Street. As I splashed water on my face and ran my wet hands through my hair, a man came over to the sink beside me. He nodded. I nodded back and started to dry my hands on my jacket. He was in his mid-thirties dressed in dark trousers, a sweater and a denim jacket. He had brown hair and was tall and thin.

'Do you want to do business?' he muttered. I looked at him blankly.

'Do you want to go in there?' he asked, nodding in the direction of an open cubicle.

I shook my head.

'How much then?' he asked before adding, 'I have a place.'

I didn't really hear the 'how much' bit, or understand what was being asked for and offered, though I knew he wanted me to have sex with him. All I heard was 'I have a place.' I was freaked out, but this might mean shelter for a while.

'Can I stay for the night?' I asked, hoping for a yes and the promise of a bed to sleep in and maybe even a bath.

'Yes,' he said and started up the stairs, motioning for me to follow.

And follow him I did. I followed him to a small room in Parnell Street, about five minutes' walk. We went up a narrow staircase and through a small door into a tiny bed-sit with old furniture.

I remember the wallpaper vividly. It was dark green with a pattern of large, stylised roses. They looked more like cabbages, which went rather well with the room's stale smell of boiled potatoes.

'All we need now is a picture of some boiled bacon,' I thought to myself, letting my mind wander as the man began to touch me.

'Cabbage wallpaper and boiled potatoes, just the bacon is missing,' I muttered to myself, forcing my mind to wander as the man started to open my trousers.

As he removed my clothes I kept staring at the wallpaper, concentrating on the bizarre pattern, trying to see what else I might discover there. I lay on my back, looking over the shoulders and head of the man, and when he was finished I turned on my side away from him, still gazing at the rose cabbages, my mind empty of anything else until I fell asleep moments later.

The next morning the man woke me up, telling me in his thick country accent that I had to go because he had to get to work. He was eager to get rid of me. He was uncomfortable and didn't look at me when we spoke. Heaven knows what his story was. He was certainly almost as wracked with shame as I was, a product of a time and a place that did not allow him to bring his sexuality out of the darkness, forcing him to hide in the stink and gloom of public toilets where he might pay for sex and never dream of love. I didn't care. I was glad of a bed for the night and even more appreciative of the shower I took in the shared bathroom off the stairs outside his room. Never before had a lukewarm trickle of water felt so luxurious. I was clean, or at least as clean as I could be.

After my shower I dressed and left without going back into his room or saying anything more. There was nothing to say.

I now had a way off the streets when I most needed it. So what if I had to let men have sex with me in order to get a bed for the night and a meal? What difference did that make? It wasn't as if I was worth anything better. This was what I knew, the one thing I could give that anyone seemed to want, so why the hell not? It was better than being cold and alone.

I'd never had the space to give much thought to my sexuality, but I assumed that my life would eventually lead to a wife, marriage and a family. I never considered that I might be gay. In my experiences so far, sex with men was not about intimacy, love or caring. It was about rape, abuse, exploitation and, worst of all, horrific feelings of guilt at my physical response to those acts. I'd come to distrust and despise my sexual self. I saw nothing good or pure or true about it. So when sex became a way out of homelessness and hunger, what did it matter? I placed no value on that part of myself anyway. My sexual self existed to be used and exploited; so why shouldn't I exploit it too?

I learned the places to go. As well as the toilet on O'Connell Street, though I hated it there and it closed in the evenings, there were various places, streets and corners. I would see other boys there, selling themselves; boys mostly in their late teens, dressed in tight jeans and tops and with bleached blond hair piled high. They looked and sounded more like girls. They even called each other by girls' names.

Donna and Paula are the two I remember most clearly. They screeched and laughed together as they stood on the street smoking and daring someone to approach them. Before long a car would pull up and one of them would clatter across the road, lean in the window for a moment before running around the other side of the car and hopping in with a wave to the other and a screech of goodbye.

I kept my distance, frightened they might see me and know I was like them, and scared I might become even more like them. I stayed on the edges of all this activity, waiting for someone to spot me and make an approach. It was safer, more hidden.

Also, I rarely got money. Well, actually, never. When I was approached I might agree to take money when it was offered but I was always insistent that I go back to their place and that I could stay the night. The next morning I wouldn't have the courage to ask for payment and they would never give it. Except once, when one man wrote me a cheque made out to cash for eight pounds and handed it to me before letting me out of his car as he drove back into town from his suburban home. I never cashed the cheque. I tried but the bank wanted identification and I didn't have any. So I guess I was technically never a prostitute since I was never paid. I didn't have the hard-nosed business head for it, unlike Paula and Donna. It's closer to the truth to say that I didn't have the self-respect for it; I thought I wasn't entitled to anything.

I always hoped that one of them might let me stay longer than one night. I hoped that one of them might see that I needed help and offer it. They didn't. I don't think it was because they were bad men, it was more that if a man goes to street corners looking for sex he isn't likely to be open to getting to know the life story of the person he picks up and offering them a leg up in the world.

I hungered for real human engagement. I was desperate for someone to really see me and connect with me as a human being. I was horribly lonely, and these encounters highlighted that loneliness.

# 8

# *On and Off the Streets*

I was desperate to get off the streets, to find a way to survive that didn't involve such exploitation and objectification. I'd been in Dublin for two months and on the streets for six weeks or so. I would get picked up maybe two or three times a week, which meant I got a bed to sleep in on those nights. The rest of the time I walked around all night and grabbed sleep wherever and whenever I could find shelter during the day.

Then, finally, I found a job. I saw an ad in the window of an Italian restaurant called The Spaghetti Inn off Grafton Street, looking for someone to work in the stillroom. I had no idea what that meant but I went in anyway. It turned out the job was making coffees and serving up desserts and wines to the waiters. I got the job. It paid ten pounds for a six-hour shift and included dinner, which was the perfect perk as far as I was concerned.

I learned how to make expert cappuccinos long before they became commonplace. I loved the smell of the coffee and the warm, sweet aroma of the milk as I frothed it with jets of steam, the clatter of cups and saucers and the glistening golden crème caramels that I turned out onto plates and served across the counter to the waiters. I loved the taste of piping hot pasta, spaghetti Bolognese, lasagne or tagliatelle carabonara, served with garlic bread and parmesan cheese. More than anything else I loved the ten pound note I got at the end of every shift. It was enough to pay for a room and a bed to myself for one night, and a cooked breakfast and hot shower the next morning. And no one to satisfy in order to get it.

I was so happy to go and do a job, do it well and be paid for honest work. The hustle and bustle of the place made me feel normal, properly part of the world around me rather than existing on the dark edges, beyond 'decent' people. When I was handed my pay, I felt good, worth something, valid. I felt hopeful for the first time in years, as if I might finally have found a way to lift myself out of the grim, dank hole I'd become trapped in. It wasn't just a job, it was hope.

If I got five shifts a week it meant that I only had to cope with the streets for two nights a week. And since I also got a share of the tips I could sometimes pay for a room more than five nights a week. The only problem was that I was in effect running to stand still. A shift meant I had somewhere to sleep that night and a meal, but it cost everything I earned to pay for a bed. I decided I would have to try and save enough money to pay a deposit and a week's rent in advance for a bed-sit somewhere. I started saving my tips. One week I got six shifts, which gave me the last ten pounds I needed to finally look for a bed-sit.

That day I bought the *Evening Herald* and opened the pages to pore over the classified ads in the 'room to rent' section. There were several bed-sits I could afford. Most were about fifteen to twenty pounds per week with a week's rent in advance and a week's rent as deposit. I had forty two pounds saved and called a number offering a bed-sit with a kitchenette and a shared bathroom, in Drumcondra on the north side of Dublin. The landlord agreed to meet me there within the hour.

This was a new area for me, it felt nice though and homely enough, like a proper neighbourhood. The houses were all built from red brick with black iron railings along the front gardens. They looked solid and warm. The bed-sit was on the ground floor at the back of a house just off the main road. It was a decent-sized room with a bed, an armchair and a kitchenette hidden away in a wardrobe. You opened the doors and there was a small fridge, a sink and a tiny cooker with two electric rings and an oven underneath. It had saucepans, cutlery, a kettle ... everything I might need. The room was a bit dark and the furniture and fittings faded and rather ancient but it was dry and warm and it was about to be mine. I took it. I had a place to live.

It was a great moment. I'd managed to get myself off the streets and had a place to live and a job. I collected my suitcase from my friend's student house and unpacked my few possessions in my new home. Everything was looking up.

But things went wrong a few months later. I had glandular fever, at least that's what my friend Alicia from Wexford thought when I went back to see her to ask for help. I wasn't able to work, and without the wages from my job I couldn't pay my rent. I was also really sick. I couldn't eat and I was exhausted all the time. I had a fever as well as awful headaches and swollen lumps in my neck, armpits and groin. I made it to Alicia's house and she kept me there for two weeks, which passed in a blur. I slept a lot, didn't eat and was in a daze most of the time.

When I returned to the house in Drumcondra I was able to get in the front door but my key to my room didn't work. I rang the landlord who told me he'd kept the room for me for the first week I was gone as my deposit paid for that week's rent, but that when I hadn't paid the rent or called the next week he'd packed my case, placed it in the hallway and changed the lock. The room was still available but if I wanted it I would have to pay the week's rent I had missed, another week in advance and another week's rent as deposit. That was over fifty pounds and I didn't have it. On top of that my suitcase, which he'd left in the hallway, was gone. I now had nowhere to live and possessed nothing, apart from the clothes I was standing in.

I was back on the streets, homeless and broke once again. This time though I was determined not to stay there. I applied for work everywhere I could. My job at The Spaghetti Inn was gone, but they promised to take me back if another became available. At night I slept in parks, on benches and beneath bushes. Eventually, in an effort to avoid sinking further, I went to the local Health Board Social Welfare office to ask for help.

I walked up to a wooden hatch behind which I could see three women working in an office. I rang a doorbell stuck to the hatch. A jaded-looking woman came over.

'Yes.'

'I need some help, please. I have nowhere to live and no money.'

She peered at me through thick glasses. 'What age are you, what's your date of birth?'

'Seventeen, I was born on July fifteenth 1966.'

'You have to be eighteen before you can claim any kind of welfare. Why are you here anyway? Why don't you go home to your parents?'

'I can't go home. I can't go back. I need help.'

'You have to go home,' she replied, already looking away and drawing the conversation to a close. 'Until you're eighteen you are your parents' responsibility, the State cannot provide for you.'

She walked away from the hatch, plonking herself down wearily behind her desk and reaching out to a pile of files.

I stood there, not knowing what to do. I wanted to cry, but wouldn't. I desperately needed help, but it appeared no one was willing to offer me any support. I turned and walked back out onto the busy road as cars and buses rattled by. I had nowhere to go, and nothing to do, nothing I could do. People walked by me, hurrying along, no doubt going to work, or school or home. Maybe I *should* go home?

But that was impossible for me. I'd moved so far beyond what might ever be acceptable to my Dad and to my family. There was no going back, not now and probably never.

It was the day before St Patrick's Day 1984. The next day I wandered along O'Connell Street and watched as crowds gathered for the parade to celebrate the national holiday. Everywhere I looked there were families, mams and dads and their children, walking together or straining to see the parade over the crowds lining the street. There were gangs of friends, people my own age, jostling each other, laughing and joking together and enjoying the spectacle, having fun. I had never felt so alone.

After the parade passed and the crowds cleared, I was still there, alone in the debris of other people's fun. I stood in the street, watching the last few families leave, children hoisted high on their fathers' shoulders as food wrappers and empty drink cans blew along the street.

I thought of my own family and wondered how they were and what they might be doing. I stepped into a telephone booth and dialled the number of our house back in Wexford. The phone rang and rang, and then it was picked up.

'Hello,' it was my brother John. The payphone beeped insistently, demanding ten pence I didn't have, even had I felt able to use it. I knew I couldn't speak to him but I just wanted to hear a voice I knew, someone safe and familiar, someone I loved.

'Hello, hello, who is this?'

A moment later the connection was cut and I was back on the street.

I'd fallen so far, so very far from my old life back on the farm. At least back then there was something good and beautiful to be found somewhere in my life. I had nature, my surroundings and the animals. I felt like I belonged there and connected to others. I felt loved and I loved. I missed my family so much, my mother, my siblings and Dad. The boy who rose early and threw his leg eagerly over his saddle and pedalled off to serve Mass on a bright, cold spring morning seemed dead to me. I could hardly imagine myself going to a church now. I was unworthy, foul and fallen.

I struggled to cope and before long I was forced to go back to finding someone who would let me stay with him in exchange for sex. It was different this time though; I made it clear that I wasn't looking for money, that I wasn't for sale. That night I met a man; let's call him Tom. He did want me to sleep with him that first night, but once he found out I was homeless he didn't just wave me off back onto the streets the next day.

Tom was a good guy. He let me stay at this flat for a few nights and then allowed me to sleep on the floor of his office for a week or two. It was shelter, and I was off the streets again.

He also helped me find a job, introducing me to Pat who ran a restaurant on Dame Street, near Dublin Castle. Pat offered me a job as a waiter. I took it gratefully, along with the offer of a hot bath and a clean bed from Pat who lived nearby with his girlfriend.

I remember being taken aback that Pat didn't seem to want anything from me in exchange for his generosity. He let me stay there for a few nights and even gave me a cash advance to get some clothes and clean myself up. That first night in their home was a godsend.

All the way to his house I was wondering if this could possibly be as good as it seemed. Surely he wasn't just doing all this to be nice to me? There had to be a catch. Maybe all that talk of his 'girlfriend' was just a load of rubbish to get me to go back to his place with him? Surely he was just like the rest of the men who offered to help me, just like Fortune?

When we got to his house I followed him in.

'I'm home,' he called, and to my relief a cheery female voice called back.

'I'm just finishing dinner,' she said. 'Are you both hungry?'

I nearly wept with relief. It was true! I was going to get a meal, a bath, a clean bed to myself and even clean clothes and I had a new job. I was beside myself.

A moment later I met Jean, a woman with twinkly eyes and an easy smile. She showed me their spare room where I would sleep and suggested that I wash my hands then come down to the kitchen for dinner.

It was amazing. That meal of roast chicken, mashed potatoes and two veg was a gourmet experience for me. It was the first home-cooked meal I'd eaten in months.

Later that night, I went to take a bath and was appalled by the stink of my feet and the open sores between my toes. My one pair of socks was stuck to my feet, and as I peeled them off I felt them tear at my skin. I was good at hiding the fact I was destitute, but this proved to me that I couldn't have hidden it forever.

I had a steaming hot bath then slipped between crisp sheets and slept like a baby. The next morning I was given a clean white shirt, black trousers and new socks to wear for my first day at work. With my first week's wages I had enough to take another bed-sit, this time in Rathmines, not too far from work.

At last I'd been given a break. I was off the streets and no longer had to let myself be used just to have a place to sleep. I was becoming self-sufficient, loving work and even making friends. It was almost too much to take in. But it was real. It was the end of living on the streets and the end of sex with people I didn't want to have sex with. I finally had some space, some safety in which I could begin to recover from all that had happened.

For the first time in ages I found myself thinking ahead a little, planning what I would do the next day, or later in the week even. On the streets that hadn't ever been a possibility.

# 9

# Coming Out

On the same street as Pat's restaurant was a pub called The Viking. It was a gay pub and lots of its customers came into the restaurant at night to eat after closing time. They were a really nice bunch of people, friendly and fun. I started to get to know a few of them and had a great banter with them all. They were also great tippers, so all the staff loved them. I still hadn't begun to address the question of my own sexuality, but slowly that began to happen, albeit with a little encouragement from others.

Homosexuality was still illegal in Ireland at that point, under the 1861 Offences Against the Person Act and the 1885 Criminal Law (Amendment) Act. Both laws were originally passed by the UK Parliament before Irish independence. Despite the fact that the same legislation was repealed in the UK in 1967, it remained in force in Ireland. The penalties under those Acts ranged from fines or a year's imprisonment with hard labour to life imprisonment.

There were a few gay pubs and a community-based club in Dublin but homosexuality was still very much taboo and a crime. There was, however, a campaign running that sought decriminalisation. Pressure was building for change, but conservative forces in the courts, Church and politics were ranged against progress.

In 1983, the year before I moved to Dublin, gay rights campaigner David Norris brought a case to the Irish Supreme Court seeking to have the laws, which criminalised homosexuality, declared unconstitutional. The court ruled against him. In a three to two majority ruling which referred to the 'Christian and democratic nature of the Irish State', the court declared that criminalisation served public health and the institution of marriage. It would be a further five years before David Norris got a hearing before the European Court of Human Rights, which finally ruled in 1988 that the Irish law contravened the European Convention on Human Rights. Five more years passed before decriminalisation finally happened.

By a rather poetic coincidence, David Norris' barrister in his legal battle was Senator Mary Robinson. Mary represented David before the European Courts. She was elected President of Ireland in 1990 and it was she who signed into law the act decriminalising homosexuality in 1993.

In fact two future Irish presidents were centrally involved with the campaign. President Mary McAleese, who succeeded Mary Robinson in 1997, was a founder of the Campaign for Homosexual Law Reform (with David Norris in the 1970s) and the campaign's first legal adviser.

David Norris was himself elected to Seanad Éireann, the upper house of the Irish Parliament, in 1987 where he has championed human rights issues for more than two decades.

Back in 1983 there was no sense that such progressive reform was even possible. Gay people were invisible in the main and kept to themselves, gathering in gay pubs and the one club in Dublin at the time, finding safe places where they could socialise together.

There was lots of banter and craic with the crowd from The Viking when they came in to eat at the restaurant. They were fun and flirty, and I started to enjoy their company, the fun and silliness of it all. They even had a language of their own.

'Vada the eek on him, he's bona,' a guy said one night as I walked by.

This was met by nods and giggles around the table.

'What are you on about?' I asked.

'It's Polari, gay speak, don't you know? He said you have a nice face. Vada means look, eek is face and bona is good.'

I laughed and walked off. Polari, a gay language, how mad was that?

Before long I was playing along with them all. If someone came in wearing a new outfit, I would chirp up, 'Love the drag [*clothes*].'

When I got to a table of people I knew it would be 'What's the dish [*gossip*] lads, any news?'

And there was always news, always some kind of scandal about who was seeing who, who had broken up, who was heartbroken this week and who was madly in love. It was great fun.

Whether or not I was gay was the subject of feverish speculation among some of that gang.

'He definitely is, definitely.'

'You are, aren't you, you are.'

I just laughed, enjoying my newfound man of mystery status.

Tom was still around. He ate lunch at the restaurant almost every day and we became friendly. We weren't involved sexually in any way, we just chatted when he came in.

One day he asked me when was I actually going to come out properly.

I looked at him a bit stunned. 'That's pretty upfront.'

'Well, all things considered, I think I have enough inside information to be entitled to ask the question,' he retorted.

'True. But I really haven't thought about it much.'

A blatant lie, I had of course started to consider that I might belong to this group, this new community whose company I enjoyed so much.

'I know it's been tough,' Tom said, 'but things are looking up for you now. Maybe it's time to take the next step, find out who you are, have some fun and live a little.'

'Maybe.'

I agreed to go for a drink with Tom a couple of nights later. I didn't want to walk into The Viking on my own, to all the heckling and calls of 'I knew it' that I expected to hear on my debut there. Tom knew that and offered to meet me and bring me there for a drink, as a friend. There was no question of anything happening between us, he was just a nice guy who wanted to help. I was grateful, but still nervous about coming out.

In the end I chickened out. I didn't go with Tom, telling him I had stuff to do at home.

'Don't tell me, you have to wash your hair,' he quipped, smiling broadly. 'It's fine, another time. Whenever you're ready, let me know.'

I was annoyed with myself. I was fed up of working and heading straight home. I wanted a life and I wanted to find out more about the gay scene, to discover whether or not I did fit in.

The next night as I left work I decided on the spur of the moment to go to Flikkers, Dublin's only gay club. I was lonely and didn't want to go back to my empty room again.

It was run by the NGF (National Gay Federation). The building was down a quiet side street behind the Irish Central Bank just off Dame Street where I worked. That area, Temple Bar, is now the scene of thousands of drunken hen and stag nights, but back then it was an undeveloped collection of second-hand shops and cobbled side streets.

I had no idea what to expect from the club, only that they ran club nights or discos three times a week, on Wednesday, Friday and Saturday nights. I rang a bell on the painted wooden door and a man showed me in with a welcoming smile. Just inside the door was a desk in an open area where I paid my entrance fee. People were sitting around downstairs chatting, laughing and drinking coffee, and I could hear the music pumping out from somewhere upstairs.

I followed the sound and the flicker of flashing lights. Just up the stairs was the coffee bar where a couple of guys my own age were working. It turned out the club didn't have an alcohol licence; it couldn't get one, and instead served tea, coffee and soft drinks. To the right, towards the back of the building was the dance floor and positioned above the dance floor, a podium where the DJ worked.

The music was loud and rhythmical, pulsating through the building as lights flashed and the crowd danced. I stood in the corner of the room, staring at all the men dancing out on the floor. I was stunned. First of all, they looked remarkably normal. Secondly, they seemed to be having a really good time. There was a euphoric air to the place, nothing dark or seedy, nothing rancid or rotten. There they were dancing, in groups and in pairs, spinning and moving, swaying and stomping to music that blared from the podium as the DJ spun his magic, twirling and whooping along himself. I stood rooted to the spot; there was no shame here, no sense of guilt. And there were so many people ... and all of them were gay. After years of isolation and darkness, it was a lot to take in. It felt like an arrival in a place where I might belong. It felt free.

That moment marked the end of a darkening period in my life. I had managed to escape the streets, found some kind of security and now I'd found a place where I might belong, with people I could relate to in a way I had never imagined. Months earlier as I wandered the streets destitute and hopeless, I thought I was lost. Instead, finding this community allowed me to let go of that life and embrace something altogether more hopeful and joyous.

I got to know people and made friends. It was a good time, a great time even, though I remained entirely estranged from my family. I couldn't go back there, not yet. But I was happier than I'd been in many, many years.

I was still too raw from all that had happened in Dublin to really understand it, so I disowned it and all the other dark parts of my history. I didn't reinvent myself especially. My life story as I told it to people was true, it was just that I left out anything I couldn't deal with. I lied by omission and stayed safe by denying a past I feared would mark me as unlovable and unacceptable.

What I recognise above all is that once I found myself in a space that was safe, I began to make decisions that were healthy and life-affirming rather than destructive and damaging. For instance, I stepped back from sex. It wasn't a conscious decision, I just stopped having sex with anyone and everyone who demanded it of me. Instead it became a choice, and not a means of survival. I valued myself on a sexual level for the first time, and sex would become something mutual, a shared experience between two people who made positive and informed choices.

A few months later, quite by chance, a school friend came into the restaurant. I was a little rattled to see someone from home. We chatted for a while, but I avoided getting into any real conversation. I didn't give much away about what I'd been up to since leaving Wexford.

A week or so later I arrived at work to hear that my sister Barbara had been in looking for me. My school friend had met her back in Wexford and told her where I was working. Barbara was told that if she came back during my shift she'd catch me. I was delighted and terrified. Delighted that I might see her and terrified of the questions she might ask. More than anything else I was terrified that I might have to go home to Wexford.

She came in a few hours later. We couldn't really talk as I was working. Instead, we agreed that I would go to see her at her place later in the week. She was attending Maynooth University, thirty minutes or so away by train, and shared a house there with other students.

I caught the train from Dublin's Connolly Station to Maynooth. Barbara met me from the train and we went to have a drink with some friends of hers. A few hours later we ended up back at her place. One by one everyone went to bed and finally we got to talk.

I was unsure about what I should tell Barbara about the months since I left Wexford and how I'd been living. In the end I decided to say as little as possible and let her take the lead.

We sat in her living room, in front of the fire. I was really glad to see her. She was my big sister, and I'd always admired and looked up to her. I'd always been willing to do anything for her. This included, aged fourteen, going into the local shop to buy her tampons and Mills & Boon novels. I was spared the indignity of it by not fully knowing what I was buying for her.

She told me things were tough at home, that Dad's business had shut down and he was trying to start from scratch again. John was now working with him and the two of them were planning to start up a new business together. Money was tight. Mam and the three younger kids were still in India and were due back that September. Barbara had been writing to them and they seemed to be doing well enough.

As we talked I decided to open up a bit. I looked at her during a lull in the conversation and saw the sister I loved and trusted, and realised I wanted to let go of some secrets.

'I think I'm gay,' I said.

Barbara hesitated for a moment, took a breath and looked at me.

'What?'

'I think I'm gay,' I repeated. 'I don't think I will ever get married and have kids.'

'Why do you think that? Has something happened?'

'Father Fortune,' I replied, shocked that I'd said it out loud.

'What do you mean Colm? What are you saying?'

'Something happened with Father Fortune, and I think I'm gay.'

'When?'

'Lots of times, every time he took me away with him. I couldn't say. I wanted to, but I couldn't.'

'Why not, why didn't you say?'

'I was scared, scared of what Dad would think. Scared about what it meant, scared it meant that that's what I was.'

Barbara looked at me closely. She looked concerned, shocked and surprised, but most of all concerned. She didn't shout at me or call me names.

'Are you OK?' she asked gently.

'I think so. I'm not sure what to do, but I think I'm OK now.'

We chatted for a bit more, then Barbara said she had to get to bed as she had lectures the next morning. She made me up a bed on the couch, gave me a big hug and headed off to her room.

The next morning the house was abuzz as Barbara and her housemates ran about grabbing books and breakfast. In the busyness of it all we didn't get a chance to talk. We walked in a gang into town and they dropped me at the station on their way to college.

Barbara was going home for the weekend and I promised to call her the next week. 'Don't worry,' she said giving me a hug goodbye, 'everything will be fine.'

I got on the train and immediately began to panic about having told my dirty secret. It wasn't that I didn't trust

Barbara, more that I was terrified of what might happen now that it was out. What if she told Dad? I could hardly expect her to keep this to herself. What if Fortune found out I had told? What would he do to me? By the time I got back to Dublin I was in a cold sweat and scared stiff of the possible consequences of breaking my long silence.

I spent the next week waiting for the sky to fall in. I fully expected Dad, or Fortune or even the police to turn up at work and take me away. I was frightened out of my mind. But nothing happened. No one came to the restaurant looking for me. I didn't call Barbara as I'd promised because I was in a state. I couldn't face her. In my fear and panic I forgot about how lovely she'd been to me and instead was caught up in imagined scenarios involving the police, the Church, Fortune, Dad and every other authority who would damn me to hell forever because of what I had done and what I had become.

A week later I quit my job. I decided to run, to avoid facing anyone at home. Work was the one place they could find me.

I found a new job working for a fundraising company that raised money for a disability charity. I worked on the street and door-to-door for a while and put all thoughts of home and family from my mind. Denial once again came to my rescue.

Before long I was back in full swing. I got more involved in the NGF, volunteering to work in the coffee bar on club nights. I was also a regular at the NGF youth group held every Sunday afternoon in the same building as the club. The group was a great space: safe, empowering, interesting, a place where young gay men and lesbians, many still living at home, could get together and talk, dance, become more informed and find mutual support. Many of the young people who came along also brought straight friends. It was a really healthy, positive environment and I felt very much at home.

There was a lot of amazing work done there, including early education programmes on the emergence of AIDS. At that point it was seen as a 'gay disease' and governments were entirely uninterested in education and prevention initiatives. It wasn't affecting 'normal society', therefore it didn't matter. The NGF youth group provided education and information, preaching the safe sex message to all the young people who attended the group and opening up important conversations about making healthy choices when it came to becoming sexually active.

There were a few of us who always made sure new people were welcomed and made comfortable. We all remembered the first time we walked into the building and knew the difference a friendly face could make. It was a very lively group, which could be intimidating for new people.

One Sunday, I happened to be looking around the room when my eyes fell on a new face. I made it my business to go over and say hello. Apart from being gorgeous, he also looked rather nervous and my heart went out to him. He was sitting alone, glancing around apprehensively as mayhem ensued about him. I went over.

'Hi. You OK?'

He looked at me and smiled a little anxiously.

'I think so.'

'It's all a bit loud sometimes,' I said, 'but we're all normal enough really, once you get to know us.'

He smiled again. I grinned back.

'So,' he said, 'you're ... ?'

'Colm.'

'I'm Alan.'

'Hi.'

I was bad at this, really bad. Then I remembered that I was meant to be the welcome committee. 'You want a coffee, or a coke or something?'

'Sure.'

We arranged to meet up again that night as he said he wanted to come back to the club. And we started dating, a new experience for me.

It was amazing. He was a year younger than me, sweet, handsome and great fun. It was everything a first love should be: tender and tentative, passionate and exhilarating, warm and loving, a real process of discovery for both of us. It was the kind of romance that most people take for granted as they grow up, but something I had never imagined.

Above all it was safe. There were no power plays, we were equals and no one was exploiting anyone.

We dated for several months and then broke up over something silly. I can't even remember why now. It was all very dramatic. I was heartbroken and wandered around like a lovesick puppy for weeks, driving my friends mad. I can't help but smile as I look back to that time. Even the break-up makes me smile. I'm grateful for the entire experience, the highs of it, the sweetness and the even the bittersweet break-up. It was all so normal, so lovely and normal.

My relationship with Alan taught me that I could love. It taught me that sex was more than a genital act, that it could be a joyful shared experience. I discovered my sexuality as something alive and vibrant, something vital, without guilt or shame. And it was fun!

By the time I broke up with Alan I was once again without work. I'd held a few different jobs at this stage, as a fundraiser, in a wine bar, even in a hair salon, but none of them lasted very long. Unemployed again I struggled to find work. Ireland remained in its recession and very little work was available. By now I was eighteen and finally entitled to claim welfare benefits. I was able to claim rent supplement and income support, which gave me enough to live on. At least it gave me enough to afford to go out a few nights a week, buy a drink and go to the club. I continued to volunteer at the club, that way I got in free at least.

By the end of 1985 I was getting restless. I'd been away from home for almost two years and had no contact with my family since talking to Barbara more than a year earlier. I didn't allow myself to think about them. There was nothing I could do to make things better and fix everything. Thinking about them just hurt.

I'd entirely reinvented my life. Gone was the small-town boy who had fled abuse and despair. I was alive, brash and full of hope and energy. I embraced this new life, I was gay and had found love for the first time. Life was now about music, clothes, going out and finding love. I had escaped all that I was and I was beginning to like who I was becoming. Fortune was gone, exiled to the dark place at the back of my mind.

But I knew that if I was to continue my voyage of adventure and reinvention then I needed new places to explore. I knew it was time to move on.

A friend had spent a few months in London and offered to get me a room in a house he'd lived in over there. It was a chance to try somewhere new and I decided to grab it. And so, in February 1986, I got on the Dun Laoghaire to Holyhead ferry then travelled on to London by cross-country bus, courtesy of my last weekly welfare payment.

# 10

# Bright Lights

It was a whole new world. Moving to Dublin from Wexford had been a big change, but London was on an entirely different scale. A real twenty-four hour city, there was always something to do or see. Ireland was still a nation of emigrants back then and very much a mono-cultural society. London was alive and buzzing, a melting pot of sounds and smells and cultures. I loved it from the moment I arrived.

I thought, when I first got there, that I might stay for a few months, or at most a few years. It was only the second time I'd ever been outside Ireland, the previous time also being a visit to London when I was in sixth class back in primary school in Wexford.

The bus ride, first across Wales and then England, took an age. I thought it would never come to an end. We travelled overnight through town after town, and I hadn't a clue where we were most of the time.

Then, as morning broke, we entered another built-up area and I saw a policeman on patrol wearing one of those weird-shaped London police hats. I had arrived!

I stepped off the bus and was met by the landlord of the house I would stay in. I felt once again like a very small-town boy indeed. London seemed vast, even bigger than I remembered. I was excited and exhilarated, pleased to have finally arrived.

The landlord arranged a room for me in the house he owned in Earls Court. It was a massive building on the corner of Warwick Road, backing onto the busy A4, the dual carriageway leading into the centre of the city. There were five floors in the house, each divided into individual rooms to let with shared kitchens and bathrooms.

Over thirty guys lived in the house, all of us gay. It was known locally as 'Fairy Towers'. My first room was an attic room known as Esmerelda's. For some bizarre reason I shared a kitchen and bathroom with the basement floor, which meant I had to heft up and down ten flights of stairs to use the kitchen or if I needed a pee in the middle of the night.

The house was a mad place. Every single one of us had come to London to get away from something, usually a small town or a difficult family. But in Earls Court, we were at the epicentre of the London gay scene. Someone in the house always knew someone who was throwing the best party, or could get tickets to a great club night. There was always someone to head out to the pub or go clubbing with. It was a riot.

Massive clubs like Heaven on Charing Cross and the Hippodrome on Monday nights drew huge crowds. Heaven especially, which was open until six in the morning, was at the cutting edge of London's emerging dance culture. It was a fantastic cathedral of a place, with enormous lighting rigs and various levels of bars and dance floors. I'd never seen anything like it.

I loved the music, the environment, the buzz of it all. My friends and I would dance all night, having a ball, then leave at six in the morning and head off back to someone or other's place to listen to more music and wind down after a mad night out. I was a very, very long way away from the farm!

My first job was working on the coat check in a club called Copa's on Earls Court Road. It was a well-known venue and packed every night. I checked coats and jackets and made a killing in tips. I only had to work three nights a week to make enough to live on and have a great social life. It was a dream start.

Later, I got work with a temp agency, usually as a waiter in hotels or as a barman. There was no shortage of shifts so I made decent money and continued to have a good social life. Then I was offered a full-time job in a hotel, as a supervisor in the restaurant.

Life took on a more regular routine then. I was working shifts on a rota, rather than just calling the agency whenever I wanted to work. It was fun though, I enjoyed the job and was pleased to have a role with some responsibility. I was twenty, time perhaps to start thinking about a career.

My family were on my mind a lot. I was happy, but now I was really beginning to miss them and wonder how they were. I thought that Mam and my three youngest siblings, Deirdre, Joy and Eamon, were probably home by then, but I didn't know for sure. I didn't know how any of them were.

I'd settled a bit, had a job and was doing well, so I decided it was time to make contact.

I wrote a long letter home. I explained where I was and that I was well and safe. I told them about my job, that I had plans to do better and that I missed them all. Then I talked about being gay. I asked them to remember I was their son, their brother and that I loved them, that hadn't changed and I hoped they could still love me too. I asked them to contact me, and said I wanted to see them soon.

I put my return address on the back of the envelope, stuck a stamp on it and walked down the street to the bright red pillar box. I stood there for a moment, reading the times of the next collection. It was 11am and the next collection was at 5pm. I worked out that the letter would arrive at my family home in Wexford in the morning in two days' time. I imagined the postman driving up the road, stepping out of his van and pushing a pile of letters, mine included, through the letterbox.

I imagined them landing with a soft whoosh on the carpet inside the front door, before someone, Mam maybe, walked by and picked them up. I saw her shuffle through the letters, seeing the usual bills and business letters, before she paused at my blue Belvedere Bond envelope, a stamp showing the Queen's head with a date mark smudging her profile. I imagined Mam's intake of breath as she read the return address when she flipped over the envelope. And then ... who knew? That's as much as I could imagine. I had no idea how she might react to my letter, but I needed to send it anyway.

My hand was shaking as I held the letter to the slot at the top of the pillar box. I couldn't let go. Then I took a really deep breath and released the letter. My stomach lurched as I heard it flutter down and land on the waiting pile.

I started to panic. What the hell had I done? I had to get the letter back! What did I think would happen when they got it? After all, if they wanted me back then surely they would have looked for me? The fact that they hadn't should have told me they didn't want to. And now I'd written to them, how stupid was I? I was in danger of opening up all that old hurt just as I was getting my life sorted.

I stood there berating myself for about twenty minutes, trying to work out what to do next. I considered waiting for the postman and then asking for the letter back. But it would be six hours before he got here. I could come back … except I knew he wouldn't let me have the letter. Once it had been posted it had to be delivered, he wouldn't be allowed to give it back to me. There was nothing I could do about it now.

I went back to the house and tried as best I could to get on with things as normal. Then four days later, my letter slid back under my door. It had been returned, stamped 'Return to Sender. No longer at this address.'

I was both dismayed and relieved. My family had moved, heaven knew where to. I had no chance of finding them now, not unless I went back to Wexford and looked for them. And I wasn't going back there any time soon. I was worried about them, wondering why they'd moved, what they were thinking about me, and most especially, if they had moved, why they hadn't tried to find me or left a forwarding address in case I tried to come home.

At the same time, the return of my letter spared me the agony of a direct rejection. At least I knew I was still safe. I breathed a sigh of relief, tore up the letter and put everything behind me once again.

In early 1987 I was offered a job in a hotel in Bath, in the south-west of England. My former manager from the hotel in London had moved there and was looking for an assistant. It was a great opportunity and I decided to take it.

Bath is a gorgeous place, a Georgian city like Dublin, with rows and rows of beautiful terraces, all built from Bath stone, a kind of limestone. The town was very proud and protective of its architectural heritage and practically every building is listed. Situated on the River Avon, just where the Kennet and Avon Canal join the river, it is a truly lovely and very English city.

I settled in well, enjoyed my new job and made friends with the staff. All the local hotel staff generally socialised together, there was an OK local club and lots of very quaint pubs, but London it wasn't. After the buzz of the capital, I took a little time to adapt.

There was no gay scene of note in Bath, which to be honest didn't bother me especially. I was happy for the break from all the manic partying and clubbing, content to slow it down for a while.

In late January that year I decided to head back to Dublin to see friends. I'd only been back once since I left and I was eager to catch up with old friends.

While I was there I met up with Alan. I was pleased to see him, pleased we were still on friendly terms, though I still had a bit of a thing for him. We were out for a drink one night when I ran into someone from home. Stephen was the older brother of a boy I went to school with.

He gave me a wave and made his way across the crowded bar towards me, looking eager to talk. I was freaking out a little; I hadn't seen anyone from Wexford for a long time. What did he want?

'How are you? I haven't seen you in ages. I have news for you. You are about to become an uncle.'

I was stunned. This was my first news from home since I'd seen Barbara that night in Maynooth three years earlier.

'Barbara is having a baby?'

'No, Deirdre is.'

The news floored me. The last time I'd seen Deirdre she was fourteen years old and heading off to an ashram in India. Now she was having a baby?

'There's more,' said Stephen. 'It's Terry's baby.'

'Terry? Terry your brother?'

'Yeah.'

Stephen told me that Deirdre had been having a rough time of it. My father's plans for me hadn't included being gay, homeless and all the rest of it. And his plans for Deirdre certainly hadn't included becoming a single mother at eighteen. She'd moved out and was staying with friends until she had the baby.

I decided on the spot that I was going home the next day. I wanted to see that Deirdre was all right. Being a young, single mother in small-town Ireland in 1987 wasn't easy. There was a lot of stigma still, and it would be very tough to cope with that. I loved Deirdre dearly. She was a loving and gentle girl with a big heart. I couldn't bear the thought of her being alone and having to deal with all of that. I suppose looking back I identified with her too, as the object of both societal and parental disapproval. I knew how that felt, and I knew how to get away from it too.

I made up my mind that if Deirdre wasn't OK, then I would get her out of there. She could always come back to London with me and I could help her manage somehow.

The next day I hopped on a train. I was determined to find Deirdre and didn't give much thought to seeing everyone else until I started to get near Wexford. As I gazed out the window and the towns rolled by, I realised I was actually going home. A short time later I looked out across the reed beds that line the River Slaney. I was only minutes from Wexford and started to feel really anxious.

I stepped off the train at Wexford station. It was all so familiar. I walked along the platform and out into the square, half expecting to run straight into someone I knew. Luckily, I didn't. I needed to get my bearings first.

Stephen's youngest brother Colin was working in a fast-food restaurant on the Quays in Wexford. Stephen told me to go and see him when I got to Wexford. He was good friends with Deirdre and would know where she was.

I walked the five minutes or so to the restaurant. Colin was a year below me in school and recognised me as soon as I came in. I asked him about Deirdre: Where was she? When was the baby due?

It turned out Deirdre had already had her baby, a little girl, a week earlier. She was staying with Colin's parents while she waited to move into a flat she'd just rented in the town.

Colin arranged for a friend of his to bring me straight over to see Deirdre. His mother Kathleen brought me into the living room and there was Dee, looking gorgeous and maternal with her baby daughter in a rocker beside her. She was busy with the baby and didn't hear me come in.

'Deirdre,' Kathleen said with a big grin on her face, 'there's someone here to see you.'

Her face lit up with a huge smile as her eyes filled with tears.

'Colm, Colm, it's you.'

I reached down and we gave each other a huge hug, squeezing tight.

'It's me,' I said.

'Meet your niece,' Deirdre said, laughing with a shaky and emotional voice.

It was great to see her. She was doing OK, as was Ashleigh, her beautiful blue-eyed, blonde baby girl.

I stayed on a mattress on the floor of her new flat that night. I'd spent the day catching up on three years of news from Deirdre. I discovered that she, along with Mam, Joy and Eamon, had returned from India as planned in late 1984. They had no idea where I was, only that I'd gone to Dublin and lost touch. Dee had tried to find me a few times, putting out an appeal on national radio, the 'Gerry Ryan Show', but to no avail. I hadn't heard it, though was heartened to know that she'd been trying to find me.

Things had been tough. Dad's business had failed and the family home sold. Mam had left with Joy and moved to Cork, a few hours away. Barbara had finished university and was now working. John and Eamon were living with Dad in a flat over a shop on Wexford's Main Street. Eamon was still in school, Dad and John were working together, in a new business they were trying to get off the ground.

Barbara had told John about Fortune and about me being gay, and together they told Dad. It had always been Barbara's burden as the eldest to be the responsible one and deal with such difficult issues. Everyone knew now, but it had never been discussed after that as far as Deirdre knew.

The next day I went to see John and Eamon. It was great to see them again. Eamon was only eleven when I last saw him. Now he was fifteen and growing up fast. John was the same as ever, slagging me off good-naturedly, laughing and gently ribbing me. I'd changed quite a lot. I was taller, much slimmer and had long thick hair, very 1980s, with earrings in my left ear, all very New Romantic.

I was watching carefully, listening to every word, waiting to hear some indication of how they felt about me and what they knew.

Dee stood up. 'Has anyone seen my handbag?' She needed something for the baby.

'Your handbag,' Eamon said with a grin. 'Which one is it? I thought that one over there was Colm's.' And he started to giggle.

When Eamon laughs, no matter how silly the joke, everyone has to join in. He laughs with his whole body, his shoulders shake and he cracks up. He finds himself very funny does Eamon. And he is. He rarely gets to the punchline when telling a joke, he just loses control, shaking with laughter as tears roll down his cheeks and he tries to catch his breath and finish his story. The joke is never quite as entertaining as Eamon telling it.

So there we all were, laughing along with Eamon. The nerve of him, breaking the tension of the moment and naming out loud the elephant in the room. I was delighted; that was that over with, at least with my brothers and Deirdre.

Then we heard the front door open. Heavy footsteps up to the kitchen on the floor below the living room.

'It's Dad,' John said. 'He's home for lunch and to collect me to head back to work.'

I could hear Dad down in the kitchen, moving about and opening the fridge. I realised I was holding my breath and let it out in a rush.

'Oh Christ, I don't know what to do.'

'Go down to him,' Deirdre said. 'Just go down and see him on your own.'

'I don't think I can face him.'

'Yes you can,' John said, 'and it would be better if you went by yourself and had a minute alone with him than if he walked in here with everyone else around.'

'Go on,' Dee said again. 'Go and say hello to him.'

I knew I had to. It had been more than three years since the day I left home, three years since I'd seen him and so much had changed. And now I knew that he knew about Fortune ... and about my sexuality. I was scared witless.

My legs were trembling as I stood up and walked across the room. My hand shook as I tried to open the door. My palm was sweating and my hand slipped on the ceramic doorknob as I tried to turn it. I wiped my palms on my jeans and took a breath, opened the door and stepped into the hallway.

Through the banisters I could see Dad in the kitchen. He was bent over slightly with his back to me, taking something out from under the grill of the cooker.

I made my way towards him, and as I started down the stairs I heard him call my brother.

'John, come on, let's go.'

I heard him start up the stairs, and as we reached the half-landing between the two floors, we met.

Dad looked at me, stunned for a moment. Then he grabbed me, pulling me to him and holding me tight.

'Where were you? Where were you Colm?'

It was the first time I can ever recall Dad holding me like that. Everything I had worried about fell away. I was home.

## II

# Mam

I was only in Wexford for another few days before I was due back at work. It was a very strange experience being home. Everything had changed. Our family home was gone and the family now scattered. Only Dad, Dee, John and Eamon were left in Wexford, and now Dee had a baby daughter too. Ashleigh was the focus of those few days. I couldn't believe my little sister had grown up and had a baby herself. Ashleigh was beautiful, and Dee was a devoted mother. I was so very proud of her dignity and the power of her devotion to her infant child. Single parenthood still carried a stigma then in Ireland. Dee though, brushed it off and got on with the job of motherhood. She was fantastic.

After that first emotional meeting Dad and I found ourselves back in our old familiar pattern. In truth, things were more difficult between us than ever. My siblings and I easily incorporated the knowledge of my sexuality into our relationships, but Dad really struggled. He didn't know what to say or how to deal with it, let alone my abuse by Sean Fortune.

His silence was caused by that internal struggle, his own trapped feelings. For me though it reinforced my belief that he was ashamed of and angry with me, that I had failed him yet again. We avoided each other as much as possible. If we were in the same room together we didn't talk unless we absolutely had to, and avoided meeting each other's eyes.

I had very little contact with Mam at this stage. She was living in Cork, trying to build a new life with my sister Joy. She learned about Fortune and me being gay on her return from India, but I'd disappeared by then. I wrote to her a few times after I visited Wexford, but it wasn't until the Christmas holidays that I got the chance to see her again. It was more than four years since I'd last seen her, at Dublin Airport.

Eamon had by now also moved down to Cork to live with Mam. I decided to surprise them all by flying to Cork on New Year's Day. I had three days off work after the busy Christmas period and thought it was the perfect time for my trip since Joy and Eamon would be off school and I'd get to spend time with them both.

Mam had rented a large detached house on the outskirts of Cork and was running a yoga centre there. I caught a taxi from the airport. The driver was a typical Cork man, very friendly, curious and chatty. Never short of words myself, I told him all about the reunion to come. The son of an Irish Mammy, he was aghast that I hadn't seen my own mother in so long, and became more and more excited about the unfolding mother–son reunion he suddenly found himself involved in. By the time we headed up the hill leading to my mother's house, we were both feverish with excitement.

'It's just up here now,' he said, 'at the crest of that bit of a hill in the road, on the left.'

I craned my neck, trying to see that far in the gloom of the darkening evening.

'We'll have you there in a minute,' he said. 'She'll get a great surprise when she opens the door and it's yourself standing there, won't she? Four years, that's an awful long time to not see your mother. Be the Lord, my own would kill me if I stayed away more than a week. It'll be a great reunion all together.'

He spoke at machine gun speed while I, for once, was wordless. I just wanted to get there.

We reached the top of the hill and as I looked to the left, there were two or three houses in a row. I was bobbing about on the seat. Which one was it? Where were they? I looked out for a give-away sign, a notice about the yoga centre or one of those window stickers that looked like stained glass, a Hindu symbol like ॐ for Om, or maybe wind chimes blowing gently in the breeze.

Then the car pulled up in front of a house in total darkness.

'This is it. Ah Lord, the lights are all off. Would they be in the back?,' asked the driver.

'I don't know, I haven't ever been here, remember? I hope so, I hope they're here.'

I got out of the car and knocked on the door, waiting to see a light hit the mottled glass. Nothing happened. I knocked again, louder. Nothing. I went to one of the windows to the side of the door and peered in, trying to make out some sign of life or movement. I knocked on the window. Still nothing.

I was crushed. Where were they? Maybe out for a walk, or at a friend's house? Maybe they were away. I should have called, made sure they'd be there when I arrived. What was I going to do now? I could wait at the house, but what if they were away for days and not just a few hours?

My taxi driver was almost as disappointed as me. But as luck would have it, he had a solution. Ireland is really a village, everyone knows everyone else, and he knew the woman who lived next door. So in we went to the neighbour's house, a lovely older lady who immediately insisted I come in for tea and something to eat while we tried to figure out this dilemma. She had no idea where Mam was, but she did know the owner of the house, my mother's landlord.

She called him and he said he would come right over. The taxi driver headed off, confident I wouldn't be left by the roadside and that he'd done his bit to deliver me back into the arms of my Mother. I sat waiting for the landlord to arrive as I was fed with freshly-made sandwiches and slice after slice of home-made apple tart, being spoiled rotten by Mam's neighbour.

When the landlord arrived he let me into the house next door. I recognised Mam's presence immediately, the smell of sandalwood and incense, the warm and colourful silk hangings, some driftwood on a shelf and hand-painted chakra charts on the wall. The house was entirely silent. I used the phone to call Deirdre in Wexford who told me that Mam, Joy and Eamon had gone to Dublin for Christmas to see Barbara. Mam had the flu and they'd stayed on. She had no idea when they might be heading back to Cork. Worse than that, the phone at Barbara's place was down so there was no way of making contact.

'Why not come down here tomorrow?' Deirdre asked. 'You can stay with myself and Ashleigh, we'd love to see you.'

'I would, but I have to fly back from Cork the day after tomorrow. I could only stay one night and then travel back to Cork airport again, it wouldn't be worth it.'

I was gutted. I was in Mam's place, her home, and she was away. All around me I could see her, see the life she had built here, see Joy's and Eamon's things too, but they were miles away and not contactable in Dublin. So much for my surprise.

Luckily, having spoken to Deirdre and confirmed that I was in fact my mother's son, the landlord gave me a spare key and allowed me to stay. I went to bed in Eamon's room that night, falling asleep cursing my desire for the drama of a surprise visit.

The next morning was spent wandering about the house, feeling like an intruder in a place that wasn't my own, but felt like home in so many ways. There were reminders everywhere of my life years earlier, not so much items from that time, but smells and images. The scent of spices in the kitchen, reminders of foods, exotic for the time, that Mam introduced us to. Cardamom pods, cumin seed, fenugreek ... spices she would roast and then grind before adding to a big pot with ginger, onions and garlic, the base for a great veggie curry fortified with red lentils. The teapot from home sat on the stove and a few other small items from the past were scattered around the house.

But it was the feel of the place, the sense of peace and calm that reminded me most of Mam. I could feel her there, her quiet gentleness. I'd forgotten how steadying that sense of her was, and I missed it.

Later that afternoon, I sat reading a book in the living room. Mam had always sworn life would be better without TV and she often hid it away for months when I lived at home. I resigned myself to the fact that I was now likely to leave the next evening without actually seeing Mam, Joy or Eamon at all. I decided to leave a note, welcoming them home and promising to come back soon. I'd already drafted one, trying to be funny and light and not play up how disastrous and disappointing the whole trip had been.

Then I heard a key in the door, and as the door opened I could hear Mam's voice chatting to Joy.

I walked out and met her as she stepped through the door.

'Hi Mam.'

I wrapped her in my arms and gave her a big hug. Mam is only five feet two and I'd towered above her for years.

'Oh my God, Colm!' She laughed and hugged me tight, Eamon and Joy grinning with delight at the two of us. Suddenly, the trip wasn't a disaster after all.

I had a great twenty-four hours with them all. Mam and I got to talk a bit. I could see that she was happier than I'd seen her in years, enjoying her new life in Cork and finally living the life she'd wanted for so long.

For years I'd known she was unhappy. Her life had taken a somewhat unexpected direction when she first began to discover yoga and the spiritual path to which she subsequently dedicated much of her life. She and Dad had grown increasingly apart and it was clear to me that they would have been happier separated but that wasn't so easy in an Ireland where marriage was supreme; divorce didn't exist and even separation was still taboo.

They were both great people but they needed not to be married to each other anymore. As their son it's not for me to dissect their relationship; I'm not sure any child can ever do that reasonably or fairly. I loved them both but they were very different and needed to find a way to leave each other in order to find their own individual ways forward. The slow and gradual ending of their marriage was an issue for me all through my teens. It wasn't nasty or cruel but it was sad to witness, and obviously painful for them both. In truth, given the time during which it happened, I'm not sure they could have handled it better than they did.

In any case, I was just happy to be back in touch with Mam again, and I focused on the good, ignoring all that had happened over the years, deciding instead to be happy about the present and make the most of the future. I was now back in contact with all my family.

I never asked them any difficult questions. I didn't ask why they hadn't tried to find me. I didn't ask them if they'd missed me or worried about me. And they didn't raise it either. It seems incomprehensible to me now that I was gone for so long, and in such circumstances, and that we never really spoke about it.

A rare occasion when my past almost forced itself on my present was my twenty-first birthday. I was out for a meal with my family when I spotted Sean Fortune in the same restaurant. I saw him heading towards the exit on a route that would take him right past our table. I was terrified he might see me and stop to say something, scared witless that he might try to re-establish some kind of contact with me. I remember shrinking into my seat and turning away as he approached. His voice boomed as he spoke to his companion, but he kept walking and headed out the door: I let go of the breath I'd been holding from the moment I noticed him. I tried not to show how rattled I was.

By now my parents knew about Fortune and they knew I was gay, but it was never mentioned. I was back and that was that.

Abuse is only possible in a silent world. And just like the rest of society, my family was silent; there were certain words that were never spoken for fear of what consequences they might bring. Instead, we demanded the silencing of truths that would inevitably tear apart our idealistic view of ourselves. The truth demands action while secrets and lies allow us to avoid taking action, they allow us to continue to pretend that everything is fine, even when it is most definitely not.

Words can cause trouble, and I was raised never to cause trouble. I never brought up anything that might cause difficulty or upset. I never once asked if they had tried to find me. I tried very hard to be good. I was just glad to be back, and I worked hard to please my family in every way I could.

That was my pattern. I was a pleaser. I didn't like anything unless the other person liked it too. If I was going to dinner with someone I would insist that they chose the restaurant. It was all about trying to make the best possible impression. I watched and waited, trying to work out what the other person might want of me, and then I gave it to them.

I related to other people as the person I imagined they wanted me to be, rather than as myself. That was one of the most difficult and frustrating legacies of the abuse.

I remember Barbara telling me once that Deirdre had said to her, 'Colm's a lovely person, but I just wish he would be himself.'

I got upset and said, 'What the hell does that mean? Be myself ... what's that about? Just tell me who to be and I'll be it!'

The very idea that I was failing to live up to my sister's idea of who I ought to be caused me extraordinary anguish. I had ceased to exist as a person in my own right. I was a mess.

I was also a tightly-bound control freak. I didn't dare let my guard down or lose control and let people see who I really was. I believed that the real me would be unacceptable to them. I avoided getting drunk at all costs. If I felt myself starting to get drunk I became paranoid. I remember once going home and getting into a shower and turning it from hot to freezing cold for a full forty-five minutes in a desperate attempt to sober myself up after I discovered the bar I was in was serving doubles instead of single measures and I'd drunk much more than I realised.

All this meant that I didn't have a real, honest relationship with anyone. No one really knew who I was, and I didn't know myself. I was so scared of who I might be, of who I had been, that I didn't go there. I lived from the neck up and the face out, avoiding the feelings that lived in my body. My focus was always on the other person, making them like me so that I'd know I was likable.

The only time when all my fears and insecurities were allowed to surface was when I was asleep. Then I would dream, dreams that had been with me for years.

In the most regular one I was back in Adamstown, living on the farm. There was no one else in the dream, I was alone apart from a huge giant who chased me across the fields, through the grove and up into the village. The giant wanted to kill me and so I ran. I had no one to run to, I was alone. The giant would tear me apart if he caught me. I ran and ran.

Up the laneway by the side of the grove, I ran past the first few houses until I got to my primary school teacher's house. I ran around the back and found a trapdoor and opened it. I threw myself down into the hole beneath the trapdoor and lay in the dark holding my breath, terrified to move. I could hear the giant crashing about outside, stomping and tearing at everything as he looked for me.

I waited, frozen in fear, not breathing, praying and hoping he would run by, tears running down my face as I lay still in that hole in the ground. Then his foot came crashing through the trapdoor, crushing me to death.

I woke from this dream many hundreds, possibly thousands of times over the years, drenched in sweat and crying. I could keep my demons at bay during the day, but at night the monsters in my past came back and got me, again and again and again.

# The Big Decision

This was a strange time for me. Being back in touch with my family was good in many ways, but it often left me feeling like a failure, a reminder of who I wasn't more than of who I was or might be. Having reinvented myself so fully, I was now struggling to integrate my new life with my old one.

Being in touch with home also meant being reminded of the past, and I wasn't yet ready or equipped to deal with that past honestly.

Bath was a lovely place, but at twenty-one it soon became just a little too quiet and sleepy for me. I decided to head back to London and got a job in Heathrow Airport, working as an assistant manager in one of the catering outlets. I was doing OK but still had no particular sense of purpose. I didn't much like the job at the airport, and after a few months I left.

I was drifting now; I hadn't lined up a new job so I decided to go back to agency work for a while. It paid reasonably and meant I was free to work when it suited me. I was back in touch with friends I hadn't seen much since I moved to Bath and started to get out and about again, and to have a social life.

One night I was in a pub called The Royal Oak in Hammersmith with some old friends I'd known in Dublin who had also moved to London. I was ordering a drink at the bar and got chatting with the barman, a guy from Dublin called Robert who had what was without doubt the scruffiest laugh I've ever heard in my life. It was throaty, deep and infectious. He was great fun and we started seeing each other. I moved back to Earls Court, to the house on Warwick Road. A few weeks later Robert lost his job at the pub and since he also lived over the pub, his home. He moved in with me for a while; a while that would become eleven years.

It's difficult to explain what this period was like. I didn't know what I really wanted to do and had very little self-confidence. I felt like I was expected to get on but had no idea what with. I tried lots of hare-brained schemes to get some kind of career going, but nothing worked. Over the course of a few years I spent a lot of time out of work, occasionally getting a job here and there, but nothing I stuck with.

Robert and I were getting on well. He was great fun and had a big heart. We were both running from demons of one kind or another, and in many ways our relationship was a safe haven, a place where we managed to gloss over the worst excesses of the hang-ups we carried with us. Being in a relationship also brought stability, and after a few years we both started to look at options for learning new skills that might help us advance in life. It was 1992, we were fed up with drifting along and at almost twenty-seven I knew I had to get my act together.

Mam was by now living in Plymouth, as was my sister Joy, who had been with Mam all along and also chosen a life of spiritual exploration. Joy is a beautiful woman with an air of calm and gentle purpose about her. At times over the years I often felt that she was the elder sibling, the one who had much to teach me about stillness and inner peace.

Robert and I went down to see them often. Mam was living in a cute little flat and Joy lived in a community in a place called Torpoint, just across the river.

Mam was a great believer in natural medicine. She'd trained as a nurse but had an instinctive faith in the power of nature and old remedies and practices to relieve pain and promote health. It obviously rubbed off on me as I was enormously interested in such therapies. I began to read more and more about them and became especially interested in physical therapy, massage in particular. I decided to study therapeutic massage and aromatherapy. Robert opted to study reflexology.

I started college in September 1993, and by the end of 1994 was qualified to practice massage and aromatherapy. I'd started to work as a cab driver to finance my studies and drove a mini-cab for about two years. That was itself quite an education.

I have no idea what possessed me to become a cab driver. Given that I was still so lacking in self-confidence that I wouldn't walk into a bar on my own, a job that required me to go into unknown bars and pubs on a nightly basis and call out the name of my fare before taking drunken, and often rowdy, passengers home might have been a bit much. I also didn't know my way around London by car terribly well and got lost on my first day as I headed to the cab office for my first shift.

Needs must though, and before long I could find my way around the city well enough and had no problem going into pubs or dealing with difficult passengers. That job served me well in so many ways. It funded my return to learning and also gave me greater self-confidence when dealing with new people. It also meant that when I qualified, I was able to gradually build up a client base while supplementing my income with driving, until I was busy enough in my massage and aromatherapy practice to give it up altogether.

As I built up contacts and referrals I got busier and busier. I was offered a regular clinic in a London university, treating students and faculty members. I loved the work; it was demanding and physical, kneading and stretching sore muscles and joints, but very fulfilling and rewarding.

It was also a very meditative process. Often as I worked to release physical tension, emotional tension emerged too. I learned that what we hold emotionally is also stored physically. There's no mystery to that in my view. For instance, I found that people who were carrying a lot of anger often experienced tight, uncomfortable tension around their shoulder blades, in the muscles around the scapula. This made sense to me since it is these muscles that react to anger, storing the power to push or punch. If that tension isn't released then it becomes pain and muscle tightness.

As I worked on parts of clients' bodies that stored such tension, emotional as well as physical release would take place. I found myself reading more and more to try and understand the connections between the physical and emotional self. It was fascinating stuff and no doubt played a large part in the emotions and tensions beginning to emerge in me too.

By now Robert had qualified as a reflexologist and was working in a drop-in centre for people living with HIV-AIDS. He was very skilled and had extraordinary compassion. He had a gentle, earthy manner and always saw the person, never the condition, he was treating. It was tough and demanding work; at that stage people living with the disease didn't have a very long life expectancy. Many of those he worked with died, and it took quite a toll on him over the years. He also saw other clients in a practice based at home, or by visiting them in their own homes. We were both steadily building up a practice, a career and a future.

I decided to rent a room in a clinic in Blackheath. I wanted a permanent base from which I could build up a decent practice. I also wanted to work with a team of therapists, to refer on clients who needed other approaches and to learn from colleagues about their own methods.

It was an exciting time. The practice began to take off, slowly but surely. I really enjoyed working with other people. I could see so many different areas that I might choose to explore in my work and kept up my training, attending workshops and courses and further developing my skills. I began to teach workshops for people interested in practising massage and aromatherapy at home. I loved the dynamic of working with a group, developing an understanding of the unique make-up of each group and tailoring my programme to their needs. I was good at it too. The groups were well attended and my practice grew steadily.

It was when I'd been in a relationship with Robert for six years and was much more settled that I finally started thinking seriously about both my future and, for the first time ever, my past. For years I'd felt an extraordinary disconnect with my past. I had no sense of it as my own history, as experiences I had lived, but rather it was like a series of books I'd read, each one a different and distinct volume unconnected to the next. I detached from anything that might make me unacceptable in the eyes of others, all the sordid, nasty truths of the past that I didn't have the capacity to deal with.

I wasn't alone in that denial of course. My family also remained silent about the past. That was itself a reflection of a powerful dynamic which existed within our society, a blanket denial to accept what we knew to be true, to see it openly and honestly for what it was, for fear we might then be forced to do something about it.

This manifested in Irish society in dramatic fashion: in the reframing of our conflict-ridden history so that one side became innocent of any wrong-doing while the other was reduced in the popular mind to barbaric monsters; in the vanishing of girls pregnant outside marriage to institutions where they were brutalised and used as cheap labour to wash the dirty linen of society, their babies taken from them. Problems and wrongs that pricked our collective conscience or didn't conform to our idealised view of who we were, were denied and then vanished, often with barbaric ferocity.

I saw that same dynamic at work in another country recently; interestingly, another society defined by its steadfast allegiance to a single faith.

In September 2007 the President of Iran was invited to speak at New York's Columbia University. Responding to questions about the execution of gay men, the president denied that such executions were happening, since homosexuality wasn't an issue in Iran.

'In Iran we don't have homosexuals like in your country,' said President Mahmoud Ahmadinejad. 'In Iran we do not have this phenomenon. I do not know who has told you we have it.'

Two months before the president's speech at Columbia, I spoke at a public protest held in Dublin expressing outrage at the execution by hanging of two gay teenagers in Iran. The boys, aged seventeen and eighteen at the time of their execution, were fifteen and sixteen when they were discovered having sex together. They were detained, flogged and later publicly hanged. Pictures of their executions caused outrage across the world.

In New York, troubled by questions about the execution of gay men, President Ahmadinejad simply denied the existence of homosexuals in Iran; denial at its most absurd and absolute.

Back in 1994, cracks were appearing in my own denial of the events of more than a decade earlier. I started to consider the risk that Sean Fortune might still be hurting other kids.

I hadn't on any rational level allowed myself to acknowledge what he had done to me. It was all abstract and unspoken. Denial is a splendid defence mechanism; a comfortable kind of ignorance I learned to embrace with all the enthusiasm of those who had taught it to me. I'm not being sarcastic; denial is a powerful, powerful defence mechanism. If you can't change something, can't escape it or defeat it and if surrender to it has its own dark horrors, then denial becomes your very best friend. You can deny what's happening even as it is happening. I always found a spot on the wall as I was being pawed at and disappeared into it, placing my entire focus on that spot or stain or cabbage rose wallpaper pattern until it was over, until it was safe to return to my body and to the world.

And then when I was back in the world I denied the reality of what had happened. I can recall how that felt even now, more than twenty-five years later. I can see and feel the adjustments taking place inside my body and mind as I stood up, gathered my clothes, cleaned myself up and dressed, all the while wiping away events only moments past as I put distance between that reality and the one I chose to live in. It simply didn't exist and only surfaced when I slept, leaving me rung out and drenched with sweat when I awoke from a deliberately forgotten horror.

It's no surprise to me now that my first conscious reasoning as to why I should do something about Fortune was all about the fact that he might be abusing other people. It wasn't about what he'd done to me.

Maya Angelou, the civil rights activist, poet and author, said in her book *I Know Why the Caged Bird Sings*, that anger turned on oneself is like a rusty nail driven inwards. It is the most powerful description of how anger suppressed becomes rage turned inwards, often as a violently self-destructive force. When I couldn't express my hate and rage, I hated myself. I couldn't punish those who had violated me, so I punished myself, not least by allowing myself to be further violated, by affirming through my own choices and the actions of others that I deserved no less.

But as time and space brought about healing, the pace of

my movement towards an open and honest realisation of all of those long-denied hurts became gradually and gently more compelling.

As I settled and matured, feelings of concern about the past – or rather fear of its impact on the present – began to surface. Just as Fortune's request that I find another boy for him to have sex with had spurred me to action more than a decade earlier, the thought of another unknown boy enduring his attentions made me act now.

I remained uncertain about what I should do, or even what I wanted to do. It was like I had an uncomfortable feeling I didn't understand; something was starting to rise from deep inside me, something I couldn't yet openly acknowledge or even name.

Barbara was instrumental once again. She was over on a visit and I broached the subject with her. I told her of my concerns.

'He might still be doing it now, today. I can't do nothing anymore. I have to tell someone.'

She was fantastically practical and strategic, always seeing beyond the moment and quickly considering the steps necessary in any given situation. She remains one of the wisest people I know. 'Think about what you need,' she told me. 'Take your time to consider the next step and then let's do whatever you need to do.'

She was never pushy and always measured in her advice, always loving and sympathetic. She listened and helped me work through what I needed to do as best I could in those early days as I stumbled my way through a minefield I hardly knew existed.

I remember walking the dog with Robert one day around

Peckham Rye Park in London, near where we lived at that time. We talked about how I might go about reporting what Fortune had done to me. It was a sunny autumn afternoon, the leaves were just starting to turn gold and the air had begun to get that gloriously musty smell of autumn. Nature was starting to wind down from the frantic activity of spring and summer.

We'd been together for more than five years at this stage, and though we were struggling individually with our own demons we tried our best to be there for each other. He was a good man.

'I should go to the police, but what if they don't believe me?'

'Why wouldn't they?'

'He's a priest.'

'Yeah but they have to listen, they have to investigate.'

'It's scary though. Maybe I should go to the bishop?'

I knew I had to do something; I knew I had to tell, to speak out and yet I couldn't quite take that step.

In the end I decided the best way forward would be to write to the bishop and tell him what had happened. Looking back, that seems daft. I hadn't had any regular contact with the Catholic Church for more than twelve years, I didn't go to Mass, didn't look to that Church for spiritual or moral guidance and yet I still saw it as a more senior authority than the Irish police or the criminal justice system.

Once I'd made the decision, I let things drift for a while. I still talked about it and struggled with it but I couldn't take the first step: I couldn't write that letter and commit the words to paper. Then in the autumn of 1994 my sister

Deirdre told me about a family wedding she and my father were due to attend. One of my cousins was getting married and Fortune was to officiate. My father couldn't bring himself to go to the wedding because of Fortune, so my sister went without him. I was very disturbed to hear about this, because it named my father's struggle with what had happened. I felt guilty that he couldn't go to the wedding, a reminder that what I had done was hurting him. I was even more disturbed by what Deirdre told me about the wedding; she said that Fortune seemed to have lots of young boys around him.

And so the pressure within me to acknowledge that dark secret grew. I could no longer ignore the risk of him still being in a position to abuse and hurt other kids.

# 13

# *Breaking the Silence*

By the turn of the year, I'd decided to report the abuse to the bishop but had yet to act on it. However, I wasn't the only one trying to find a way to break my silence, as I found out on New Year's Day 1995. Dad was also struggling to cope with what had happened. In the end it was my relationship with him that would trigger my finally reporting Fortune.

I'd always believed that Dad was puzzled by me, that he couldn't understand or relate to me, and that it was because there was something wrong with me. My sense of his disappointment, and more particularly my belief that I was responsible for it, was an ever-present and powerful force that further crushed my self-confidence. I wanted him to see who I was and be proud of me. I desperately wanted him to tell me that I had done something, anything, right.

That was why, all those years earlier, I was so scared he might find out about what had happened with Fortune. And why, when he did find out, I just couldn't discuss it with him. I was terrified that this only confirmed what he believed, that I was unworthy to call myself his son, that I was a pervert and that the acknowledgement of these awful truths would finally and fully alienate us.

Interestingly I never had the same fears about Mam finding out. I think much of that has to do with the masculine nature of the relationship between fathers and sons. I never felt my mother demanded that I be tougher, stronger or manlier. Mam never seemed confused or irritated by my sensitivity and the gentle side of my nature.

In the end of course I never did tell Dad myself. That had fallen to Barbara. Now, despite how grave an issue it was and how much it burdened us both, we remained silent, never broaching those hard truths. We avoided speaking because we couldn't say the things we needed to say the most.

On New Year's Eve of 1994, there was a party at Barbara's house in Wexford. Dad and Deirdre now lived there too. After the New Year was rung in, Dad called Barbara and a friend of his into his room. He broke down as he told them he could no longer live with the knowledge of what had been done to me and that he needed to do something about it. Twelve years had passed since Barbara told him and he'd never spoken of it again, not because he would not, but because he could not. He said that he hadn't been able to sleep for all those years without waking up and thinking about it. He wept.

The next day Barbara called me and told what had happened. In many ways this was my nightmare, that my father was so hurt by what had happened. But when she told me about his desire to do something, it actually spurred me on to take that final step and report what had happened.

I phoned Dad that same day, and for the very first time we spoke about the past.

'Dad, it's Colm.' I was nervous, and didn't know how to start this long-overdue conversation, so I just charged ahead. 'Barbara told me about the party, about you wanting to do something about Sean Fortune.'

He didn't answer.

'I want that too. I've been talking about it for months now, I want to do something.'

'No, you don't,' he replied. 'You've never spoken about it before, you never even talked to me about it.'

'I do. I'd already decided to do it. I know I haven't spoken to you about this before. I couldn't. And you never spoke to me either, you never mentioned it once.'

It was tense. He seemed angry with me for never having spoken to him about the abuse.

'You never said a word to me about it. Never. Why would you want to do something about it now, after all this time?' he asked.

'I couldn't say anything to you. I just couldn't. That's not fair, you can't just blame me for that. And I will do something, I have to.'

I think we both realised that this first conversation was in danger of turning into an argument.

'OK,' I said. 'We both obviously wish we'd done something sooner, but we didn't. We both want to now, and we can. Let's just work out what to do next.'

'I put windows into the bishop's house last year,' Dad said. 'I was there, in that house, and I wanted to talk to him about it then, but I didn't. I couldn't.'

I could hear the emotion in his voice now, and it cracked as he said again, 'I couldn't.'

He was admitting to me that he hadn't been able to speak

about it either. He was angry, but perhaps with himself more than me.

'It's OK Dad. We can do it now and we can do it together. Barbara will help us.'

We agreed then and there that the best way forward would be to talk to the Gardai, the Irish police.

'I'll talk to Barbara,' Dad said, 'and we'll arrange it.'

And there we left it. It was the first time we'd ever spoken about anything real in many, many years. As I hung up the phone I couldn't quite believe it had actually happened.

Barbara was fantastic as ever and made all the necessary plans for me to make my complaint to the police. A month later I flew back to Dublin from London. She was determined to do everything she could to limit the awfulness of what I had to do. She met me from the plane and took me out for dinner and on to a show. Her care and concern touched and lifted me. I knew I would not be alone.

Later that night we drove back to Wexford and the next day Pat Mulcahy, the detective who would handle the case, came to her house to meet with me.

I was nervous and unsure of what to do and what to say. It was one thing to have made the decision but it was another thing altogether to find the words and the courage to actually do it. Pat was fantastic. He was careful and considerate and told me that we could take all the time we needed to get my statement down on paper. He assured me that he was taking this very seriously and that he would personally work to do his best to discover the full truth. More importantly, he believed me.

Over the next few hours we drew out as much as I was able to give on that first day. I haltingly talked about how

I had met the priest and how he had begun to take me away to his house for weekends. Slowly and with great reluctance I began to say the words I never thought I could say as I told Pat what had been done to me. Barbara sat by my side, offering solid and loving support. I couldn't have done it without her.

As I told the story and said the words I'd avoided for so long, the awful reality of it began to hit me as if for the very first time. Saying the words out loud made it real, and that uncovered the feelings I had hidden and buried for so long.

It was so hard to find the words. After so many years I struggled to allow myself to say them out loud. And when I did, they sounded so wrong. It was precisely because I'd worked so hard to keep everything buried, that I now felt like I was doing something very, very wrong in exposing it all.

As I started to talk and remember, it was as though I was back there in that room thirteen years earlier. I was shaking as I stepped back in time but I managed to stay focused and get the words out. I found myself having to translate and use words very different to the ones in my head. They were the words of a fourteen-year-old boy, but I couldn't use them now, not in a police statement.

I told Pat how we had both ended up in that double bed, how I was dressed in my new pyjamas. I found it hard to go beyond that and hesitated. I was also struggling not to panic as the images, sounds and smells of that night replayed in my head.

'And then?' asked Pat carefully.

In my head the words I heard were, 'He felt me up.' But I couldn't say that. Instead I said, 'He put his hand on my genitals.'

I looked at Pat, I wanted to get out of there and end this. I wanted to be anywhere else in the world but there. I felt the blood drain from my face and I started to shake again.

'Take your time,' Pat said. 'We're in no rush, we can take as long as you need to do this, and you can take a break whenever you want to. OK?'

'OK ... He touched me, and then he got me to touch him. He tried to kiss me, but I wouldn't. I couldn't.'

I could feel the stubble scratching my face and his slobbering attempts to kiss me. I started to feel sick. I had to stop.

I had to take a lot of breaks as I battled to describe the pictures flashing inside my head. I used words like 'masturbate' and 'oral sex', words I wouldn't have used back then and that felt strange to me, heavy and unfamiliar despite my adult understanding of them. When it got to telling about the rape, I couldn't express the force used, the violence of what he did. Instead I said 'He got on top of me and put his penis in me.'

I was cringing with shame as I spoke. I was horrified, both by the pictures in my head and the words coming out of my mouth. I balked at telling all of it; I couldn't go there, not like that, not that first time. I wasn't ready to admit to myself all that had happened, never mind to anyone else.

Pat could see I was struggling and he left the room, allowing me time alone with Barbara. I was leaning against the cooker, with my arms wrapped around my waist. I stared at the floor silently as Barbara put the kettle on to make us all a cup of coffee. She touched my arm. 'How are you doing? Are you OK?'

I looked at her and started to sob, swallowing hard to try and hold down the grief and shock that was rising up my throat. It felt like an enormous lump, forcing its way up from my stomach. I felt like I was choking.

I looked at Barbara, her eyes were warm and soft, full of compassion and concern. I cracked.

'Look what he did to me.' I started to cry, hot tears falling down my face.

Barbara put her arms around me and held me. 'I know. I'm sorry Colm. I'm so sorry.'

It took about two days to get out as much as I could remember; two days to produce a statement two pages long. At the end of the process Pat told me that he would take it all away and see what else he could discover. At that point I was certain it would come down to my word against the priest's and that I was the only one it had happened to. I was wrong.

There were miracles happening that week too. Dad and I looked each other in the eye for the first time in years, maybe the first time in our lives. We went out one night to the pub for a drink and began to really talk. We broached subjects we never thought we could ever discuss. Dad was comfortable in this environment, and seemed anxious to talk.

'Why didn't you tell us what was happening Colm? Why didn't you tell us what he was doing to you?'

'I didn't know how, and I didn't really understand what was happening ... and I blamed myself for it. I thought I was doing something very wrong and I thought you would blame me.'

'How could you think that? How could you possibly imagine that I would blame you?'

'He told me it was my fault. He told me that I had a problem, and I already felt sick with guilt when it happened. I didn't know how to make sense of it all, and he was a priest. I never thought you would believe me, that you would believe him instead.'

Dad was visibly upset. He looked at me with tears in his eyes.

'I'm so sorry Dad. I'm sorry that I let this happen.'

'Stop that,' he said. 'You have nothing to be sorry for. You were only a boy.'

'I know, but I let it happen.'

'No, I'm sorry. I'm sorry that you couldn't tell me. I'm sorry that I wasn't there and that I didn't stop it. You're my son, it was my job to protect you, and I didn't.'

'Don't, it's not your fault, you didn't do anything wrong.'

'I didn't see and I didn't stop it. I should have, and I didn't. That's for me to deal with, not you. I feel so sad for you, for what you went through, what you went through alone. And I am so very sorry.'

It was an extraordinary moment, one of the most important in my life. I'd been terrified of how he would react, that he would blame me and be ashamed of me. Instead, he sat with me and told me of his grief *for* me, not *because* of me. He talked of his sorrow, not for me to console him, but because he needed me to know. As my father he needed to tell me that he was sorry for what he saw as his failure to protect me.

That night Dad gave me the best of who he was. It was a powerful moment among a time of a great many powerful and life-changing moments.

We also talked about the other things that had kept us distant from each other. We spoke about my sexuality. He'd never been able to come to terms with me being gay. No surprise there; it had taken me a long time to get even halfway there myself and I still had a distance to go. We ended up having a bit of a row about it, but at least we were talking, really talking.

'There are men and women and that's how it was meant to be. Anything else is not natural. Anything else is just wrong,' he said.

I looked at him with raised eyebrows. 'Ah come off it, what does that mean? Natural, wrong ... what does that mean and how do you decide who those words apply to?' I said. 'Give me a break, for fuck's sake. Do you think I chose this? Do you think I woke up one day and decided, I know what I'll do, I'll be gay. That sounds like a bit of a laugh. Do you really think I'm that stupid? You didn't raise stupid kids Dad. I'm not stupid and this wasn't a choice. I wouldn't have chosen this.'

Dad sat looking at me, but listening. I was pissed off and I kept going.

'You do realise that there are people who would cheerfully kill me for being gay don't you? Do you think this is easy? It isn't. It's just who I am and I can do nothing about it, nor do I want to. It's just who I am.

'You always taught us to stand up and be true. To be who we are. And that's what I'm doing. You taught me that.'

Dad looked at me and smiled. He didn't say anything much in response. 'Let's leave all that for now,' he said. 'There'll be time for more talk later.'

I needed to understand that he was just saying the things he needed to say. This was how he felt and what he believed. He meant no disrespect; he just needed to have it out with me.

It wasn't a fight but it was the very first time that we'd really spoken about anything important and so very personal. And it was the first time I'd stood up to him and said damn it, I can't please you if it means denying who I am. You taught me better than that. Strangely, just being myself was what finally brought us together.

Later that night we were on the way home. Barbara was driving, Dad was in the front seat and I was in the back with Deirdre. We stopped at a bank as Deirdre needed to get some cash from the ATM. She hopped out of the car and Dad started to chat to Barbara. I think he thought that I'd gone with Deirdre because he started to talk about me.

'That was a good night. Myself and Colm had a good chat.'

'Yeah,' said Barbara, 'everything OK?'

'It is. He's a great man really isn't he?'

'He is,' said Barbara laughing, 'and he's still in the back of the car.'

I laughed too, my heart bursting. Dad joined in, chuckling along with us both.

'Well, you are,' he said flipping the rear view mirror to look at me, 'you are.'

The next day I left Wexford to travel back to London. Dad came rushing home at lunchtime to see me off. He wanted to say goodbye and see me before I left. I was delighted; this was new, this pleasure in being together. Barbara took a photo of us before I left. Dad was wearing his work clothes, a shirt beneath his overalls. He insisted on putting on a jumper to cover the overalls. I love that picture, it sits on my desk and I look at it every day. We are captured there forever in that moment of affection, our arms draped over each other's shoulders, both of us smiling, happy and at home with each other. It is the picture I never expected to see, the two of us comfortable together, father and son.

A few days after I got home Barbara called me to see how I was. Dad was there and asked to speak with me. He got on the phone and after asking how I was he brought up our conversation of a few days earlier.

'Remember what we talked about in the pub that night?' he asked me.

I said I did remember.

'Well, forget all that, forget what I said. You are my son and I love you.'

And then he started to sob. And once he told me he loved me it was as if he couldn't stop.

He said it over and over again; sobbing and telling me he loved me, that he was proud of me. I sobbed back, telling him that I loved him too.

A little while after our conversation ended Barbara went to look for him. She found him in his room sitting on his bed, crying with a towel to his face. And all he could say was 'I told him I loved him.'

During that week Dad gave me the freedom to face my own demons by naming his. His courage in facing what had happened to me, in speaking from his heart of his love for me and his grief as my father at what had happened, set me free. He showed me that I was not to blame, that it wasn't my fault. He didn't turn away from me as the truth was finally spoken and all the awful secrets of those years began to emerge. He turned *to* me and held me. He told me he loved me. He was there and stood by my side.

His determination to see this through, whatever that might mean, gave me the strength to begin to believe that I could do this, that I could confront the past and face whatever the future might bring.

Back in London I tried to get on with the day-to-day but I was raw from the telling and tender from long-suppressed feelings that had begun to rise to the surface.

I was still afraid on many levels and turned to my old friend Denial to help me cope. Putting the investigation out of my mind was essential. It helped me keep those uncontrollable feelings from erupting into the world where everyone would see them.

I needed to stay busy and in control. I was very conflicted. I needed to act like nothing was happening and at the same time find a way to deal with everything I had allowed to escape from my hidden past.

In truth, both tactics failed. The secret was out so denial would work no longer and I had no real role in the police investigation once I'd made my statement, so I could do nothing more than wait to hear from Ireland and hope things would move quickly.

After a few weeks I heard from Pat. He told me he'd found other men who had been abused by Fortune, and they were telling the same story as me. I was shocked, horrified and relieved all at once. Horrified to hear that this had happened to others and relieved that I was not alone, that my evidence would be strengthened by the collective power of these other statements.

Things moved rapidly from this point on. Before long there were six men who were prepared to make statements and the police approached the diocese and the bishop to inform them of the investigation. Around this time I began to hear the first rumblings that there might be even more to the story and that the Church itself may have failed in some way to prevent Sean Fortune from abusing boys. I remember hearing this and not really getting it. Why would they do that? What possible reason could they have for allowing him to abuse kids?

A few weeks later stories about Fortune started to appear in the papers. He had by now been temporarily removed from active ministry and was, I understood, no longer allowed to work as a priest. At least that was the idea, but he refused to be limited by any order from his bishop. Before long I heard that he was visiting children at the local hospital, telling their parents that his prayers could heal their sick child. He also arrived at a funeral and insisted that he co-celebrate the funeral mass, donning his vestments and taking his place at the altar.

The press stories were not focused on any allegation of sexual abuse. Instead they suggested financial impropriety and other abuses of his authority. I remember opening an Irish paper at Heathrow Airport to see the headline 'The Misfortunes of Fr Sean', over a photograph of Fortune and a story detailing a string of allegations of improper behaviour which ranged from threatening to curse those who defied him in any way to running a dubious media studies course at the premises of RTE, the Irish national television and radio broadcaster. There were suggestions that he'd made a lot of money from running useless courses that awarded meaningless qualifications.

It was all a bit bizarre. I was shocked to see Fortune's picture in the paper and I knew that the whole story would soon be reported. I was anxious about the exposure this might bring and the public reaction to what I had started by making my statement.

I'd decided when I first came forward that if and when the story became public I would not hide behind anonymity. I would allow myself to be publicly identified when the time came.

I remembered as a boy reading a story in a Sunday newspaper. It was about a boy who had been befriended by an older man. The man used to take him away for trips. On one such trip the man showed the boy his penis and asked if he knew what it was for. The boy answered that it was for going to the toilet. The man laughed and put his penis away. Over successive trips the man began to undress the boy and touch him. Despite what was happening to me at the time I didn't understand the story. I didn't understand why the man had laughed at the boy's answer, but more than anything I didn't understand why the article went on to say that the boy couldn't be named in the story. I remember thinking that he must have done something very wrong if he couldn't say who he was.

As an adult I was determined that I wouldn't allow my story to tell any child who might be going through abuse that I was ashamed, and that they should feel ashamed because of what was happening. I wouldn't be party to that.

I talked this through with Barbara, who found it very difficult to deal with. She'd been so very supportive and loving, but it speaks volumes about the stigma attached to the experience of sexual victimisation that she was horrified at the idea of my speaking publicly. She saw it as an invasion of her and the family's privacy. She was angry and upset that I was insistent on not relying on anonymity.

It's very difficult for families in such circumstances. Dealing with the existence of such trauma and pain within one's immediate families is incredibly tough, and to then also have to deal with it publicly is very exposing. We were from a small community, and Dad was a very private man. I know that Barbara also feared how any publicity might hurt him.

It takes great love and great courage to stand by someone who has decided to go public over such an issue. Despite her fears, Barbara stood by me. I was blessed to have such support. It was tough for everyone at times but my family were there for me.

Before long the story did move on. Other journalists began to ask questions about the diocese and the role of its bishop, Dr Brendan Comiskey. Their interest was heightened by the high public profile of Comiskey, and of Fortune who was at that time considered to be a high-flier himself, a charismatic and modern cleric.

Questions began to emerge about the level of co-operation the bishop had given the police in their investigation of as yet unnamed priests who were the subjects of child abuse allegations. It was suggested Comiskey might not have been especially co-operative in his engagement with the police and that he had refused to be interviewed. The police made no public comment and the bishop denied any wrongdoing. The focus then moved to include other aspects of Comiskey's management of the diocese and suggestions that Church funds had been used to purchase an apartment in Dublin in the bishop's name.

Then, in September 1995, Comiskey left the country in dramatic fashion. It was announced that he'd gone to the US to seek treatment for alcoholism. It was clear that things had started to get too hot for the bishop, and no doubt this added to his now acknowledged struggle with alcohol.

At this point I also began to learn much more about Fortune and his long history of conflicts and trouble. Over the next eighteen months I discovered that the parish where he'd taken me all those years earlier had been deeply divided as a result of his placement there. Not long after his appointment to Poulfur, Fortune began to place himself at the centre of all social activity in the parish. This wasn't unusual in a small rural parish, but he'd done so with little regard for the feelings or sensibilities of those already involved in such work. Within a few months he was involved in an acrimonious dispute with the committee that ran the local hall. That dispute began to spill over into other areas and before long there was a significant faction within the parish who were outraged and angered by his behaviour and in open conflict with him. Fortune responded to such challenges by publicly denouncing those involved, using his position to condemn and undermine them.

Anyone who defied him was subjected to vicious attacks. One local organisation refused to allow him to take over their committee. He responded by publicly cursing the first-born of the members of the committee. The threat of a curse placed by a priest was terrifying to many of those he dealt with. They were very religious people who saw their priest as all-powerful. In fact when one of his public challengers was paralysed in a car accident it was widely believed that it was the inevitable result of him 'going up against the priest'.

And so I began to hear more about the conflict that followed Fortune wherever he went. At that point it was all just whispers, short on detail and fact. What began to emerge clearly, however, was a suggestion that the diocese and the Catholic Church at a high level had been made aware of concerns about Fortune long before I ever reported him to the police.

I was really troubled by this. I'd started out thinking that what he had done was to me alone. I believed that no one else was involved, whether as a victim or as an authority complicit by a failure to act to protect children. Now I knew that at least six others had been abused by Fortune and that there might be more to come. It was becoming clear that the Catholic Church itself might have questions to answer about what it knew about the abuse of children by one of its priests. It was a very confusing time. So much changed so quickly and I struggled to keep up, to understand the significance of what was revealed as a result of my reporting the abuse to the police.

And then, in the middle of all of this confusion, I heard that Dad was unwell. We were in touch a lot at this time and enjoying getting to know one another. It was a great joy in the midst of a really difficult time. His love and his support gave me so much strength, so much encouragement to keep going with the battle that was emerging.

Little did I know that soon I would have to find even greater strength.

# 14

# The Death of my Father

My father had been ill for a long time before he let anyone know anything about it. He was typical of his generation; he never went to the doctor and never attended to his ills. I don't know if he was fearless or terrified ... or both.

The first I knew of his illness was a call when I learned he'd been to the doctor because of stomach pains, a discomfort that made work and sleep difficult. Perhaps it was ulcers, the effects of years of over-working and a more than casual relationship with stress. It would be OK, even a good thing if it meant he had to take better care of himself.

That was July. In November I received the call from my sister Barbara to tell me that it wasn't ulcers and that it would not be OK. It was cancer. The malignancy was so progressed that there was no way of telling where it had begun. It was in his liver now and there was but one outcome. They could operate to discover where it had started but no more.

We were told it would be twelve or at best eighteen months. Even as I write I'm frozen as I try to remember the moments that followed that call. I'd come in from the garden, then stood in the kitchen with the dead phone in my hand.

How can a constant end? How can it be possible? He'd always been there, somewhere, a solid presence in a world of uncertainty. My father had his failings but he was constant, everything else and everyone else changed but he was true and unchanging. He'd emerged over the years from behind my childish perceptions. He was not the disapproving, cold, disappointed man I had imagined. The idea of his death was unthinkable, ridiculous and yet now inevitable.

The tragedy is, as I now know, that we were more alike than different. Dad loved ferociously, but unlike my own, his was a hidden love. He was a boy taught not to show his heart. I never really knew him when I was a child, and as a result I never knew myself either. I'd wanted to learn from him how to walk and talk and love and live.

Now when I look at my hands I can see his. I see my body become like his, the shape, the tone and feel of it. The mystery of his adult self becomes less mysterious the older I grow. All those fantasies of infallibility, strength, certainty and righteousness are exposed, as I experience how it feels to be me now.

As a child, I loved him … I adored him. I wanted to place my hand in his and bring him close. I could feel and see his unease, his lost heart. I wanted to touch it and bring the warmth alive. I wanted that for him. It was simple then, at three or four or five. I couldn't speak it aloud but I could see and know it. I knew there was a place where he sat, distant from me, quiet and alone. Not waiting as such; he'd given up waiting when his father died, when he left and didn't come back. There sat the boy he was and the man he feared to be, blind to the world and certainly blind to the love of this boy he had brought into the world, this boy with the same heart.

Death is such an intimate process, so deeply, intensely personal. Especially when one is dying from an illness like cancer and death happens slowly, even though the news may have been greeted by a steely determination to beat the odds. I remember Dad telling me that he planned to get five years more out of life, this after being told he had eighteen months. He found hope in the idea that he might extend the deadline, that he might make it beyond that point in the too-near future.

We were told six to twelve months, he was told twelve to eighteen, and yet the truth was despite his positive, even cheery determination that he would get five more years, he died three weeks later.

We often complain about doctors not telling us the whole story about our health, or more pointedly about our disease, our imminent death. But imagine being told you have twenty-one days left. How could you find a foothold on the bank of that roaring torrent as you figured out how to navigate the flash flood pulling you out of life? How could you even begin to find a way not to be dragged under the swirling water tearing you from the arms of family and friends, away from everything you know towards an uncertain and frightening landscape?

I know my father's doctors were right to give some sense of future, of hope. Our minds can find ways to deal with most things, and Dad simply reframed his idea of life expectancy and found hope in the idea of five more years. It gave him some control and purpose, some point of reference to begin to navigate the process of his dying.

He was amazing. After that call from Barbara we all came home to be there for him when he was told and to receive and hold this terrible news together. My youngest brother Eamon and I travelled from London on a cold November morning with ice and snow on the roads of the city.

We set out knowing the road we had to travel, but shaky and emotional, the ground beneath us was unfamiliar and unsettled. We only knew we had to get there for Dad, that he would need us close when the news arrived.

We arrived the next morning. Dad was still in hospital. That morning Barbara met with his doctor and together they went to tell my father he would die. We waited outside the ward; the sight of us all together would have been too much and betrayed the news before he'd been allowed that small moment of privacy to receive it.

I don't know how long Barbara was with him before she called us in. I sat there waiting, wanting to be with him but knowing he needed that moment. We sat and waited … and then we went to him.

We all walked in together. He sat in his bed, propped up against a pile of pillows, looking lost and small. He looked at us all as we walked in. The first word he said was 'Sorry.'

He was sorry he was leaving us, he apologised for the pain he knew this would bring … I was sorry too. We'd just gotten close and begun to meet and talk and know each other for the first time in our lives … and now he was leaving, finally and forever. He was sorry and so was I.

After a little while Dad and I were alone. He was sat up in his narrow hospital bed, dressed in his pyjamas. He seemed so out of place to me there. The curtains around his bed were drawn, a pretence of privacy in a very public place.

'I just want enough time to see this through with you,' Dad said. 'If I could just get five more years maybe?'

He looked at me, his eyes pleading for some kind of hope, some way to defeat the death sentence he'd just been handed. I didn't know what to say. I held his hand. He held on tight for a moment.

'Do you think a liver transplant might work?' he asked.

He was looking at me intently, looking for something. My Dad, the strong one, here he was trying to find a way to face the fact that he was dying.

'I don't think so,' I said gently. 'We can ask the doctor, but I don't think so. The liver cancer is secondary. It started somewhere else and spread. It's unlikely they would consider a transplant.'

He nodded. But he was determined to find a way to live a little longer.

'I will get five years yet, if I can have five years more that will be fine,' he said.

He was out of hospital the next day and home.

The day after that, Eamon and I drove to Cavan, to a little house on a near-deserted lane on the border between the Irish Republic and Northern Ireland. Mam was living there, spending a few months on retreat. We drove up to tell her that Dad was dying and to bring her home to see him for the first time in a decade or so.

We drove for over fourteen hours from one end of the country to the other, up and down narrow country roads in the middle of nowhere. We were determined to get there and back in a day, not to lose any time.

When we got back to Barbara's house Mam and Dad had a few hours together, talking in his room where he was in bed. I've no idea what they talked about. They'd shared twenty years of life together, many sorrows and many joys, they had six children and now he was dying. I'm sure they had a lot to say to each other and I was glad they got the chance to have that conversation.

The next day I went back to London. Dad was up and about when I left. He hit the ground running and surprised us all with his energy and determination.

That was the middle of November 1995. Dad died at twenty minutes past noon on 8 December 1995. He died with us all around him.

It was a difficult night. Dad returned home to his own bed to die. We all knew that this was how it would be and we all travelled home to be with him. They were journeys of extraordinary purpose for all of us. Dad had visited my sister Joy in Cornwall for a week, as part of his process of checking in with each of us before he was able to leave, putting his house in order. He had deteriorated rapidly in the last few days of that visit, so much so that the doctor in Cornwall advised us to get him home quickly before he became too ill to travel. He flew back the next morning with Barbara. A one-hour flight to Cork and then a drive of three hours home, a last journey.

Earlier that week, I was at home in London and drove down to Cornwall to see him. I was shocked by how much he had deteriorated in less than a week. As I travelled back to London I knew he was getting much worse and feared how quickly the end might come. Shortly after I arrived home Barbara called to tell me I should head to Wexford as soon as possible. It's a strange thing to get a call telling you to come home, not for a wedding or a birth, a funeral or a party, but to be with your father as he dies. I remember the calm I felt following that call, the determined calm that was the result of one focused thought, one clear and powerful purpose: to be with Dad when he died, to hold him however he wanted to be held as he made his way out of this life. That was my purpose, my responsibility to him, my final act as his son, the honour he was due as my father.

That night was hard. I stayed up with Dad and sat by him as he struggled to rest. Sleeping pills had stopped working but he relaxed and rested if I massaged his feet. He slept for an hour or so before he became restless and troubled. By midnight his breathing was laboured, fighting for each breath, and I could feel his fear as he battled to stay alive. At 2am I held him to give him a drink and talked softly to him. It was so distressing to see him fight. I wanted to breathe for him, to take the weight that was dragging him under and allow him to break the surface and breathe deeply and freely. It was like watching him drown, unable to rescue him.

I sat close to him, holding his hand with my head resting on the mattress near his pillow.

'Dad, you don't have to do this, you don't have to fight like this. Not for us, we'll be OK. Don't do this for us, it's too much. Don't fight for us anymore, but if you want to fight for yourself, then fight like a bull. Fight as hard as you can, but only for you.'

He fought. I thought he would go that night as I sat waiting for his breathing to stop. Each breath demanded such effort. Each time he took a breath in I waited to hear the exhalation, not breathing myself as I sat there not knowing if the next breath would come, if this would be his last. I remembered hearing that the body is at its lowest ebb between midnight and 4am ... now I saw it for myself. Those were the hours the battle raged. At 4am Dad seemed to still and rest. His breathing became less laboured; he had made it through. I went to bed and slept, certain that he'd reached a place of rest and recovery on his journey.

I slept for four hours or so and awoke to a house full of life. It didn't feel like a death watch, it didn't feel morbid. We all focused on what we needed to do for Dad. There was medication to get, the doctor to call, everyone to feed ... the everyday demands even in the midst of what was an extraordinary day, a day we will never see again, that changed all our lives for ever. The mundane grounded us. Humour takes its place, allowing us to connect beyond fear and a rising feeling of grief. Anything can be funny, anything can bring a smile, a smile returned with gratitude for its touch of warmth.

Barbara was with Dad when I got up. She'd just helped him to the bathroom. It was incredible that the man who had battled for every single breath only hours ago was up and walking, albeit with help. He was exhausted by the effort though, and Barbara helped him back to his room, holding him all the way.

We all stood and sat around my father's bed mid-morning as he began to fight again for breath. Our distress built as we watched, waiting to see if his chest would rise and fall again breath by breath. It seemed that he was no longer with us, that he was somewhere between life and death.

He sat propped up in bed with his mouth open and his eyes closed, breathing raggedly. His false teeth had slipped down, making him look pathetic and dishevelled. John wanted to help, to preserve his dignity. He reached forward to take Dad's teeth out, and as he did Dad's eyes shot open and threw John a look as he snapped his mouth shut. 'Not yet,' his eyes said. 'Not yet, back off.' There was a smile in his eyes. We laughed and savoured his presence as he stepped back into the room for that moment. He was in charge of this process; he was still in the driving seat and would make the decisions.

He died an hour or so later, and we were there with him. I would wish for a death like his, surrounded by those I loved, given the space to make my own decisions about how and when I chose to let go.

Within minutes of his death Barbara opened a window, clearing the air and creating an exit. It was an unconscious action but one that had deep meaning, an aspect of the ritual of death ingrained in our unconscious.

After he died I knew there was more I needed to do for him. I looked at his body; he was so clearly gone but I knew his body needed to be honoured and cared for. It was due proper respect.

The rituals of death were now important, for him but especially for those of us left behind. They were part of how I worked through this enormous event, this uncharted territory where I was no longer any man's son. That thought kept going through my head, 'I am no-one's son.' It stuck and repeated in my mind, like I needed to keep seeing it, hearing it, if I was to grasp the reality of his death, of the passing of my Father.

There were practical things that needed to be done, Dad needed to be 'laid out'. I knew that this meant blocking the body's orifices so that fluids didn't escape as the body let go of life and began to return to the earth. Writing the words 'fluids' and 'orifices' seems very clinical ... it was far from that. I felt very strongly that no stranger should be allowed to perform those duties; no person for whom this was an everyday function. I wanted my father's body to be held gently, carefully, prepared and dressed with love. I wanted us to do this for him, to usher him from this world as a final act of love.

Evelyn, a friend of the family who was a nurse and familiar with the process, helped me. I closed his eyes. I was surprised it was nothing like the gentle closing of the eyes of the dead as portrayed in films, no single, soft sweep of the hands downwards that gently closed the eyelids and brought rest. It was harder than that. It took time and care, closing his eyes and waiting until they were ready to stay closed. We undressed him gently and I stood looking at his naked body. It seemed so vulnerable and delicate in death. He was naked, bare and helpless, almost like a newborn in an odd sort of way. Death and birth are perhaps not so far apart.

We washed his body. Evelyn was lovely, talking softly to Dad as she worked, apologising to him, gently for the indignities he would no longer care about. It mattered to me though, it mattered that there was gentle care. I was glad I was with him for this, glad that this was happening like this, in his room, in his bed, with those who loved him.

I can still recall the scent of him, that familiar smell I'd known all my life. I remember thinking that when we washed his pyjamas, the clothes he'd worn as he died, that it would be the last time I would sense that smell of work and strength, of authority and respect, of my father. Every moment was a final moment of sweetness and grief entwined. For the first time I realised that grief was how I would now love him, how I could hold that love close. That grief was an extension of that love ... and the expression of the grief an expression and experience of love.

We dressed him in a new suit. He had no use for vanity now but we needed to continue to honour his body. He could never choose a shirt and tie to go with a suit; someone would always have to approve or choose the combination for him. He wasn't colour-blind – not that you would have known if you'd seen some of the choices he made over the years – but rather blind to the idea that certain colours and patterns really should never see the light of day together. Now once again we would choose his suit, select his shirt and tie and make sure he looked great. And he did! He was a handsome corpse. All the pain and struggle, the weariness of illness and the fight to survive left his face when he died. He took on instead a gentle smile, his cheeks, which had been grey and sunken, now became rosy and full. It was extraordinary. He looked like his old self, the man he was before cancer began to take him from us.

The final act was brushing his hair, his thick silver hair that had mistakenly assured me I would never lose mine. All this went through my mind as we prepared him.

We laid him back on his bed, hands folded together, his thumbs no longer twirling around each other as they had when he sat thinking or talking ... something else I've found myself doing over the years. Instead his hands were clasped together and a set of rosary beads entwined around his fingers, a reminder of the faith he was born into and had held true to in his own fashion throughout his life. That faith would be a central part of the ritual of his passing, though we were determined not to allow it to take over.

We all agreed to make sure there were no more than two or three chairs in his room at any time. We wanted to avoid a morbid atmosphere if it became the focus of repeated rosaries and prayerful vigil. We wanted that too and knew it would be important for others who had loved him ... but we wanted to try to ensure that the rest of who he was could live and laugh and be remembered in that room too.

We worked together, almost silently at times. As soon as Dad was ready and laid out on his bed, visitors began to arrive. It was enriching and disturbing at the same time to meet for the first time so many people who had known him so well, people I'd never heard of but who spoke of their love and respect.

I will never forget one man, in his sixties like Dad, who came to the house and walked to my father's bed. As soon as he saw him he fell to one knee and lay his forehead on my father's arm and sobbed. This man of my father's generation, of the generation of men who did not show such love ... it shocked and moved me deeply.

My Father's death was an enormous event in my life. It marked the end of a time where I worked so hard to be acceptable to him, to gain his approval. By the time he died I knew he loved me and was even proud of me, and I know if he had lived he would have been tremendously proud of me. But we had only found each other ten months before he died. We had only begun to know each other and I had only begun to realise that I didn't have to work hard for his approval; I only had to be me.

His death was a huge loss and yet it also demanded that I grow up, move beyond my need for fatherly approval and stand on my own two feet, alone. He was no longer there as a reference point. I miss him still. I miss the talks we could have had and the things we could have learned from each other. I miss being my father's son.

# 15

# Suing the Pope

After Dad died I was left reeling by the events of the previous twelve months. I'd broken my silence, dared to speak the unspeakable and begun gearing up for the battle of my life: I'd found my father, only for him to be snatched from me less than ten months later. I was a wreck and functioning on autopilot from one day to the next. I couldn't allow myself to feel the impact of what had happened; if I did, I might never escape a place full of tears. And so I reverted to doing rather than feeling.

I was now back at home in London. I decided that a positive response to everything that had happened was to become a therapist. A more considered and reasonable response would have been to go into therapy, but not for me.

I needed to prove to myself that I was not broken. A part of me was terrified that I was, and that I would never be able to deal with it. One way to prove it was to become the fixer. Better that than the one needing to be fixed.

My training lasted from January 1996 to June 1998. I was lucky enough that the people who trained me, the extraordinary husband and wife team of Anne Geraghty and Martin Gerish, were tough, and determined that any trainee of theirs would undergo the personal therapy necessary to work professionally.

It was a really difficult and demanding time. I had to fall apart and slowly rebuild myself with my newly informed sense of who I was and of the past I had worked so hard to forget.

I'd been running from it for so long. Each time I escaped one dark event or place I had to run forward as if it had never happened. I never spoke of it or consciously thought about it again. But I buried all those experiences inside myself as if they had never happened, and there they sat in isolation. I never allowed myself the compassion to look at each incident honestly and objectively, to know that the boy I was could not have prevented those men in the village from hurting me, or that the teenage neighbour, himself a victim of the same exploitation, was nonetheless responsible for his actions. I never let myself acknowledge how powerless I was, or see the power of the priest and the vulnerability of the boy he abused. I never allowed myself to feel my sorrow at how I had been failed by those who loved me and were unable to protect me.

And beneath it all was a well of shame so deep I couldn't even allow myself to look at its surface for fear of drowning. None of this was intellectual, none of it conscious, it all lived below the neck, in my body. I didn't allow myself to feel, feelings were too dangerous.

Intellectually, I knew I wasn't to blame for the things I was powerless to prevent. At least I knew it in an impersonal kind of way. When my therapist or my teachers told me that the abuse wasn't my fault, I would nod and agree with them. They were the experts and they were trying to help me; they were the good ones. I owed them the 'right' response. After all, they held my salvation in their hands, they would tell me I was OK, give me their stamp of approval and then I would be redeemed.

And they were right; it wasn't my fault. I had nothing to feel ashamed about. Nothing. If I did allow myself to acknowledge my shame I would be letting them down. So I nodded and agreed and gave them what I thought they wanted from me.

It didn't work though. Each time I told them what I thought they wanted to hear they didn't seem to approve at all. I repeated my familiar mantra: I was abused, it was awful, they were bad, it wasn't my fault, I needed to heal my 'inner child', I would learn to love him, he/I deserved to be loved.

Then one evening, as I droned on as usual in a group session, Anne looked at me. She had a way of looking at people with incredible intensity but without being intimidating or threatening.

'Colm, when I hear you speak about all of this I can hear the words you say but I have absolutely no idea what you're talking about.'

Initially, I didn't know what to think. My words made sense. There were sentences, a narrative, I was speaking English ... what could she mean?

But somewhere deep inside me, something hit home. She could only mean that she didn't believe me or that I was talking rubbish and getting it all wrong. I was devastated.

After class, Anne and Martin took some time with me. I was hurt and angry, scared and confused. I didn't know what to do. I didn't know how to get it right. Slowly and patiently they told me that there was no right.

Over a long period of time, I began to understand what they meant. I allowed myself to move beyond what I thought and instead explore how I felt.

I allowed my feelings to exist and expressed them without censoring them first. I tried to stop questioning whether they would be acceptable to the people around me.

I remember a group session when we were talking about uncomfortable feelings. Alan, another tutor on the course, was listening to me talk about how I knew the abuse wasn't my fault. He gently stopped me.

'Colm, you're right of course,' he said. 'You know it's not your fault, intellectually at least. But that's not working for you, is it?'

I shook my head.

'The thing about shame, and about most feelings, is that they don't always appear to make sense. You have such a well of shame inside you. You know it's not your fault, and yet that doesn't drain the well and get rid of the shame, does it?'

Again, I shook my head. I listened, holding my breath, frightened of what he would say next and at the same time desperate to hear what he might offer me.

'Instead of avoiding your shame by staying in your head with what you know to be true, or at least true for everyone else, you have to dive right in there and swim in it. You have to get to know it and face it. Accept it as how you feel.'

And so it was. If I was to move forward then I had to go back to where so much of me was still trapped, caught in a past disowned and abandoned. And I did. Little by little I learned to allow myself my feelings, my fears, my shame and guilt. As time passed and I faced honestly and openly what had happened, I got angry. And that anger became outrage. And outrage drove me forward with purpose and a new clarity.

Before this stage of my life I hadn't been much of a strategic thinker. From the time I was abused by the priest, any plan I might have had for my life, university and a career went out of the window.

But by 1998 this outlook started to change significantly. My decision to report the priest was based more on fear that the abuse might be happening to someone else than any sense of outrage about what had happened to me. But the act of reporting the crime, combined with the loss of my father, made me look deeper inside myself.

It led to me training as a therapist and resolving to use my learning to work with others struggling to deal with experiences of trauma. My training gave me so much on a personal level that by the time it ended I knew it was the single most important thing I had ever done for myself. Even if I'd never gone on to work as a therapist, those two and a half years would have been worth every penny and all the effort I put in. I emerged with a much greater understanding and appreciation of myself.

I was also in love with the process of therapy. I learned that healing is not some external procedure granted by the intervention of another, but rather a drive to health that is an essential part of who we are.

Life is resilient and drives us forward through seemingly impossible situations and experiences. When we find ourselves in times and places from which we feel unable to escape, then survival becomes all. Life's primary drive is to exist and, once survival is secured, to work towards ever more healthy and self-actualising living.

When we experience physical injury our bodies respond to protect and defend life and then to heal from any physical trauma. We use medicine to create the optimum conditions for recovery and healing to take place. When these are achieved, and where the damage is not totally catastrophic, then healing is not only possible – it is inevitable.

Just like medicine, psychotherapy creates the optimum conditions for recovery and healing. In my training and in my work as a therapist I learned how to create an environment where the person I was working with could emerge and sort through the trauma that had so far defeated them. In such circumstances I saw Life take over and drive onwards through pain and struggle as that person worked to emerge fully into being.

Sometimes we seem intent on our own destruction. We might use alcohol or drugs to deaden pain we don't know how to heal and cannot live with. That self-destructive drive is an attempt to make the pain bearable.

Therapy creates a space where new ways of coping emerge and new skills are developed. Feelings gradually begin to surface. Interventions from the therapist are not interpretative or directive, instead they prompt a personal questioning of old patterns and behaviours, a consideration of whether or not they serve us well today. Therapy is not about the past; it's all about the present. When it does examine the past, it is in an effort to understand how the past is impacting on us today, and how it can sometimes remain unresolved and often destructive.

For me, therapy was both an extraordinary and yet also a profoundly ordinary process. Life as a force with its own power and purpose was something I had a deep and instinctive connection with when I was a boy back on the farm. I saw it in the lambs, cattle, wild cats and the rats in the hay barn, in the fog of my breath expelled into the cold spring morning air as I mounted my bike and pushed off up the hill to serve Mass. It was everywhere then and I embraced it.

I lost it when my own life lost its sweetness. Of course it was never really lost to me. That part of me that was so in love with life was simply hiding from a world I feared.

Therapy allowed me to emerge from that fear and discover that I had, in fact, survived. It offered an environment where that part of myself hiding from the all-consuming trauma could gradually get to know the world again. In time, and with a lot of work, I learnt that I could allow the power that was Life within me to emerge, confident that I was now able to protect myself and move beyond just coping and surviving, to live life to the full.

And as I learned to trust that force, call it Life or God or whatever it is to you, I began to let myself be taken forward by it. It was like water that carried me, happy and trusting, on to an unknown destination. I didn't feel any need to worry about the way ahead. Instead I watched and responded to what Life presented.

By the time I qualified as a therapist I had a growing private practice. I had qualified as a physical therapist first and my work as a massage therapist paid for my training as a psychotherapist. I was already getting referrals and didn't need to advertise for clients.

Back in Ireland, the criminal case dragged on slowly. At the best of times, it seemed like some distant event I only connected with when it was demanded of me. But in the bad moments, it was there like a dark storm on the horizon, waiting, but never actually arriving.

I'd made my first statement to the police on 9 February 1995. Following a major criminal investigation, an arrest warrant for Sean Fortune – relating to twenty-one charges of various sexual offences – was issued on 1 November, but it couldn't be served at that time because he had left the country. He was arrested and questioned in relation to my complaint in March that year and was fully aware of the case developing against him. He'd tried to withdraw a large amount of money from a bank in Wexford, then fled to Brussels and refused to return. The Irish authorities made it clear to Fortune that if he did not return to Ireland and face the charges they would seek his extradition from Belgium. He returned to Ireland and handed himself in to the police. He was arrested and charged on 15 November, and appeared in court the same day and was arraigned on twenty-two sexual abuse charges. He was granted bail and forced to surrender his passport.

He appeared in court once more, on 6 December 1995, and was once again remanded on bail. My father died on 8 December, two days after this court date, and I was entirely unaware of this or the next few court appearances.

On 18 January 1996 Fortune appeared in court again and was charged with a further forty-four offences. The case was adjourned on a number of occasions over the next nine months until 23 September, when the case was finally sent forward for trial at Wexford Circuit Court. I remember

feeling elated and at the same time anxious. I was relieved
to finally see an end point to the criminal process, but also
afraid of what it might bring. I understood very little about
the criminal justice process and had no idea that Fortune
could delay and drag out the whole thing for months or
even years. He could, and he did.

Fortune's lawyers launched a High Court challenge to
his prosecution, claiming that it was unfair to prosecute
him for crimes alleged to have taken place years earlier. He
asserted through his lawyers that he could not remember
events from that time well enough to offer a fully effective
defence and that this would not allow him a fair trial. It
seemed crazy to me that he would suggest he was unable
to properly defend himself against charges arising from
events that had happened less than fifteen years earlier. But
that was his assertion and he had a right in law to make
a challenge against his prosecution. In fact it was entirely
possible that he might succeed and secure an order from
the High Court blocking his prosecution on some or even
all of the charges.

So just when I thought an end was in sight a whole new
battleground opened up before me. And yet again I was
outside the process and had no control over what might
happen. I was a witness in the case; only the State and
Fortune had any control. Once again I was forced to sit
and wait for a trial that might never happen and which
could be years away if it did finally take place.

By this time I'd begun to think about the wider
implications of the case. I was aware of the suggestions
that the Bishop of Ferns, Dr Brendan Comiskey, had not
co-operated fully with the investigation and had refused to

be interviewed. It had also been suggested, and confirmed to me by people close to the investigation, that the bishop had refused to grant the police access to diocesan files. I'd seen evidence that at least one complaint about Fortune sexually assaulting a young man had been made directly to Comiskey in 1985, almost ten years before I came forward. Just how much did the Catholic Church know about Sean Fortune?

By late 1997, I heard of another case where a victim had made a direct complaint to the Church about Fortune, claiming that the priest had abused him during the same years he had abused me. He'd written to the bishop in October 1987, at the suggestion of the priest appointed to replace Fortune in Poulfur. The letter explained that this man was worried that Fortune might still be harming others.

I started to get really angry. I'd assumed the Church would have questions to answer about how it had failed to see what Fortune was doing, but I never imagined for a moment that they might have actually known what he was doing to children, that they ignored complaints and concerns and simply allowed him to carry on. I began to suspect that the Church was in some way complicit in the abuse.

I knew how I ought to respond, but found myself hesitating before going to see a lawyer. This was such a huge step. It was one thing to report a priest and name what had happened, but now I was considering suing a bishop – taking on the Catholic Church, the most powerful institution in Ireland. It seemed unthinkable. I didn't want to imagine how people might react.

Dad was still very much in my mind whenever I tried to work out what to do next. I missed him terribly and wished he were with me to advise and support me. I would recall how on the day he discovered he was dying he told me he wished he could be there to see this through with me. That, and the memory of how facing the past honestly together had helped us find our way back to loving each other, made me certain that getting to the truth of everything that had happened was the only way forward.

And so in the autumn of 1998 I went home to Wexford again, this time to seek advice from a lawyer who was already acting for other men who had made complaints against Fortune. Trips home for meetings like this demanded that I dredge through the details of the abuse again and again as part of some legal process or investigation. I hated having to explain to new people what had happened. Their professional curiosity was of course absolutely appropriate, but I always felt horribly exposed. The thought of having to face Fortune in court for the criminal case and be questioned and challenged by his lawyers was terrifying enough. If I took a case against the Church there would surely be even more questioning. I would probably have to see some kind of medical specialist or psychiatrist, someone who would ask me questions about my sexuality, who would prod and pry to find ways to say it was all my fault. I was very anxious and uncertain about whether I could do this. And yet I was also angry and knew I had to at least try.

I saw my sisters Barbara and Deirdre again in Wexford. They were always great during times like this. Theirs was a quiet but powerful support. They rarely talked to me about what was happening unless it was to help in practical ways, like organising a trip or setting up a meeting of some sort. If I wanted to talk they were there, ready to listen and to hold me when I needed it. I always knew they would be available in an instant if I needed them, but they gave me space and time, they made sure I didn't forget that there was more to who I was than the abuse and the case. They kept life normal and real in an unreal time. All my sisters and my brothers were magnificent.

The next day I met the lawyer, Simon Kennedy. I was uncertain about what to expect and knew nothing of how this would work. I did know that if I wanted the Church held to account I would have to do it myself, and that meant hiring my own lawyer.

The offices were in a side street off the Quays in New Ross, a coastal town about thirty minutes drive from Wexford. They were a bit faded and unimpressive and I found it difficult to see how this place might contain the steely resources necessary to take on the Roman Catholic Church. Simon's office was fitted with black ash furniture. His desk was covered in files, with shelves of law books on the wall behind it.

'So, why do you want to take a case against the Church?' Simon asked.

'I want the truth. It's that simple. I want to know what they knew, when they knew it and what they did or didn't do about Sean Fortune abusing me and other kids. They won't tell me, so I want to make them tell everyone. I want this exposed and dealt with.'

'You do realise what you're taking on, don't you?'

'Yes. I know who they are and I know this won't be easy, but I still want to do it. I have to do it.'

'Are you ready for this to end up in court? Are you ready for cross-examination and all that it could bring? It won't be easy and they won't take this lightly. They will fight and fight hard.'

'I want this to get to court. I don't want, nor will I take, some secret settlement. This isn't about money. I want them to have to answer my questions. This is about the truth, nothing else.'

It turned out that Simon was already acting for the man who had written to the bishop in 1987. I was stunned as I heard more about the case. It seemed that a few years after he'd written the letter, the man, then a teenager, was taken to a Catholic Church College in Dublin and questioned by a Church investigator. Nothing was known about the outcome of that investigation, other than that Fortune had continued to work as a priest. I learned that Comiskey had written to the boy's mother apologising for what had happened to her son, and that the mother had destroyed the letter in anger and distress.

Here was more evidence that the bishop had received complaints about Fortune sexually assaulting boys up to ten years before I made my complaint to the police. Ten years in which it would appear he did virtually nothing to respond to those who had been abused, or to ensure that Fortune could not abuse others.

As I look back to that day in Simon's office all I see is the betrayal of the boy I was, of my family, my community and even of my faith. The depth of that betrayal left me breathless.

Vivid memories flashed before my eyes. Me, lying naked and obscenely charged as Fortune leaned over me;

depressed and suicidal at aged seventeen; on the streets of Dublin alone and desperate, lost to my family; Dad and I, our shared hurt ... As I look back I see the cost of it all: the loss of myself for so very long; the lost relationships with my family and especially with my father; the years lost to running from myself and what happened to me. Those were years that ought to have been filled with opportunity and fulfilment. They were not.

Somebody once said to me that perhaps what happened to me happened because it would eventually lead me to do the things I have done. She believed that the things I have achieved and the battles I have won have somehow made sense of what happened. For her, the abuse is somehow less tragic in the context of what she sees as my triumph over it. I don't agree. All I see is hurt and pain that should never have happened. This was a battle I should never have been forced to fight.

Over the years I have realised that what healing there has been for me has come not from a sense that I have been able to put right what was done to me but from a realisation that I cannot and must not try to put it right. Healing lies in an acceptance of the truth of what was done to me and allowing myself to let it be.

I cannot fix it.

I cannot go back in time and make it so it never happened and no victory over any of those responsible for the abuse can change the nature of what happened to me.

Any attempt to fix it, to make it better, to bring hope or redemption would be a betrayal of the truth of my experience. For me, the experience of rape was one where there was no hope of rescue, no way of making it all ok, no escape. It was entirely hopeless. To pretend otherwise is to corrupt that truth and once again abandon myself.

'How could they bury and hide this, stand by and allow it to happen?' I asked Simon.

I thought of my father and me. I thought of how allowing the truth to be spoken had finally brought us together. I sat with the realisation that had the Church spoken out in 1985, or in 1987, on either of the occasions when I now knew they had knowledge of complaints of abuse, then I would have come forward.

Their power kept my father and me silent.

Their authority caused those who had been abused to be silent. Their word could have broken that silence and brought comfort. And yet they did not speak. They, who were outspoken on so many other things, who challenged wrong and demanded virtue of all others, were silent on the sins of one of their own.

I was furious.

Simon explained that it could take up to three years to get to court but he felt I had a strong case against the diocese. His view was that the diocese had a responsibility as Fortune's supervisors to make sure he did no harm in his role as a priest.

He also felt there was much more to discover about the extent of the Church's knowledge of Fortune's abuse of children prior to his assaulting me. He explained that if we could prove they knew he had a propensity to abuse boys before I met him, and did nothing to prevent him from abusing me, we would certainly win our case.

I resolved to do whatever was necessary to expose the truth. I knew enough even then to be convinced that the

Church had knowingly covered up abuse and rape by one of its priests. I was certain this went beyond my case and beyond my diocese.

'Who else would have known?' I asked.

'The Vatican perhaps. Every bishop must report to the Vatican directly every five years on the state of his diocese, his people and his clergy. They either knew or should have known.'

'So what do we do?' I asked.

'You could add the Vatican to the suit,' he said. 'You could sue the Pope.'

It had been a long journey to get to the point where I could take such a huge decision. I often wonder if I realised what it was I was taking on. Did I understand that I was about to challenge the oldest and one of the most powerful organisations in the world?

I told Simon that, if the evidence suggested that the Vatican did know, then I would indeed sue the Pope. It was a momentous decision and I hated the idea that it might take another three years. I am not convinced that I really did realise back then the scale and significance of the challenge I was taking on. No one knew where this would end, not the lawyers, not the Church and certainly not me. All I knew was my truth and my sense of what was right. I knew what the truth demanded of me too. And that was enough.

# 16

# The Court Case

I was now involved in two parallel legal processes, the criminal case against Fortune and the civil case I'd started against the Church.

The Fortune case dragged on and on. Every now and again I would get an update, a call to tell me that his latest attempt to have the case dismissed was due before the courts. More often than not it would be followed by another call explaining that there would be yet another delay due to some new legal technicality.

Finally I got a call telling me that the case was scheduled. The trial would begin at Wexford Circuit Court on Tuesday, 2 March 1999, and I was to present myself to give evidence on the second day. Almost four years after my initial complaint, the case would finally reach court.

After all this time a jury would hear the evidence and I could hand what had happened over to those responsible for working it all out. After more than fifteen years, I might finally be free of the burden of secrecy. But it also meant I would have to step into the witness box and tell it as I remembered it all. No hiding and no dodging by making it something other than it was. I would have to lay it all out, every sordid, awful, humiliating detail.

If what I said was accepted as the truth, then Fortune would be found guilty. His only way out was to discredit me in some way. If he was innocent then I had to be a liar. I had to be ready to face his lawyers as they worked to defend him by undermining me. I was frightened of what that might be like, of whether I could keep it together and stay clear-headed. I was scared of messing it up, of getting it wrong and allowing him to avoid the truth of what he'd done to me and to so many others.

I really had no idea what to expect. I'd never been in a court before and had never seen a criminal trial, apart from on TV. The police told me I should make myself available for up to three weeks, though they didn't know how long it might last.

I got back to Wexford a few days before the trial was due to start. My family, as ever, did everything they could to support me. They took me out to dinner and Deirdre held a party at her place. It wasn't to mark the upcoming trial but to allow us all, me especially, a diversion from the stress and worry.

The day before the trial Pat Mulcahy, the detective who had investigated my complaint, came to Barbara's house to see me. We sat in the kitchen, the same room where four years earlier I'd broken my silence and made my police statement. He told me that Fortune was prepared to offer a guilty plea to some of the minor charges, but not the most serious one – the charge of buggery, which related to the time he raped me.

I was torn. An offer to plead guilty would avoid the

need for a trial and mean that Fortune would acknowledge his guilt before the court. At the same time I knew that dropping the most serious charge would probably mean he would get a light sentence, possibly a suspended term. More than that, it meant I would have to accept the official and legal validation of a lie.

For all these years I believed that only through the full and honest disclosure of the truth could this whole awful mess be finally and fully addressed. I promised myself that I would tell the truth and be guided by it and committed to it. When secrets and lies have caused so much hurt, truth matters. I remembered Dad. His wish when he found out he was dying to live just long enough to see this through with me.

I owed him the truth. I owed it to myself and I owed it to others. Lies and half-truths were what allowed abuse to happen in the first place.

The system was looking for a tidy way out, to avoid a trial and the telling of the brutal and uncomfortable truth. Sean Fortune was looking to avoid the truth of what he'd done. No doubt the Church wanted that too. Then we could all go home and get on with life. There would be some damage, a conviction and scandal for the Church, but without the mess and drama of a public trial. The truth would be suppressed. I could have none of that. I told Pat that I would be completely opposed if the State agreed to the dropping of any charges.

The next morning I got up and with a calm and steady sense of purpose showered, shaved and dressed, had breakfast with my family and headed down to the courthouse in Wexford.

As we walked up the steps of County Hall Barbara asked me if I felt nervous.

'This isn't my day to be frightened or anxious. It's Fortune's day for that. This is the day I get to give it all back to him.'

It had been such a long road to get this far and I was ready for whatever might come at me now. I had carried all that shame for so long and finally, after years in therapy and a lot of tears and frustration, I knew that it wasn't my shame. It was his. And this day, he would have to take it back.

When he abused and raped me there was shame in that room, in that car, in every place it had happened. But Fortune was shameless; he refused to own the wrong that he had done, to take responsibility for the sin and the hurt. He left it there, smeared all over me, and I had no choice but to bear it. No one else would, so it became mine.

But now, in a court of law, before the State and a jury of his peers, he would hear what he had done, spoken loud and clear as the charges were put to him. He could dodge no more. He would have to respond, admit the fact of the accusation and hear me speak from the witness box as I showed him that I had broken free of his threats and control, free of his collar and of the fear he instilled in me. I would name what he had done and he would have to answer.

I remembered his words all those years ago. 'You have a problem, I am a Priest and I have a duty to do something about it.'

He had used my fears – of who I might be and of disappointing my father – to make me go back there time and again. But in the end, my father loved me. He loved me. As I headed into that courthouse, Dad was with me. We would face him together.

I wasn't frightened of what anyone might think anymore.

My own legal team was there to greet me. Simon told me that Fortune was still arguing to find a way to prevent the trial going ahead. That made sense to me. He was a powerful personality; his ego was enormous and he was used to getting his own way. He believed in his absolute authority and would not easily permit anyone to hold him to account. After all, he had managed to do exactly as he wanted for years without anyone stopping him or controlling him.

The prosecution team wanted to meet with me to discuss another plea bargain. Simon explained that Fortune was now offering to plead guilty to most of the charges, including a charge of attempted buggery, in place of the existing charge of buggery. At this point I didn't know whether to laugh or scream. It all seemed so ridiculous.

'What does that mean, *attempted* buggery? Does it mean he tried but couldn't get it in? He only half-managed it? Is there a measurement, a degree of penetration that means attempted buggery rather than actual buggery?'

I was ranting now, appalled that this was happening. When the charges against Fortune were first formalised I struggled to get to grips with the fact that he'd been charged with buggery rather than rape. He had raped me. But the law at the time of the offence did not recognise rape of a male. Instead the only offence he could be charged with was buggery. I was very upset about that.

The charge related to an offence created to criminalise consenting sexual activity among adults. I struggled to deal with how others might interpret that charge, particularly since I was gay. I cringed every time I heard the word used in the context of the case. In the end I made my peace with it as best I could and accepted that there was no other way for the law to frame what had been done to me.

But now it was being suggested that the charge be reduced even further to *attempted* buggery. I was furious.

'This is how it works,' Simon replied. 'His guilty plea will mean there won't have to be a hearing and you and all the others will be spared the ordeal of the witness box.'

'But it's not the truth. That's not what happened. I thought this was all about the truth. I thought that's what justice meant!'

'It's how it works, Colm,' Simon repeated, looking at me over his glasses. 'There won't be any need for a trial. He will plead guilty. You will have won.'

'Who says I don't want a trial? I want my day in court. After all this time and all these games, I want to stand up and tell the truth. I want him to hear me say the words and to face me as I say them. That's what matters most to me now. It's been too hard and taken too long to get this far to back down now. Tell me they won't do this without me.'

Simon knew I was upset. 'You need to talk to the prosecution Colm. Hear them out and tell them what you think. Try and stay calm and listen. It's a good thing that he's offered to plead guilty to at least attempted buggery. It's a good sign.'

He did his best to calm me down and suggested I talk to the prosecution before making my mind up about how

I felt. Though I knew how I felt and was certain I would not be prepared to accept the charge being dropped or reduced, I knew I had to listen to the prosecuting barrister.

I reluctantly agreed and met the prosecution team in a small, austere room in the courthouse. There were two barristers, the senior and the junior counsel. They were dressed in black robes with white collars, which I remember thinking were not dissimilar to the vestments of clergy. More symbols of authority, of expert understanding of a code that was beyond the appreciation of mere mortals like me, though this time on an intellectual rather than spiritual level.

The senior counsel was a decent man. He talked me through their position, explaining that an offer of a guilty plea was always considered as it avoided the expense and the risk of a trial. It would also mean that all the victims would be spared the experience of giving evidence in open court and of cross examination by the defence.

The one thing that rocked me a little was that if I refused to support the dropping of the charge then I would in effect be forcing all the other victims and their families, and Fortune's family, to go through the ordeal of the trial. I felt the weight of that and struggled with it for a moment. At the same time I knew I had to avoid taking responsibility for anyone other than myself in all of this. I had to be guided by the truth and I would at least ensure that everyone else involved would be free to make their own choices on the same basis. If I deviated from that, everything was in danger of becoming distorted and unreal, and I did not feel safe with the idea of that.

The barrister explained that they were discussing this with me in order to take on board my views. 'The case is essentially one taken by the State against Fr Fortune,' he explained. 'As you know, you are a crucial witness, but it's the State that must decide how to prosecute the case and not you.'

I looked at him as he walked around the room. He wasn't being unpleasant or unsympathetic and his tone was measured, warm even, but he needed me to understand how this would work, and to test me to see how I might react.

'We are, however, interested in your view on the matter. We would like to take on board your view and your feelings should the State decide to accept the plea from the defendant.'

He went on to explain that there had been another high profile case involving the killing of a police officer in which a guilty plea to a lesser charge, without any consultation with the family of the victim, had caused a public outcry.

I respected how upfront he was with me and I was equally upfront in return. I knew that this was also a high profile case. The media were present in droves with TV cameras and photographers waiting for a shot of Fortune, and reporters desperate for any snippet of information. I knew the State would be particularly concerned about dropping a serious charge against the wishes of the victim.

I took a breath and looked him in the eye. 'I would be vehemently opposed to the dropping of any charge,' I said. 'And I would be very vocal in my opposition.'

He nodded, and that was that.

\*　　\*　　\*

The rest of that morning was taken up with jury selection. I sat watching the process. Each man and woman chosen would be responsible for hearing the evidence and deciding a verdict. After all these years, it would all come down to these twelve people.

I hadn't seen Sean Fortune so far that day. I hadn't actually seen him for twelve years, since that close encounter in the restaurant on my 21st birthday. But as I sat in the courthouse that day I was acutely aware that he was also there, somewhere in the same building. I knew that at some point, within minutes or at most hours, I would face him across a room.

By lunchtime the trial proper was yet to start. An argument from the defence sought to further delay the trial on the basis that the senior defence barrister had not arrived at the court as he was delayed on another trial. When I heard this I expected the judge to order that the trial would, once again, be put off. Thankfully he didn't. He reminded the defence that they'd had notice of the commencement of the trial for some time and that it would begin as scheduled later that day. And with that the court broke for lunch. Half the day was gone. Two issues that might have prevented the court from hearing the case or delayed the trail had been averted. It was nerve-racking. I wanted it to begin ... so that it would be over.

After lunch we all headed back to the courthouse. I still hadn't met any of the other victims and didn't recognise anyone. I didn't really want to meet any of them at that point. I'd come so far but the idea of having to talk to someone else who had been abused by Fortune was still too much. I could deal with what he'd done to me but I didn't think I could cope with what he'd done to anyone else, at least not up close and personal. I didn't want to see the hurt in the eyes of another victim. I didn't want to get entangled in their feelings and fears in a way that might blur my focus.

At one point the father of one of the victims approached me. He asked me if I would agree to an effort to have the trial moved to Dublin and away from Wexford. He looked mortified by the whole experience.

'It's easier for you lads that live away. We have to live here, we have to live with this, you don't.'

I didn't know what to say to him. This was exactly the sort of thing I needed to avoid. 'I'm so sorry that this is so difficult for you and your family. It's difficult for my family too. But we've all waited so long now and I couldn't cope with another delay. It's hard for everyone. I'm so sorry.'

He nodded without a word and walked away. It was an awful moment.

Apart from concerns about a further delay, I also felt it was very important that the trial took place in Wexford. This was where it had all happened. This was the community that had denied it happening right before their eyes. It was vital that the truth be brought out, clearly and uncompromisingly, before the very people who had sought to dodge or deny it for so long. Nothing can be dealt with until it is acknowledged.

As we waited for the trial to begin I kept hearing suggestions that Fortune was refusing to come into the court, that he was still trying to find a way to prevent or defer the trial. Finally, after what seemed like hours, we were told to make our way into court.

I sat at the back of the courtroom with Barbara, Eamon and Deirdre. It was packed. At the front sat both teams of lawyers, plus my own legal team who were there as observers. Below the judge's bench sat the various court officials and in front of them the media, notebooks and pens at the ready to record the unfolding drama. To my right were the police witnesses and the investigating team. Someone pointed out a woman who was there with Fortune, his housekeeper I was told. I had no idea if any members of his family were there or not, I wouldn't have known them if they were. Looking back it must have been a truly awful time for them too. There were no winners here, no victory to be had. We had all suffered and we were likely to suffer more as the trial unfolded.

After a few minutes the doors to the court opened, just to the left of where we were sitting, and Sean Fortune entered. I was shocked by his appearance. He was as tall and intimidating as I remembered but he was now also obese. He was dressed in full clerical garb, with the black suit and roman collar but he also wore small, round sunglasses that hid his eyes. He limped into the court on crutches and sat beside his lawyer. I didn't know what the crutches were for, though I heard he'd been suggesting his health was bad.

A moment later a court official called out, 'All rise.'

Judge Joseph Matthews walked from his chambers across the courtroom and stepped up to take his seat behind the raised bench. Above his high-backed chair was the emblem of the Irish State, a golden harp. Then everyone else sat down and the trial was under way. My stomach lurched as I realised that this was finally it: it had begun.

After some preliminary comments the judge asked that the defendant rise to hear the charges before him. Fortune stood, leaning on his crutches and looking wretched.

'Are you Sean Fortune?' Judge Matthews asked.

I could feel a flash of irritation from Fortune, outrage at his having been addressed so casually.

'I am *Father* Sean Fortune,' he corrected, his chin in the air and his voice clear and strong.

The charges were then put to him.

I held my breath. There were sixty-six charges in all. Not all of them were read out in court but twenty-nine were put to him, one by one.

Each time a charge was read so was the name of the victim. Fortune was charged with sexual offences against named victims.

Mine was the first of eight names read out in the long list of charges: 'That on a date unknown between June 1981 and September 1983 you did commit an act of gross indecency upon one Colm O'Gorman. How do you plead?'

Barbara held my hand tight, giving me a squeeze of support.

I looked over at Fortune, standing there staring at the clerk of the court.

'Not guilty.'

The clerk went on, reading out all twenty-nine charges. It was a huge moment for me. This was a big part of what I needed, to see and hear him face each charge, to hear him accused of acts of sexual assault, gross indecency and the final charge of buggery. There could be no more secrets now, no more half-truths. It was out and it would have to be dealt with.

After each charge Fortune was asked how he pleaded. 'Not guilty,' he answered each and very time.

As the sixteenth of the twenty-nine charges was read, he asked: 'I'm getting very weak. Can I sit down please?'

Once granted permission, he sat, clattering his crutches as he lowered himself, all fuss and bluster before he replied: 'Thank you, my lord.'

He answered to the remaining charges from his seat.

When the last charge had been read, the defence lawyer began to put further legal arguments to the judge. I was fixed on Fortune, watching him intently from the other side of the court. He started acting very bizarrely. At one point he looked like he was falling asleep, his eyes closed and he started to lean precariously out of his seat. I thought he was going to fall over until a police officer tapped him on the shoulder and he seemed to wake up with a start, letting out a forced-sounding yelp of surprise.

He then called out to Pat Mulcahy, the police detective who had investigated the case. 'Pat, tell them I didn't kill anyone. They are saying I killed someone.'

The judge told Fortune's barrister to keep him quiet. In reply, the barrister informed the judge that he was seeking a hearing to assess Fortune's ability to stand trial. His lawyer said that he was both physically and mentally unfit to be tried. I felt sick. Only an hour or two earlier Fortune had been arguing and trying to negotiate a plea bargain. Now all of a sudden he seemed incapable of coherent thought and unable to properly answer the charges he faced. My stomach turned as I realised this might stop the trial dead in its tracks.

To his great credit the judge tried to wade through the arguments being presented. He dismissed the jury, explaining that in law this was not a matter for them. The defence offered expert testimony from a psychiatrist who had been treating Fortune. The psychiatrist said that Fortune was under very great stress and had been under his care for some time. The judge listened carefully. He pointed out that it could not be disputed that Fortune was under great stress, he had after all been charged with very serious and despicable offences and it would only be human to suffer the effects of stress. What he wanted to know was whether or not his mental health was affected in ways that were more serious than stress. During this time Fortune continued to act bizarrely. It was a terrible and distressing drama and I had no idea where it was headed.

In the end the judge ruled that he'd heard sufficient evidence to suggest there was a question as to Fortune's competence to stand trial and that there would need to be a separate hearing to decide Fortune's capacity to stand trial. He informed us that a jury, and not he as judge, would decide the issue and that it would have to be a separate jury to the one already selected. Since the pool of around one hundred people from which the trial jury was selected had been released, this hearing could only take place once a new pool was called and a new jury selected and sworn in. As a result he had no alternative but to suspend the trial subject to the outcome of that hearing.

I was stunned. The trial was once again delayed, and worse yet it might not go ahead at all if Fortune and his legal team could convince this new jury that he was unfit to stand trial.

Fortune's barrister rose and informed the judge that he was seeking the continuation of bail until this hearing could take place. It looked like he would walk out of court having delayed the trial again, and I would return to London to wait, again. To my mind, he had played the system and won, just as he always seemed to win.

But Judge Matthews had a surprise in store. He told Fortune's barrister that he would not be granting bail since, when Fortune presented himself before the court, his bail was surrendered and he was therefore not automatically entitled to continuing bail. In fact, he explained, as Fortune's lawyers had asserted that he was psychologically unwell, the judge was ordering that he be remanded into the care of the Central Mental Hospital, a secure institution in Dublin. If he was as unwell as was suggested the defence could have no cause to object to his being remanded into the care of the hospital where he could receive the best available treatment.

Fortune himself appealed to the judge not to be remanded into custody and undertook to subject himself to any treatment or supervision the judge suggested. In one moment he'd gone from a rambling, incoherent wretch to a clear, lucid man appealing to the judge.

The judge rejected his pleas and the objections of his lawyers, and Fortune was led from the court. I watched as he was led away by the police, praying that this turn of events would result in an early hearing and an end to the drama, hoping against hope that this latest twist might mean that things were moving forwards and that Fortune would not be able to manipulate the system for much longer.

As we left the courthouse I was exhausted. I was so used to the endless delays that it was both shattering and familiar. I spoke briefly to *Irish Times* journalist Alison O'Connor, who asked me if I would be prepared to talk to her on the record at some point. I told her yes, once it was legally possible, I would talk to her.

I'd taken two weeks off work for the trial, with arrangements to take more if necessary, so I decided to stay in Wexford to rest before heading back to London.

I went to Barbara's house and spent the next few days trying to get my head around what had happened. The case was reported in the news, saying only that an unnamed Wexford priest had appeared in court charged with sexually abusing boys and that he had been remanded to the Central Mental Hospital for psychiatric evaluation. The media had to be very careful about what they reported in case it prejudiced the trial.

A few days later, on 5 March, Fortune applied for and was granted bail at the High Court in Dublin.

The conditions attached to his bail were that he live at an address in the town of New Ross in County Wexford and that he sign on weekly at the police station, as well as undergo psychiatric evaluation. And so he was out again. Before he could be transferred to the Central Mental Hospital, he was sent to Mountjoy Prison where he was assessed by a psychiatrist. It appears, though it still remains unclear, this assessment found that he did not need to be referred to the hospital.

There happened to be a strike at the hospital so he was held in Mountjoy for almost a week. It must have been a sobering experience for a man who knew he was facing a prison sentence of some kind.

In any event, he was granted bail and returned to the small terraced house he was renting in New Ross. The house was like a fortress, with shutters and closed-circuit TV cameras, evidence of his fears for his personal safety.

He was right to be anxious, though he still had a great many supporters. Some people refused to believe that a priest could be guilty of such awful crimes.

Not long after his release, kids kicked the shutters of the house while he was inside. The papers later reported that he called the police. When they arrived he showed them the video of the incident as captured on CCTV. In the video he was seen running down the street after the boys. This was the same man who had appeared in court a week earlier on crutches, with a wheelchair waiting at the foot of the stairs.

As that week came to a close I mentally prepared myself to head back to London, for yet another journey back with nothing resolved and no end in sight. Then, at around noon on Saturday 13 March, I got a call. It was the journalist Alison O'Connor.

'Colm, I have some difficult news,' she said. 'Sean Fortune was found dead at his house in New Ross this morning. He's killed himself.'

# 17

# New Beginnings

'What?' I said. I could not make sense of the words I was hearing. I didn't understand.

'He's dead,' Alison repeated. 'He was found in his bed this morning by his housekeeper. He appears to have committed suicide.'

I couldn't breathe, panic leapt up inside my chest. I felt sick.

'Are you ok? I wanted to call and tell you before it came out on the news.'

I mumbled something in reply. I was in shock. This wasn't possible. I started to cry without knowing why or who I was crying for.

After I hung up the phone, I stood in the hallway with tears streaming down my face. Then I started to shake and sob out loud. A friend was there with me and I told him what had happened. A moment later Barbara and Deirdre were there and I told them too.

I was horrified. I couldn't believe or accept that it was going to end like this. This was no ending, no resolution. This was worse than anything I might have imagined.

'You know this isn't your fault,' Barbara said. 'You know you are not responsible for this.'

'I know that,' I replied.

She looked at me quizzically, trying to make sure I got it, really got it.

'No, really I do,' I said. 'He chose this. He had a choice to make and he chose this. He could have decided to face it, to take responsibility for what he did to all of us and taken whatever sentence he received and done something about it. But he didn't. Instead he chose this. This is nothing to do with me. This isn't what I wanted, not even for a moment. I didn't want to destroy him. I just wanted the truth.'

I sat down on the bottom step of the stairs. 'I hoped the truth would show us all a way forward. I even hoped that one day, somehow he might be able to face me, honestly, and tell me why. Tell me what it was all about. That's why I'm so upset I think. I hoped that there might be some kind of healthy closure for us all, even him. Now that's impossible.'

'It was the coward's way out,' someone said.

'No it wasn't, it wasn't cowardice. It was ego. No one could be allowed to hold him to account, no one. He would not permit that.'

I realised that I was crying for all of us then. For me, my Dad, my family and all we had endured over the years because of this. For the other boys, now men, and their families, and all the others who had remained silent in their shame at what had been done to them. For his family, for the brothers and sisters he left behind to bear the shame of what he had done, for their loss of a brother in such circumstances.

And even for him, for him as the last victim of his psychopathic nature that would sooner destroy him than be limited by rules and by the law.

This was no ending.

I was of course also devastated that I would now be denied justice. As Paul Molloy, one of his other victims, said later that week: 'I was upset at the thought that my story would never be told and he would never be formally found guilty. I wanted him to show remorse, to look down in the courtroom as I told my story. That won't happen now.'

Alison rang me back later. She told me that Sean Fortune appeared to have killed himself with a cocktail of whiskey and prescription drugs. He was found in his bed with his hands crossed as if in prayer, dressed in full clerical garb and with a set of rosary beads entwined in his hands.

Alison asked me if I wanted to say anything on the record about what had happened. I agreed to talk to her, to be photographed and allow her to name me in her story. It was vital now to be clear and public. There would be a lot of reporting, speculation and innuendo; I had to do what I could to name the truth, to make the voice of victims heard.

The following day I explained the background of my case to her, how I'd met Fortune and what had happened to me as a result. I spoke of my father's role in my decision to report the abuse and my hopes for what that might achieve.

'All I wanted from the court case was to be able to say what happened and to have a reaction from the justice system, and from society, an acknowledgement of it. To have all those charges read out in court was an incredible moment. But then it was back to waiting and wondering how much longer he could manage to stretch it out. It's been a long four years and I think I'm probably going to start to realise now what it has taken out of me.'

The previous day Bishop Comiskey made a statement to the media. He refuted any suggestion that he had failed to act on complaints of abuse and denied reports that he had 'simply moved the priest from one pastoral assignment to another'. He promised to provide documents, which would prove this, once the case had run its course and he was legally permitted to do so.

His spokesperson went on to say that the bishop wished 'to extend his sincere sympathy to the family of Fr Sean Fortune and he wishes for people to remember him and them in his prayers at this difficult time'.

I told Alison, 'I think that the Church has an opportunity now to put right what happened, not just in this case. The Church must lead the people in this. They have an opportunity to do what they are supposed to do, to act with love, compassion and respect. I read a lot in the papers this morning about how the bishop asked for prayers for his (Sean Fortune's) family.

'There was no mention of the rest, obviously there may be legal constraints, but he could have asked for prayers for the others affected. It is sad for me, my family and for all the boys abused and their families. I am praying for Father Fortune too. Yesterday I wept for him. He was a human being, the tragedy now is that he is a victim as well.'

The papers that Monday were full of the story. I was alone in Barbara's house that morning. There was a knock on the door and when I answered it a taxi driver handed me a note asking me to ring a number at RTE, the State broadcaster.

When I rang I spoke to a researcher who asked me if I would go on air to talk to Pat Kenny, the presenter of the main morning show on RTE Radio 1.

'How did you get my address?' I asked.

'We looked in the phonebook and sent taxis to every house where anyone called O'Gorman lived.'

That was my first experience of just how tenacious the media would be in chasing this story. I got more calls that day too, from newspapers and radio shows who worked hard to get me to give interviews. Some of them were very pushy indeed, others understood how difficult it all was and were kind and sympathetic. I felt overwhelmed and didn't know what to do.

My lawyer Simon told me I should decline all interviews. He felt very strongly that I shouldn't be in the media too much, that the one interview with Alison was enough. I was grateful for a reason to say no and not deal with the volume of calls, so I took his advice.

Comiskey returned from the United States when Fortune killed himself. I was surprised he'd been away from the diocese at all. One of his priests was on trial for abusing boys and it was a crisis for so many people, but he wasn't there. I hadn't had any contact from him or the diocese in the four years since I made my original complaint.

A few days later the bishop officiated at Fortune's funeral. In his homily he spoke of hope.

'Father Fortune's hope, like the hope of all believers, lies in the mercy of God, and God ... is rich in mercy.'

As I watched the bishop on the TV news being driven from the church back to the palace in a big black BMW,

I remember wondering what Christ would have done had He been there.

My outrage at the bishop's response was the fuel that drove me forward. In that moment I knew this wasn't over. Fortune was dead, he would never see justice, never be afforded the opportunity to face his crimes, but Comiskey and the Roman Catholic Church still had a great many questions to answer. Over the days and weeks that followed we learned more and more about how much was known of Fortune's actions.

On the 23 March, ten days after his suicide, the criminal case against Fr Sean Fortune was struck out at Wexford Circuit Court. Pat Jackman, another of his victims, said later: 'We will always be his *alleged* victims now.' And that was how it seemed to me too. It all felt hopeless.

I affirmed anew to pursue truth and justice and force the Roman Catholic Church and the Pope himself to be accountable for their part in the crimes committed against me and countless others.

When I got back to London more challenges awaited me. Robert and I had decided to split up after eleven years together. I felt that our relationship no longer offered us a space to grow from. I had changed so much over the past four years, and we'd grown apart. I loved him, I still do, and leaving was harder than I can describe. I knew I was hurting him, and that was hard to deal with. But I knew I didn't love him in the way I needed to if we were to be together.

Work was changing too. My practice had grown and developed. I was now working almost exclusively as a psychotherapist and did little physical therapy. I loved the work. I was amazed by people's capacity to heal, to face and confront difficult histories and emerge from them, stronger and more alive than ever. I'd experienced that for myself and knew it was possible.

More than two-thirds of my clients were presenting with experiences of childhood sexual abuse. It was challenging and inspiring work, but I felt I was limited in what I could offer them. Often, when a man or woman began to step back into that history their day-to-day lives would suffer. The hurt, which already impacted so much on their adult lives, became more acute as they struggled to manage it.

The boundary essential to a therapeutic relationship meant that I could not offer the kinds of practical support many clients needed. I found that difficult, especially as it became clear that there were no other organisations that provided such support.

I needed professional peer support myself. I had a clinical supervisor to discuss my work with, but I felt I needed to be part of a team, to have my work informed, questioned and supported. I looked around for an organisation within which I might work, a support service for women and men who had experienced sexual abuse, but I couldn't find one.

Having developed a sense of the sort of organisation that was needed, and discovered it didn't yet exist, I decided to set one up.

It was a big task to take on. Where would the money come from? Did I even have the necessary skills to start something from scratch? How would I get others involved? There are always reasons why one might not take on a challenge like this, but not one of them was important enough to put me off doing what I believed needed to be done.

When you know the true potential of life, when you have experienced the awesome power of life working to fulfil itself, then very few things seem impossible. There really isn't much to fear. Faith, in life and the endless potential for good that lies within us all, conquers fear. It was in this spirit that I founded One in Four.

I read research that said around 25 per cent of people experienced sexual abuse in childhood. It was a shocking statistic. I thought this astounding fact needed to be more publicly revealed. The name was meant to provoke questions, and it did.

I recruited friends and colleagues. My friend Beth, my clinical supervisor Aleine and another friend, Rahanna, who worked with the local social services department, all got involved. They agreed to be trustees of the new charity and volunteered their time to help me set it up. In early September 1999, we began to see clients at One in Four's newly refurbished offices, over a beauty salon in Catford, south-east London.

There was no news from Ireland about the civil case against Bishop Comiskey and the Vatican. Things had quietened down within a few weeks of Fortune's death and the media attention shifted to the next big story. Simon told me he was advancing the case as quickly as possible, but that it might take another three or four years to get to court. I despaired at the thought. That would mean it could be 2003 before it was all over, a full eight years from when I first made my complaint. I'd always done my best to get on with my life and not be dragged down by it all, but I knew it was having an impact. I was tired, and I wanted it to end.

At the same time I knew this was how it was. Cases like this took forever. I suspected it might be a tactic on the part of the defendants: drag it out, make it as tough as possible and it might just go away. I was determined not to go away. However long it took I would see it through.

I got on with life. I'd learned over the past four years that I couldn't let my own healing and recovery be dependent on a victory in some courtroom. I put the case to the back of my mind and dealt with it when I had to, when some new development meant I had to speak to Simon or meet with him, though that was rare by this stage.

I was rebuilding my life and making active choices about my future. Setting up One in Four was perhaps the best example of that but I wanted to do the same in my personal life.

I decided it was time to get out in the world and date. I realised I'd never really done that. I'd been with Robert for eleven years, since I was twenty-two. We met and within weeks were living together. I didn't want to step into another serious relationship; I didn't think I was ready. Neither did I want a succession of one-night stands. I just wanted to have fun, to go out and meet new people.

Most of my friends were couples. I hardly knew any single people at all, and I didn't have any gay male friends. I badly needed to widen my social circle.

I had a few dates with different people, nothing serious and nothing at all sexual. It was good fun though, meeting new people and doing new things. It was all very grown up, theatre, films, music and dinner at new restaurants, exactly what I needed. Then one night, on Friday, 13 August 1999, that all changed.

I went on a blind date. I had rules about dating, and this one broke them all. No men under thirty, because the chances were they would have issues. No one from a 'difficult' background, because who needs the hassle never mind the almost inevitable co-dependent relationship?

Paul was from Northern Ireland. He was twenty-three, a full ten years younger than me. I thought he was way too young for me. My friend Beth didn't agree. She thought my rules were stupid.

She was helping me redecorate One in Four's new offices and heard a message he left on my phone and thought he sounded nice.

'He has a lovely voice, really warm and interesting,' she said.

I laughed. 'Shut up.'

'He does, he sounds lovely.'

'Shut up! He's way too young,' I said. 'All men under thirty are messed up. I need to date people who are at least a little settled and secure.'

'My God, you are so pompous! Get over yourself and your rules. Go out and have some fun.'

That night I headed off to Soho to meet Paul. We arranged to meet in a pub called The Yard for a drink, quite late on a Friday evening. I'd only been to The Yard once before and it took me forever to find it. I drove around with my map on my lap trying to find a parking space. I finally arrived at 10.45pm, convinced he'd be gone, and that a beer alone would be the end result of my poor map-reading. I went in anyway and headed upstairs to the upper bar where Paul said he would be. I had no idea what to expect or what he looked like.

I couldn't spot him at first, so got myself a beer and walked out onto the balcony of the bar. There, I saw a man leaning over the balcony, looking downstairs. I knew it was him. I don't know how, I just did.

I walked over. 'Paul?'

He turned around, looked at me. 'Yeah.'

I don't know what hit me first. It wasn't how he looked, more the way he looked at me. He was warm and open and something clicked. The bizarre part is that I started to panic. It sounds so corny now but I was struck dumb. A voice in my head was shouting, 'Now you're in trouble, now you're really in trouble!' My brain was addled, trying to catch up with what was happening and failing miserably. I stuttered and held out my hand.

'I'm Colm, sorry I'm so late. I got lost.'

'That's OK. You made it now. Let's go downstairs where we can talk.'

We went downstairs and stood chatting in the courtyard of the pub. Or rather he chatted and I babbled incoherently. It was all quite mad. This had never happened to me before. All I knew was that life might never be the same again, that this man was someone really special.

It was late and the bar was about to close. I didn't want to say goodbye and didn't want to head off to some noisy club. Paul felt the same and suggested we go to a nearby coffee shop.

It's pretty rare for me not to have anything to say. I've been called articulate, I've also been called a big mouth, but when I met Paul that particular curse, or quality, abandoned me. I couldn't put a sentence together that didn't sound like total gibberish. The evening went from terrifying to embarrassing as I spilt coffee over Paul. Twice.

Thankfully Paul had the same feelings for me that I had for him. My new life of bachelorhood came to a rapid and frankly unexpected end. I was completely captured. Paul worked a few hours out of London so we only saw each other when he was off work. It was very exciting, living for the weekend or his next few days off.

Paul made me love with a passion I had never imagined. He opened my heart, and that's what caused the panic and terror. When I looked into his eyes, some deep part of me knew that this man would demand new levels of honesty and commitment from me. I knew in an instant that I would love him.

It was alive and compelling. It was inevitable. All I could do was surrender to it and let go.

This was a time of powerful healing for me. The part of me that had loved freely had been so crushed by the abuse that it remained hidden, so lost that I didn't even know it was missing, until I met Paul.

Loving Paul has been the most challenging thing I've ever done because he makes me be real, warts and all. I'm capable of hating him in a moment as passionately as I love him. No one gets to me the way he does, no one sees me the way he does and demands so much of me. We have challenged each other in ways I never would have believed possible. We've also grown together in ways I could never have imagined.

As another new year approached, I reflected back on twelve months of extraordinary events. Sean Fortune's suicide and the collapse of the criminal case, the end of my relationship with Robert and moving to a new home, setting up One in Four, and above all, falling in love with Paul.

As Big Ben struck midnight on 31 December 1999 and the twentieth century drew to a close, I stood with my arms around him on London Bridge. The sky was lit up by brilliant flashes of glittering light as thousands of fireworks exploded above us. All around us couples kissed and friends embraced as the crowds drank champagne from overflowing bottles and toasted the dawn of a new millennium.

# 18

# One in Four

Despite all the dire warnings that the Y2K computer bug would cause planes to fall from the sky and the world banking system to collapse, the dawn of the twenty-first century and the third millennium saw the world continue much as it had before.

Work was going really well, though money for One in Four was very tight. We had no funding for the new service and depended on donations from clients to keep it going. I still saw other clients from my old practice which also brought in a bit of income, but it was Paul's generosity and support that meant I could still pay the mortgage and continue working to properly establish One in Four.

We had a great team of enthusiastic volunteers who gave their time to keep everything going. It was time to announce the new organisation publicly and we planned a press launch for the second week of February. Unintentionally, this coincided with the launch of the Waterhouse Report, an inquiry into horrific sexual and physical abuse in 'care' institutions in North Wales. It exposed appalling abuse and failures on the part of social services and other agencies. Before long there were numerous large-scale investigations into child abuse in care institutions across the UK.

I was struck by the similarities between the North Wales cases and my own. A group of people, those running the homes, had been granted unquestioned authority over boys placed in their 'care'. No one checked how they exercised that authority, no one questioned what might be happening even as evidence of truly horrific levels of abuse emerged. The local social services department and the local authority didn't investigate and deal with the abuse; instead they seemed to have covered it up in an effort to protect themselves from any liability. Reports about the homes were hidden and those who tried to speak out were threatened with legal sanctions.

Unaccountable and unquestioned power had abused the vulnerable. The authority responsible for stopping that abuse had acted to protect itself rather than protect children. Institutionalised power protected the institution, not those it purported to serve.

As a result of the publicity surrounding the report, our launch generated national media interest. I found myself doing interviews about One in Four on BBC Radio 4 and many regional stations. We were featured on the evening news in London and I was interviewed in the studio of the main weekend current affairs programme on London Weekend Television. It was all very new to me.

But I learned quickly, made only a few mistakes and soon realised that the media could be a powerful tool in my work. I also discovered that I had an instinct for it.

I knew how to deliver a point in strong, straightforward language, and that it was best to stick to one or two points, reinforcing them throughout an interview to ensure the audience took them fully on board. I could coherently deliver a reasonably complex point in just thirty seconds, and the camera or the microphone didn't intimidate me at all. These would turn out to be important skills in the years to come.

All this media attention meant that One in Four became very busy. I recruited a few more therapists and we also developed an advocacy programme to offer practical support, such as reporting cases to the police or social services and helping with housing or legal advice. Often we needed to find an understanding doctor or health service that appreciated the impact of childhood rape and abuse, and for women who needed cervical smears or other gynaecological services. It was incredibly busy and demanding but there was an amazing sense of the possible about the place. Each and every day we saw miracles, women and men overcoming a legacy of abuse, getting back to life, step-by-step and day-by-day. It was extraordinary.

One day I got a call from a woman who identified herself as Shy. She needed help as no one would listen to her. Shy Keenan lived in Essex, about an hour's drive away, and I suggested that she come in and meet me so that we could go over her case.

I didn't appreciate at the time just how difficult this would be for Shy. She didn't tell me she was agoraphobic and rarely left her house because to do so brought on enormous anxiety and panic. It's testament to her courage and tenacity that she defied her fear and came to the office to meet me.

A few days later, I sat on the floor of one of the counselling rooms with Shy, surrounded by files and documents. They told a truly staggering story of decades of abuse by her stepfather and numerous other men, and in children's homes where she was sent after her mother died. She had reported the abuse to the police and to social services, but to no avail. She had written to her Member of Parliament, the Health Secretary and the Prime Minister, again to no effect. She had even written in desperation to Prince Charles and the feminist writer and academic Germaine Greer, neither of whom could do anything to help.

'I've told everyone bar the slugs at the end of the garden, Colm. And no one will do anything,' she told me.

Shy had even recorded her stepfather in a telephone conversation with her sister Sandy, talking about the abuse in detail and naming other victims and offenders. But still no one would do anything.

It was clear to me that her case was not just about the abuse she had experienced as a child and the failures of social services and the police to protect her, but also about the continuing failures of the system to respond to her complaints and ensure no children were at risk from those offenders today. I knew the only way to force an investigation and expose these gross failures was to get the media involved.

I contacted BBC Television's flagship news programme, *Newsnight*, and took Shy to meet their researchers. They committed to an in-depth investigation of the case. And so for the next nine months I travelled with Shy back to Birkenhead on Merseyside, as we worked to tell her story and gather evidence on camera. The story would also be told in her powerful memoir *Broken*.

Making the film was harrowing. Working with and watching Shy as she stepped back into the nightmare world of her childhood was inspiring but also dreadful. She should never have had to do it in the first place, not if those charged with investigating her complaints had done their jobs properly.

We discovered that the things done to Shy, her sisters and other family members across three generations were possible not because no one knew about them, but because they were denied and ignored. Only when they became so appalling they could no longer be ignored did anything happen, and then the intent appeared to be to make it all go away rather than deal with it. Shy's social services files painted a picture of a trouble-making, attention-seeking young girl who brought the abuse on herself. She, the victim, was blamed for seducing her stepfather, not he for raping and abusing her.

Sarah Macdonald, the director of the film, and I became good friends over those months. Sarah is a courageous journalist and film-maker and has huge integrity. Most of the time it was just the three of us – Sarah, Shy and myself – travelling up and down to Merseyside for three or four days a month to do local research or record Shy, using a hidden camera, as she tried to capture her abusers talking about the past. We developed a great bond of trust and were determined to expose the truth and force a proper investigation.

One day as Sarah and I sat outside Birkenhead library waiting for it to open so we could trawl through microfiche records, we talked about my own life. It was a grey morning and we'd spent a heavy few days working with intense and distressing material. Shy was back at the hotel and would join us in a little while. We were all tired and not especially looking forward to hours sifting through decades-old newspapers in search of small but vital snippets of information.

Sarah had learned a little about my history by this stage and knew that I was involved in a case back in Ireland. I told her about Sean Fortune and his suicide, how his death had ended the criminal case and forced me to focus exclusively on the civil suit against Bishop Comiskey.

'What are your chances of succeeding?' she asked.

'It's hard to say. I just want to use the case to force them to reveal what they knew. I want to find out when they first heard about Fortune abusing boys and why they did nothing about it.'

'What if they only found out after he abused you?'

'That will matter to my own case, obviously, but it's not just about that. They definitely knew before I went to the police in 1995. I want to know when and who they passed that information to, both inside and beyond the Church.'

'Who do you think they might have told about it?'

'Well, they should have told the police and social services for sure. If they did, then the State failed to act on that. He remained a priest and in ministry until I went to the police. He was working in schools and with kids all that time. If they knew, then it's another whole mess. And my lawyer believes they would have also told the Vatican.'

Sarah sat bolt upright. 'What?'

'Every five years a bishop has to submit a report on his diocese to the Pope. He has to report on his priests, the faithful and the state of the diocese. Simon, my lawyer, believes that if the diocese knew about Fortune then they would have told the Vatican. So I'm suing the Pope.'

Sarah stared at me, wide-eyed. 'You're suing the Pope? Oh my God, that's huge! You have to let me tell that story!'

I was a little taken aback by her reaction. When the extraordinary becomes your everyday it starts to be, well, ordinary. I was so used to the case by now that I often lost sight of the scale of it. And I hadn't considered that it might be of interest outside Ireland; the media had already covered it in great detail at home.

'I don't know. What's the point and how could it be told anyway. We just don't know enough yet. That's the point of the case.'

'Let me take a look at it and see if we can get some interest and the resources to do a really good investigative job.'

Sarah said she'd speak to a few people and talk over the idea before getting back to me. I didn't think much more about it beyond that. Apart from anything else we were still very much caught up in making the film for *Newsnight*.

Shy's case eventually became a BAFTA award-winning documentary, *A Family Affair*. It aired later that year on BBC2, with *Newsnight* devoting an entire broadcast to that one film. It caused a sensation. I found myself back on *Newsnight* just after it aired to take part in my first ever live studio debate, facing the Chief Constable of Merseyside Police, the head of Social Services and a government minister as they struggled to explain the gross failure, going back many decades, of their collective systems in this case.

I might have been intimidated by the debate if I wasn't so outraged by the case. I was determined to push hard, and we did. In the end, more than a hundred years of prison sentences were handed down to the offenders.

It was a powerful example of how effective the media can be. I learned a lot from the experience, and I will never forget Shy and her incredible courage in going back to demand truth in the face of such absolute denial.

Sarah got back to me later that year to discuss making a film about my own case. The BBC was very interested and wanted to film it as part of their *Correspondent* series. I was still worried that the film might not be possible for legal reasons, but Sarah and the BBC agreed that they would not broadcast it until either my legal case ended or I agreed to it going out.

I trusted Sarah totally and agreed to work with her. And so, a few months later, in October 2001, she accompanied me to Ireland to meet with my lawyer and talk over the project. We were there to meet with people who could help us piece together the story. Even at this stage, there were a great many questions to be answered before we could set about making the film. We hoped we would find enough people with knowledge of the case to tell the story.

As it turned out we didn't have to dig very much at all, it was there waiting for us, a story desperate to be told.

We had quite a lot of information already. We knew that many complaints about Fortune had been made to both Bishop Comiskey and his predecessor, Bishop Donal Herlihy. Many of them were about Fortune's treatment of people in his community. He had a reputation as a bully who would countenance no opposition to any plan of his. He believed that as the local priest he should control every local body and community structure.

We didn't yet know if any of the complaints made to either bishop related to Fortune abusing boys, apart from the one made in 1987, just after he left Poulfur, by Simon's other client. We did hear a suggestion that he was accused of abusing a group of boy scouts when he was in training to become a priest at St Peter's College, the seminary and boys' boarding school across the road from the residence of the Bishop of Ferns in Wexford. If we could prove that a complaint had been made at this time then we could prove that the Catholic Church had knowingly ordained a paedophile and appointed him to posts where he continued to abuse with impunity.

Sarah and I spent three days in Wexford meeting with people who we felt might have something to tell us, building the story in preparation for shooting the film.

A month later we were back, this time with our cameraman and a number of interviews lined up. We planned to stay a week and had several new leads to follow up and further interviews we were desperate to get if only we could convince the people to agree to talk on camera.

Sarah drove us out from Wexford towards Poulfur. It was freezing cold and the leaves fell from the trees, swirling in the wind as they laid a blanket of gold and bronze along the hedgerows. It was a surreal experience driving down that long, narrow road again – the same road Fortune had driven along as he brought me to and from his house almost twenty years earlier.

It was as if I was tumbling back in time. I looked out of the window. Bright yellow ribbons flashed past, the flowers of gorse bushes turning into vivid strips of colour as we sped along.

The cameraman had his lens trained on me from the passenger seat, watching my struggle.

'Are you all right?' Sarah asked, looking at me in the rear view mirror.

'Not really. I hate this. I don't want to be here.'

I looked out the window again, took a deep breath and tried to calm myself.

I knew I had to do it. I knew that it was the right thing to do. I felt sick, but my anxiety was not about today. It was old fear, the fear I'd felt as a boy driving along this same road; fear of what I knew was about to happen. I reminded myself that this was different. I was on this road to face down that fear, to name what had happened and to challenge those who had allowed it.

Sarah didn't say anything more. I caught her eye as she looked in the rear view mirror. 'I'm fine,' I told her. 'Don't worry, I can do this.'

After about half an hour we pulled around a sharp right-hand bend and there on the left I saw a small corrugated iron shed. It had been a shop back when I was a regular visitor, open after Mass in the church across the road. Now its roof was covered in dead leaves and moss. It was closed and shuttered. An old ice cream sign faded with age hung next to the door.

Then the house came into view. It loomed up at the end of a driveway about a hundred metres from the road. It was an ugly house, pebble-dashed and still painted the same sickly peachy-cream colour. It was two storeys high with another floor hidden from view, the basement Fortune had converted into a youth club during his time there. I could see the roof of the church in a deep hollow to the left of the driveway.

Sarah parked at the end of the drive next to a set of steep steps that led to the sacristy, the priest's entrance to the church. We walked down and went into the church itself. I felt anxious and half-expected Sean Fortune to jump out from some corner, looking just as he did all those years ago. At the same time I was desperate to get into the church, to see it again and remember. I expected to see myself as I was then, pale and quiet, sitting in the front pew to the left of the altar doing as I was told. I wanted to take that scared, silent, fifteen-year-old away from here, away from him.

St Aidan's Church was exactly as I remembered it, simple and beautiful, an historic building set in an isolated wooded hollow. A stream runs by it to the left of the graveyard and past the side of the priest's house, which sits high above the church.

I looked up at the house, at the window of what had been Fortune's bedroom. The graveyard smelled of autumn, musty with the scent of damp leaves blown against ancient headstones covered in lichen and moss. I could almost feel Sean Fortune up there, dressed in black, his angry eyes glaring down at me from behind dark glasses, warning me to stay silent.

I would be silent no more though. As the film-making process went on we found more and more people willing to talk to us, including three other victims who were prepared to tell their stories on camera. It was tough asking them to lay out what they had endured for public scrutiny, but I knew that if we were to tell this story, it had to be told honestly, brutally even. Because it was brutal.

Pat Jackman was one of those victims. He was from Wexford town, the same age as me, and we'd mixed in the same circles as teenagers. I was shocked when I heard his name read out at the criminal trial back in 1999. I hadn't seen him in years and we'd never spoken about Fortune.

Pat had gone to school at St Peter's College. He had been in the scouts when Fortune was a scout master. I went to see him with Sarah and sat to the side as she interviewed him on camera.

'We went away on camp together and we were in a tent one day when Sean started playing with one of the boys. When I say playing I don't mean football. He was interfering with him sexually in front of us. There were about six kids in the tent, ranging from about ten to twelve.'

This first shocking experience of Pat's led to a complaint being made to both St Peter's College and the Catholic Boy Scouts of Ireland in early 1979. Fortune was barred forever from the scouting movement. It didn't prevent him from becoming a priest in May of that same year, however, when he was ordained by Bishop Herlihy.

This was the evidence we'd been looking for.

After his ordination, Fortune was appointed to serve in the Holy Rosary parish in Belfast. There, he continued to abuse. Damian, another of the victims who talked to us on camera, was a teenager in the parish.

'He asked to play a game, and the game was patting each other in the groin area,' Damian told us.

'I was maybe thirteen, fourteen, didn't know what I was at, so I agreed and thought it was a game. And then all of a sudden, like after a couple of minutes, he started groping. You know, literally rubbing me up, and that went on for another couple of minutes until I turned and said stop. As I stood up he more or less tried to force me back to the ground'.

It appeared that Fortune caused his superiors in Belfast all sorts of problems. There were other rumours about him behaving inappropriately with boys. Damian told us about the time he and a friend were approached by a young priest who asked questions about Fortune.

'He'd ask me the question: did I see any strange behaviour was going on with Father Fortune, or any funny games? You know, strange games? And I denied ever knowing anything about Father Fortune playing games. It was just because my friend was there with him, I didn't want to get embarrassed.'

In May 1982 Fortune was appointed curate in Poulfur. I met him within weeks of his appointment and he began to abuse me. He also established contact with Pat Jackman's family, befriending Pat's mother in his established pattern. By that time, Pat was fifteen and very much aware of the rumours surrounding Fortune and even other priests at

St Peter's College. He did his best to stay away from Fortune but, like me, Pat wasn't able to defeat the power of the collar in the Ireland of the early 1980s.

One day Fortune arrived at Pat's house. Both his parents were away and the priest manipulated the situation to ensure he could get Pat's aunt to let him take Pat away with him to Poulfur. Pat was trapped.

As I listened, I heard how he had suffered just like me. The same pattern emerged: coercion, charm, bullying and power, until he was trapped in that house for the priest to paw at him. The next day Pat waited desperately to be taken home, to escape.

'He took you home?' asked Sarah.

'Eventually, yeah, after dragging me round the parish. And those parishioners were looking at me, like you know, another little boy, as if I was kind of encouraging him in a sort of way. Having to face them and having to be normal.'

Then he told us about the conversation they had as Fortune drove him home.

'"Ah you know Pat, myself and your mother, we're getting on great. We're great mates. You won't say anything to her, it'll kill her. It'll hurt her feelings and you'll ruin our friendship."'

'And I said to him, "Look Sean, if you promise not to do to anybody else what you did to me I'll have no problem in not saying anything." And he just smiled at me and he says, "Ah come on Pat."'

'The man was unrepentant. It wasn't even a question of lying about it. If he'd lied to me at that moment, if he said, yeah you're right Pat, I'm very sorry, it won't happen again, I wouldn't have said a bloody word. But no. He planned to continue and he made no bones about it.

'Right, bugger you, says I. I'm going home and telling bloody everybody. I didn't tell him that but the minute, the second I was in the door, I went up to my auntie and told her Sean Fortune queered me up.'

Pat's father was close to Bishop Herlihy. He went to him and told him about Fortune's sexual assault on his fifteen-year-old son. But Herlihy refused to accept that a priest could behave in such a way. 'The bishop thought it was ludicrous that a man of the cloth would act like that.'

After Herlihy died in 1983 and Brendan Comiskey was appointed Bishop of Ferns, Pat's father repeated his complaint. Yet again, nothing was done.

I was reeling, from the emotional impact of Pat's story and as I struggled to make sense of what I was hearing. I'd always suspected that the Church had failed me, covering up the fact that Fortune had abused boys. But now it was confirmed beyond question. They knew, and yet they still ordained him. They had received complaints about him before and then again, during the time he was repeatedly abusing me.

Pat had managed to tell. He told and his Dad acted. He'd tried to stop Fortune from abusing others. Pat was at least saved from further abuse, but still nothing was done.

The problem wasn't simply that no one told about the abuse, but that no one in the Church was prepared to act. No one in authority did anything even when they did know.

It's not enough to speak out. Others have to be prepared to listen and acknowledge what they have heard. They have to believe it, no matter how threatening or troubling the facts might be. And, most importantly, they have to be prepared to act.

I was especially concerned to hear how Pat believed that Fortune's parishioners had known what was going on and had done nothing. He even suspected that some of them blamed Pat himself for what was happening to him.

It was painful hearing Pat's story, but also affirming. I knew I was doing the right thing.

# 19

# Many Kinds of Silence

I believe in the power of truth. Naming the truth in difficult circumstances is *always* the right thing to do. If we have the courage to hear and accept the truth of who we are and what we have done, to face it and own it and find a way forward from that place, then we can change the world.

Truth in this context challenges us to face the worst of who we might be, but also to discover the best of ourselves. So often, we run from the things that we feel mark us as bad. I know that feeling well.

I ran from my life on the streets, the nights where I allowed myself to be exploited in exchange for a bed. I ran from the abuse, my physical reactions to it and my powerlessness to prevent it. I believed that these shameful experiences named the truth of who I was. But they didn't.

The truth of who I am is to be found in the way I responded to the events I experienced and how I chose to deal with them once I was free to do so.

The things we do as we struggle to survive unspeakable trauma name the power of our instinctive desire to survive, but they say very little about who we are – what we believe and feel and the principles and values we hold dear. It is only when we have the space to make free and informed choices that we discover who we really are.

This was why I chose to make the film. I knew it was time to uncover and publicly name the truth of everything that had happened. I knew it would be difficult for a lot of people, but I also knew that in facing the truth we stood our best chance of finally dealing with it. Seven years earlier I broke my own silence; now it was time to break the silence of others.

Silence in the presence of very great wrong has a deeply corrupting effect. It diminishes and cheapens us all, and denies us the opportunity to confront that wrong and make it right. And yet, so often we stay silent in the face of abuse. If we can make it invisible and secret, then we don't have to do deal with it.

But our silence has victims, and not always obvious ones. A hurt denied and ignored can rarely heal. More likely it will fester for years after the event.

Monica and John Fitzpatrick had a son called Peter. He was a good-looking boy who became a handsome but troubled young man. Peter died at twenty-three; he shot himself in the chest. There were many rumours about the cause of his suicide. Some people said he killed himself over a relationship break-up, insisting this was the case even when they knew the truth to be much darker. Peter died in the late 1980s, within a few years of Sean Fortune's departure from Poulfur.

There were others too. By 2001, four men, all of whom were boys when Fortune was their priest in the early to mid 1980s, died by their own hands: four men in a community of no more than two hundred families. Sometimes silence can be impossible to live with when you're screaming inside. Monica and John remained silent too. They didn't have permission to speak, to name the truth in a society that was determined to deny it. I knew I had to talk to them.

They agreed to see me right away, to talk about Peter and how he died. They wept when we met. But it quickly became clear that their tears were not because of a rekindled hurt, but those of a hurt held close which could now finally be released. Monica agreed to speak about Peter on camera, to finally name the fear she'd held since the day she found his body.

She was a small woman, with short hair and sad eyes. She had a lovely, gentle air about her and a warm manner, but she was also cautious. It was plain to see hers was an old hurt that had settled into her.

'Peter had a caravan just at the bottom of the garden there, because he wanted his own bit of space.' she said. 'And when I went down, I called at the caravan door, there was no answer. I stepped up into the caravan and Peter was lying back on the bed.'

I sat to one side with her husband, John. He was a big broad-shouldered man, a former soldier, with thick grey hair and a moustache. He sat with his head bowed as he listened to his wife speak, his forearms rested on his thighs and his hands clasped together. I could feel the intensity of his listening as I sat next to him.

'I just screamed and came tearing up the garden,' Monica continued. 'And I got my son Patrick and my husband and they came down with me to the caravan. And I said, "What happened to him, what's wrong?" And Patrick said:

"Mummy, you didn't see, it's on the floor." I didn't see the gun on the floor.'

Peter was already dead.

Later, she spoke about the priest. Fortune had by now left the parish, but returned for Peter's funeral.

'I didn't want Father Fortune near the house. I didn't want him near the place, but he came that day, that Saturday night. He was laughing and joking the usual way, and I said to him, "Father Fortune I didn't want you here."

'And he said, "Oh we can't talk about things like that now. This is not the time to be talking." I said "I specifically said I didn't want you here and I don't want you at the funeral either."'

Then she named her fear, and the agony of her years of silence.

'It just keeps hitting me all the time – did he abuse Peter? Was Peter involved with Father Fortune? I do keep thinking about that, and would that have brought on this? I don't know. I don't know.'

Monica broke then, sobbing, her head in her hands.

'Have you contacted the bishop or anything?' Sarah asked.

'No. No, he didn't do anything when the youngsters and their family told him about it. There is no point. But I think the bishop knows most of the answers and I think he should be answering the questions for the people.'

I looked at John. He still sat silently, but his head was raised as he looked at his wife with tears running down his cheeks.

They both seemed liberated by having named their fear. The relief shone out of them and they smiled and wept at the same time as Monica busied herself making tea and John brought out a bottle of home-made damson liquor. It was a beginning for them, the start of a process of finally coming to terms with their loss and grief.

They had much more to face. On later visits I made alone over the next few years, Monica allowed herself to remember more.

She told me of the time Peter returned home from a weekend away with Fortune on some kind of youth event. Peter was unable to walk properly, and over the following days she was shocked to find a lot of blood on his clothes, in his underwear and on his trousers. Peter told her he had bleeding haemorrhoids but he didn't want to go to the doctor.

In a moment of panic, fuelled by the rumours in the village, Monica asked Peter if the priest had touched him.

He said no. But Monica said he'd given her a troubled look, as if asking, 'What do you know?'

Silence has many victims.

As we went on with our interviews and investigation we met other examples of silence too.

We met the woman who told us how people joked about not bending down in front of Fortune in the churchyard. We met other victims, some of whom could finally talk, like Donnacha MacGloinn who had been brutally raped by Fortune at the age of fifteen, and others who didn't feel able to break their long silence so publicly.

It became even more clear that Fortune was allowed to continue to work as a priest by the Catholic Church despite their knowledge of so many individual complaints about him sexually assaulting and abusing boys.

It's not that the Church did nothing. They did react to several complaints. They put internal investigations in place, and referred Fortune to specialist psychiatrists to have him assessed. In fact, they took steps that clearly identified he was a threat to minors, should he be allowed to continue to have access to children and teenagers in his work as a priest. And then they let him continue.

In 1981, a professor of logic and psychology from University College Dublin, having carried out an assessment at the request of Bishop Herlihy, reported that Fortune's 'personal history during his seminary years ... gives rise to grave cause for concern'. He went on to say that while Fortune dismissed his behaviour with the boy scouts as 'just messing', it was, in the professor's view, behaviour that might 'even be classified as indecent assault in Civil Law'. But within a year of this report, Herlihy appointed Fortune to his post in Poulfur.

One of the first things Fortune did on his appointment to Poulfur was to establish youth groups in the basement of his house and a 'reconciliation room' for boys who were in trouble at home. He did all this under the eye of the diocese and with their knowledge.

It wasn't long before a group of parents and parishioners wrote to the bishop again worried at his failure to properly address their concerns about Fortune. This time though they also wrote to the Papal Nuncio, the Pope's ambassador to Ireland. In the letter they raised many issues, mainly referring to improper conduct, bullying and abuse of the sacraments. They also made reference to things of a sexual nature involving a retreat held for young people. Given the information already held by the Church about Fortune this should have caused real concern that children were at risk.

In a letter in response, the Papal Nuncio told the parishioners that the Pope had been made aware of their concerns.

In 1987, another specialist, Dr John Cooney, saw Fortune and recommended as a matter of urgency a lengthy period of in-patient treatment with close supervision. He referred Fortune to a psychologist who confirmed his concerns.

In October 1987, on the pretext of leaving his parish to go to London for a media course, Fortune finally left Poulfur. Bishop Comiskey would say later that he sent him to London to receive assessment and treatment for sexual problems.

He did receive some counselling, but refused point blank to attend assessment and treatment courses. One of his counsellors strongly recommended to Comiskey that Fortune attend a residential treatment course and described him as a 'pathological liar'. Fortune never attended the course.

In 1988, he was back in Ireland. Comiskey arranged for him to see yet another psychiatrist. On this occasion the bishop was advised that Fortune be put on a course of sexual suppressants, and be allowed to return to parish work on the conditions that he have no responsibility for any youth organisation and was subjected to ongoing supervision.

Fortune continued to refuse to engage in any meaningful way with the professionals to whom he was referred. Instead he chose a psychotherapist of his own, who disputed the findings of the clinicians who had previously assessed him.

He even went so far as to suggest that no progress could be made in treating Fortune unless he was restored to ministry in the diocese. He suggested that Fortune be subjected to an independent assessment and that Comiskey agree to accept the outcome of that assessment. The bishop agreed.

As a result, a consultant psychiatrist in London saw Fortune later that year. During this consultation, Fortune presented a very particular record of his life up to that point. He spoke about his happy childhood and told the doctor he achieved much greater success academically than was true, something that could easily have been checked against the official records and earlier assessments. He said he coped well with his time in the seminary and in his role as a priest.

He told the doctor that before he took his vows as a priest he had a number of sexual relationships with women. He said he had never had any homosexual interests or experiences.

The consultant psychiatrist was not informed of the serious allegations made against Fortune over the previous seven years. He was not given copies of any of the previous medical reports obtained by the diocese. His assessment was based almost entirely on the picture painted for him by Sean Fortune himself.

The psychiatrist's report said that he could find no evidence of current mental or psychiatric illness in Fortune's behaviour. It declined to advise the bishop whether or not Fortune was suitable for a position as a curate in a parish, saying that was best left to the bishop.

The doctor drew the bishop's attention to the information missing from the material used to carry out the assessment and ended the report by saying: 'If there is any further evidence available bearing on his condition or on my conclusions, I would be happy to consider that evidence, seeing him again if necessary.'

Comiskey didn't respond to the report, nor did he provide the doctor with the missing reports or notify him of the numerous complaints against Fortune.

He did, however, appoint Fortune to a new post, this time as a curate in the small community of Ballymurn. Like Poulfur, Ballymurn was a 'half-parish', it had its own church and the curate had his own house. Fortune was technically under the control of the parish priest of Crossabeg, but Comiskey didn't inform that parish priest about the complaints of sexual abuse made against Fortune, or brief him on the need for close supervision.

No advice was given to ensure Fortune was kept away from young people. In fact, the bishop appointed Fortune chairman of the board of management of the local primary school, a post that made him responsible for the governance of the school and manager of all the staff, including the school principal. He also gave classes in religious instruction in Bridgetown Vocational College, a secondary school, attended by children aged between twelve and eighteen.

In 1991, parents from the school complained that Fortune was encouraging the children to tell lewd jokes, using sexually inappropriate language and asking intrusive and prurient questions while he heard the children's confessions. Another messy and protracted process took place, including a meeting between Comiskey and the parents that the bishop insisted Fortune also attend.

It must have been very difficult for those parents to voice their concerns effectively with Fortune sitting in the same room. In the end, he resigned his position at the secondary school, but remained the curate in Ballymurn, working almost daily with young people. He also remained the manager of the local primary school, a position he continued to hold on the direct nomination of Comiskey.

Fortune continued to give classes, unsupervised, to children in that school until the police arrested him in March 1995 following my complaint.

At no point in more than fourteen years that the Roman Catholic Church received complaint after complaint about Fortune did they inform any civil authority of the crimes he was accused of. They didn't inform the police and they didn't inform social services to ensure a proper child protection assessment. They didn't inform the Department of Education that a person appointed by the Church to teach in schools had been accused of the rape and abuse of children. Never, not once.

When the police approached Comiskey to interview him as part of the investigation that followed my complaint in 1995, he declined on three separate occasions to make a statement. It took the diocese over a year to offer the police access to their files on Fortune, by which time he had already been charged and arraigned on sixty-five other charges and the book of evidence for the case had been finalised. By that time, there was no point in the police even looking at the files.

When making the film, we also approached Comiskey, asking him to explain why he had failed to prevent

Fortune from abusing young boys. He declined to answer our questions. So we decided to go to him direct and ask him on camera.

One day as his big black BMW pulled into the car park of Rowe Street Church in Wexford, the bishop got an unexpected reception. Sarah was there, camera switched on and recording.

As he opened the door, Sarah called out, 'Bishop Comiskey!'

The bishop stepped out of his car, bizarrely singing, 'We will survive.' Then as he walked towards Sarah, he said 'How are you?'

'I'm fine thanks. Sarah Macdonald, BBC television.'

'Sarah, how are you?' the bishop repeated, making a beeline for the door of the church.

'Very well, thank you. I've come to ask you a question about Sean Fortune ...'

'I'm going to have Mass at half past six ...', he said, still moving but looking increasingly uncomfortable. He wasn't used to being treated in such a challenging way. He headed up the steps towards the church door.

'We just wanted to know why didn't you stop Sean Fortune abusing young boys? Bishop Comiskey?'

The bishop paused for a moment, turning towards Sarah and the camera.

'I, I, I moved him, when it was brought to my attention. I moved him out of the parish and sent him on treatment for two years ...'

And off he headed again, up the steps.

'Not for six years, you didn't move him out of the parish. Why didn't you stop him?'

At the top of the steps, he paused again and turned to Sarah, nodding goodbye. 'Thank you very much.' And with that he hurried through the door, closing it with a thud in Sarah's face.

There are many kinds of silence, and then there is the truth.

# 20

# London, March 2002

*Suing the Pope* aired at 11.15pm on 19 March, on BBC2 in the UK. Given its late slot, and the fact that not many people back in Ireland might watch BBC2, I didn't expect much of a response. I was wrong.

I wasn't even sure the film would be broadcast until a month or so earlier. Simon was very firmly of the view that the Court might find that I had prejudiced my case and feared that all of our hard work to get to the truth would count for nothing. For a while it seemed the film might sit on a shelf for a number of years.

I really struggled with that. After all, I'd started my case in the first place to try and force the disclosure of the truth. I couldn't now allow it to impose yet more secrecy and silence. The film exposed much of the scale of the cover-up by the Church, and that had to be told, whatever the potential impact on my case.

In the end I decided to consult another lawyer. I was referred to Pearse Mehigan, who had a lot of experience in taking on the Church in cases such as mine. Pearse was fantastic and completely understood where I was coming from. He was calm, measured and clear, and his integrity and determination were obvious. I was immensely impressed by him and decided to move my case to his firm. Given how strongly I felt about it, he agreed that the film should be broadcast.

I watched it at Sarah's house. Paul was with me, and back at One in Four the staff of therapists and volunteers were geared up to take calls from anyone who had been affected by the film. The BBC gave our helpline number to viewers after it aired.

Watching the film on TV was a surreal experience. I was pleased that it was finally airing, but cringed as I saw myself so exposed on screen. My outrage, never far from the surface, boiled again as I watched Pat, Damian and Donnacha tell their stories. And my heart broke all over again as Monica wept as she spoke about Peter.

Her testimony had moved me to express my anger in particularly frank language in one part of the film: 'I'm still now forced to be in a position where I have to fight to get somebody to acknowledge what they did or didn't do and the responsibility that they had for that. And I meet up with other men who are in exactly the same position and I find out that young boys and men have died, have committed suicide, I believe because of what he did to them.

'And you have, frankly, bastards like Brendan Comiskey, hiding in his nice palace in Summerhill, behind his alcoholism and his regret and his inability to understand or to do anything about it. It's not good enough. It's not good enough anymore. People have died. People are dying. People are hurting.'

I was shocked to hear myself so angry, and to hear myself call the bishop a bastard! How would people react to that?

Paul and I headed back to One in Four at about half past midnight. When we got there the office was busy with calls steadily coming in from men and women talking about their own experiences of abuse when they were children. I got stuck in, taking calls myself and offering support.

The first call I took was from an eighty-four-year-old man. 'I was six when he did it to me, the priest. I was only a little boy. It was a long time ago. I never told anyone.'

He started to sob loudly, gulping in breaths, trying to talk.

'It's OK. Take your time, I'm in no hurry and I'm not going anywhere. Take your time and tell me whatever you want to tell me.'

He settled a little. 'I was six. He raped me, and I was only six. I didn't even know what had happened. I never knew, not all those years, I never knew. I never even told my wife, or my kids. I never told anyone. But I never forgot.'

'What do you need now?' I asked.

'Nothing. I just needed to tell someone. It helped to just tell someone. There's nothing to do now, he's dead and gone, thank God.'

'He is, but you're not. And I'm glad you could call and tell me about it.'

'I had to, after I saw the lad in the film. I had to tell someone.'

'That was me.'

'It was you? Oh my God, I am glad to talk to you. You know, don't you?'

'I do.'

'I might call again?'

'Do that. Call when you feel the need or if you want to say hello. We'll be here.'

We exchanged first names and he hung up. He called a few more times after that night, each time opening up a little and telling me more. He didn't want therapy, he just wanted someone to hear his story, to end eight decades of silence. It was powerful.

We kept going until 3.30am, listening as people spoke about years-old hurt and referring them on to therapists and support services wherever possible.

The next morning, my own phone kept ringing. This time it wasn't only those seeking support, there were dozens of calls from the Irish media too. The film had caused uproar in Ireland, and the diocese and Bishop Comiskey were coming under severe public pressure.

Over the coming days, the story grew and grew. There were calls for the film to be aired by RTE, the state broadcaster in Ireland, as many people hadn't seen it on BBC2.

There was no real response from the Church. Comiskey said that he intended to write to the four of us who featured in the film. I immediately faxed him my address and telephone number, and waited to hear back.

I never got a reply.

On 25 March I wrote to the Irish Minister for Health and Children and to all the politicians who represented the Wexford constituency, asking them to comment publicly on the case. I highlighted the failure of the State to proactively intervene, and asked the Minister to establish a State inquiry into the handling of complaints of sexual abuse made against priests from the Diocese of Ferns.

Such an inquiry would be a big deal in Ireland. The lines between the Church and the State remained very blurred. The Church was the main provider of education, centrally involved in the Irish health service and a powerful political force. Few politicians were prepared to challenge the authority of the Church. But a number of them publicly supported my call for such an investigation.

It was announced that RTE would broadcast the film on 2 April. I agreed to fly back and take part in a studio discussion as part of the broadcast.

I continued to do interviews with the Irish media and the story began to get international attention. *Time* magazine ran an article about the film and the case I'd taken against the Pope. The story continued to build.

The film was shown across the world. One friend who was on holiday in Australia told me how he saw the film on TV in a pub in New South Wales. *Suing the Pope* was aired on ABC in Australia and I was asked to take part in an online chat following the programme. I received many emails from victims there in the weeks that followed, another clear indication of the global nature of the scandals.

In the meantime calls from Ireland kept pouring into the One in Four office in London. More and more victims of abuse by clergy were making contact with us and we were struggling to keep up with the volume of calls. Worryingly, many of them were from people who had never notified the authorities about their experiences of abuse. We worked hard to ensure that as many of those cases as possible were notified to the civil authorities.

Many people asked if I would consider opening a One in Four office in Ireland. That would have meant moving back to live there again, a decision I didn't feel able to make easily. Paul and I discussed it a lot, and decided to see how things evolved in the coming months.

I did start a One in Four website for Ireland, however – a point of first contact for those seeking help. It was decided to launch the website at a press conference in Dublin the day after *Suing the Pope* aired on RTE.

On 1 April, the day before the broadcast, I received a call from a journalist who told me that Comiskey intended to resign as Bishop of Ferns later that day. I was stunned and deflated. I never for a moment imagined that he would actually resign. There had been calls for him to step down, and opinion polls in the diocese suggested that well over 80 per cent of people felt he should go. But he had seen other crises through. I remembered his singing out 'We will survive' on camera a few months earlier. It appeared he wouldn't after all.

I've never been a fan of the call for heads on plates in the face of scandal. More often than not it's no more than a bloodletting, a superficial if dramatic response that achieves very little. I didn't want the bishop to resign and walk off the pitch; I wanted him to deal with this whole sorry mess once and for all. I wanted him to answer questions and tell the truth.

I feared this might have a negative effect on my quest for justice. If the media and public felt satisfied by the resignation and saw it as some sort of resolution to the case, then I might never force the Government to agree to the investigation I felt was so necessary.

Prime Minister Bertie Ahern was asked for his views on the scandal. Perfectly reasonable and appropriate you might think given that the case was essentially about child protection and very serious criminal offences. In fact, Mr Ahern was eager not to get involved at all.

'I haven't really been following that at all,' he said. 'It's really a matter for the Church, it's not a matter for politicians. I'm not going to cross politics and religion.'

So the leader of the country believed that the State had no business getting involved in the case. And it appeared that senior Church figures felt exactly the same way. They began to suggest that it would not be possible in law for the State to investigate the Church. They expressed the view that Canon Law, the internal code of law of the Roman Catholic Church, was superior to Civil Law, the Law of the State.

I was used to such legal manoeuvrings. The Church's only response to my legal action against the Pope was to declare that the Papal Nuncio, the office I sued as the representative of the Pope in Ireland, had full diplomatic immunity and could not be sued in an Irish court. The Vatican were using legal dodges to avoid telling what they knew about Fortune.

It wasn't the first time that the Catholic Church had used Canon Law to redefine the meaning of truth. A few years earlier, in the case of the notorious paedophile priest Fr Brendan Smith, his superior told a journalist that he had not discussed the case with Cardinal Cathal Daly. That was a lie. But when he was caught out, he declared that in Canon Law it wasn't a lie at all, as he didn't have permission from the Church to tell the truth!

This position, while patently ridiculous and perverse, was a good illustration of the Catholic Church's policy in dealing with sexual abuse perpetrated by priests. Their overarching priority was to prevent scandal and protect the reputation and authority of the Church. No issue was of more importance to the Vatican, not even the safety of children. Absolute secrecy was demanded from everyone involved – victims, witnesses, perpetrators and Church investigators.

I spent so much of my time working to combat the spin put out by the Church and trying to force the hand of politicians. In the face of political impotence and Church arrogance, I knew that forcing a situation where the State would take on the Church would need massive public support and pressure. Politics in Ireland, just like in many other countries, reacts to public opinion, rather than leading it. The media would be key in this.

The story remained in the headlines for weeks, from the first screening of the film on the BBC to its broadcast on Irish TV. Comiskey's resignation raised the coverage even more.

I spent hour after hour, day after day with my phone pressed to my ear, dealing with the media and answering calls from people offering support or seeking help. And all the while I could feel something building, a mounting pressure I knew would lead us to achieve something tremendous.

On 2 April I headed back to Ireland for the broadcast. I hadn't been back since the film aired on the BBC and I still wasn't sure what kind of response I might receive from people in the street. The media frenzy continued unabated. I did two live radio interviews from Stansted Airport as I waited to board my flight, and by the time I landed an hour later I had another twenty-three voicemail messages from journalists. I drove to a friend's house and began to prepare. I had an urgent press release to write, a press conference to organise and two national newspapers had asked me to write articles for the next day.

Later that night *Suing the Pope* finally aired on Irish TV, preceded by a live panel discussion programme on the RTE current affairs show *Primetime*. For the first time, the Church allowed a spokesperson to comment on the film.

Bishop Colm O'Reilly said, 'I have to say that woeful mistakes were made for certain and that from now on things need to be done very differently. And that the starting point is that acknowledgement and finding out exactly what the full picture is.

'So I long for, just as much as anybody else obviously, for the day to come when both for the Church and for the people who have been victims, that a point is reached where reconciliation and healing is possible for everybody.'

I repeated my view that resolution could only happen if the truth was fully and independently established. I made it clear that the Catholic Church had to take full responsibility for its own failures, and not simply focus on the crimes of individual priests.

'We are talking about the responsibility of a Church that failed to act in these cases, that failed to prevent abuse, that failed to acknowledge it when it happened and that facilitated it and allowed it to continue.

'That's the responsibility that we need the Church to acknowledge. Not the fact that sexual abuse and the rape of children is an evil awful crime, everybody knows that. What we need the Church to acknowledge is that they failed in their responsibilities and that at times they knowingly failed in those responsibilities.'

Both programmes recorded massive viewing figures. There was no sign of the public uproar abating. I would press on with my campaign to secure the inquiry.

The Church remained stubbornly silent. Prior to the appearance of O'Reilly on the *Primetime* panel there had been little or no official comment from the Church. Both of Ireland's most senior Catholic Church leaders, Archbishop Sean Brady, the Catholic Primate of All Ireland, and Cardinal Desmond Connell, the Archbishop of Dublin, declined to make any substantial comment on the crisis.

Cardinal Connell actually said that he didn't know very much about the story and therefore couldn't comment. A rather incredible statement given the profile of the film, the acres of newsprint about the case over the preceding seven years and the fact that the journalist Alison O'Connor had published her book, *A Message from Heaven: The Life and Crimes of Father Sean Fortune*, about the case in 2000. His comments were greeted by derision and disbelief. One enterprising newspaper editor, Ger Colleran at the *Irish Daily Star*, fed up of 'no comment' from bishops who said they didn't know enough about it, sent a copy of Alison's book to every bishop in the country and then called again for a comment. He still didn't get a response, but it did highlight the ridiculousness of their position.

The day after the broadcast I headed into Dublin city centre. The parents of another victim of abuse in the diocese would be joining Pat, Donnacha and myself at the press conference. Pat and Josie Gahan were from the village of Monageer, a small community shattered by the abuse of a number of young girls by the local priest as they were prepared to make their confirmation. Their presence was important, to highlight the fact that ours was by no means the only case that warranted investigation.

This would be the first time I was out in public since the film was shown. I didn't know how people might react to me and I was anxious that I might get a smack for how I had spoken. I didn't expect everyone to be happy with what they might perceive as an attack on their Church, no matter how careful and measured I'd been.

I stepped out of the car near the press conference venue. As I walked across the street a few cars honked their horns and people wound down their windows to call messages of support. I was extremely relieved and very moved. Without real public support we would never win this battle for justice, but we had it and this meant a lot to me. It kept me going.

Of course not everyone was so supportive. Thankfully, the negative reaction was less direct. A letter to the local radio station in Wexford made it clear that the smack I expected might well come my way, and maybe even worse. It was sent to Alan Maguire, the presenter of the mid-morning show on South-East Radio, on whose programme I had appeared a few times. It read:

*Dear Alan. When you have Colm O'Gorman on your programme tell him I hope he rots in hell for what he has done to our lovely Bishop. He'd better keep looking over his shoulder for the rest of his life.*

Other callers suggested that I should 'go back to pagan England'.

Another message recorded on the radio station was from a rather sneering and smug woman. 'I would like to just comment on Colm O'Gorman, to cast any stone particularly the first one. And I say sin with a big S, thank you.'

I was pretty certain that this caller was referring to the fact that I was gay. I'd expected such ignorant comments and that some people would suggest that since I was gay, I must have invited the abuse. Another caller said, 'Colm O'Gorman knew what he was doing when he climbed into bed with that priest.'

But the majority were very positive. As Alan Maguire told the BBC: 'Most decent people were so full of sympathy for them. I mean we had people ringing in crying. Women in tears, mothers who were concerned about their own children and they knew the terrible evil that this can bring into people's homes. So the community at large I think were very good and were very angry towards the Church.'

Ireland was embracing the truth, and in doing so, Ireland and Irish society was changing.

# 21

# Rewards and Awards

Ireland was indeed changing, and in many ways for the better. People were no longer too frightened or reluctant to challenge the absolute authority of the Catholic Church, in fact the tide changed so far in the opposite direction that at times it became inappropriate and unfair.

An elderly nun walking down Dublin's O'Connell Street was verbally abused and spat at. There were reports of many other nuns and priests feeling anxious about wearing clerical clothes in public. I was appalled that to some people's minds, the actions of the institution of the Catholic Church somehow justified an attack on an elderly woman, or on any group of people based solely on their role in the Church.

The spin used by the Catholic hierarchy didn't help. Speaking in October 2002, Cardinal Desmond Connell said, 'We must judge what has happened against the background of the many hundreds of good and faithful priests over all the years who have served their people with complete integrity and unselfishness.' It seemed like a reasonable point to make, that those who abused children represented only a small minority of those in religious life, and that the majority were decent men and women working hard for the good of society.

However, this argument also infuriated me. To me, the issue was not the work of ordinary members of the clergy, and I had never suggested that they were responsible en masse for the sexual abuse scandals. The issue was no longer the vile acts perpetrated by an undoubtedly small minority of priests, but the gross failure of the institution of the Church and its leaders, up to and including the Pope, to deal properly with them. They were guilty of an appalling level of negligence, having denied the abuse in the first place, then covering it up and allowing abusers to continue raping and assaulting with near impunity.

In December 2002, Cardinal Joseph Ratzinger – now Pope Benedict XVI – made a statement suggesting that the scandals were in fact some kind of grand conspiracy to bring down the Roman Catholic Church.

At that time, Ratzinger was Prefect of the Congregation for the Doctrine of the Faith, a powerful and influential role for which he was variously nicknamed the Pope's Bulldog, God's Rottweiler or the Vatican Enforcer. His position as head of the department once known as the Holy Office of the Inquisition, placed him in charge of managing and responding to cases of priests who abused children. Apart from the Pope, he had more authority and knowledge than any other senior Church figure to fully appreciate the scale of the problem. Pope John Paul II said that the role of the Congregation for the Doctrine of the Faith was '*to promote and safeguard the doctrine on the faith and morals throughout the Catholic world: for this reason everything which in any way touches such matter falls within its competence.*'

Speaking to journalists at a Catholic Congress in Rome, Ratzinger said, 'I am personally convinced that the constant presence in the press of the sins of Catholic priests, especially in the United States, is a planned campaign, as the percentage of these offences among priests is not higher than in other categories, and perhaps it is even lower. In the United States, there is constant news on this topic, but less than 1 per cent of priests are guilty of acts of this type. The constant presence of these news items does not correspond to the objectivity of the information nor to the statistical objectivity of the facts. Therefore, one comes to the conclusion that it is intentional, manipulated, that there is a desire to discredit the Church. It is a logical and well-founded conclusion.'

I was especially interested in his use of the phrases 'objectivity of the information' and 'statistical objectivity of the facts'.

What information and which facts? For years senior Church figures had told us they didn't understand that priests could or did sexually abuse children. They told us that they had little or no understanding of the phenomenon of child sexual abuse and were therefore just as ill-equipped and ignorant as the rest of society when it came to responding to its revelation in recent years.

That the head of the Vatican's investigation and enforcement department was in a position to assess and judge the 'statistical objectivity of the facts', suggested to me that the Catholic Church possessed much more information than it was publicly disclosing.

His assertion that less than 1 per cent of priests in the US were guilty of abusing children certainly suggests that he had some in-depth, historical understanding of the situation. At that stage, the civil courts in the US had prosecuted very few priests and the Catholic Church used its own legal code, to investigate and prosecute priestly crimes and misconduct. So was Ratzinger's 1 per cent referring to priests found guilty by his own department, the Catholic Church courts and tribunals? I believed it was and, if so, he was exposing previous Church protestations of ignorance and innocence as blatant lies.

In any case, his figure was entirely discredited by research in the US. In June 2002, American bishops commissioned independent research into the scale of the problem. The research was carried out by the John Jay College of Criminal Justice and found that clerical sexual abuse was 'widespread' across the US Catholic Church, affecting some 95 per cent of dioceses and involving between 2.5 and 7 per cent of all diocesan priests. Overall, the research discovered that 4 per cent of all priests in active ministry in the US between 1952 and 2002 had been accused of sexually abusing a child.*

The study also revealed that of the 10,667 people who made allegations of rape and abuse by priests, two thirds were made prior to 2002. This means that in the US alone, the Catholic Church was aware of more than 7,100 cases of children allegedly abused by its priests prior to the public emergence of the issue. The scale of the cover-up was becoming clearer.

At the same time, I was learning more about the history of clerical sexual abuse and the Roman Catholic Church.

---

* The Nature and Scope of the Problem of Sexual Abuse of Minors by Catholic Priests and Deacons in the United States, *John Jay College of Criminal Justice,* 2004

I met an amazing man, a Dominican priest called Fr Tom Doyle, who was an expert on the issue. Tom had been a senior official in the Vatican Embassy in Washington in the early 1980s when he wrote a paper warning of the threat sexual abuse of children by priests posed to the institution of the Church. He warned that a continuing failure to address the issue would do untold damage to the reputation of the Church and could cost it millions in damages to victims.

As Tom's warnings were increasingly ignored, he became convinced of the existence of a concerted high-level cover-up and challenged the Church even harder. As a result he was fired. Rather than leave the Church, Tom became a chaplain in the US Air Force, recognising that as a priest and Canon Law expert he could work to champion victims of abuse. He would go on to give expert testimony in cases worldwide and his research and analysis was central in forcing the issue into the open. To me, Tom is a shining example of priestly courage and integrity, a man who not only refused to be silent in the presence of great wrong but also worked to do what was right.

Tom's research revealed startling examples of the Catholic Church's historic awareness of child sexual abuse throughout its two thousand year history.

Early Church law makes many references to sexual offences committed by clergy, including sex with adult women and homosexuality, and there are frequent references to the crime of sexually abusing boys. In early Church law, sexual sins are ranked as high as homicide and idolatry, the three gravest sexual sins being adultery, fornication and the sexual corruption of young boys.

In fact some of the earliest laws refer explicitly to that crime.

The earliest mention of forbidden sexual behaviour in Church literature dates from around the end of the first century. The *Didache*, which set out structures and rules for the newly emerging church, condemns many sexual practices and includes a specific ban against 'corrupting youth'. Canon seventy-one of the Council of Elvira, in the year 309, condemns men who sexually abused young boys and sets out the penalty for such crimes.

In 1051, St Peter Damian, a monk who became a bishop and later a cardinal wrote extensively about the sexual crimes and immorality of the clergy of his day. He was especially critical of homosexual activity by clergy, but clergy who abused young boys particularly angered him. He condemned Church superiors who ordained offenders and failed to expel from the priesthood those who abused. He also made a direct appeal to the reigning Pope, Leo IX, to take action.

In 1568, another Pope explicitly acknowledged the issue of clergy abusing minors. In his papal order *Horrendum*, Pope Pius V said that priests who offended were to be stripped of the priesthood, deprived of all income and privileges and handed over to the secular authorities.

There are scores of other references throughout Catholic Church history that expose as lies the many statements made by the modern Catholic Church hierarchy claiming innocence and ignorance. They have known for centuries that priests could and did abuse children. They simply failed to do anything of any real significance to prevent it.

In Ireland, there was no real indication that the Catholic Church was any more prepared to take responsibility for its mismanagement and negligence than the early Church. Instead, in what I believe was clearly an effort to contain the scandal and pre-empt a State inquiry, the bishops set up a Church investigation into the scandals.

The Independent Catholic Church Commission on Child Sexual Abuse mirrored the approach adopted by the Church in other countries when faced with similar scandals. The US bishops set up a similar body, as did the Australian Church. Quite how a Catholic Church-established and -funded commission could be seen as truly independent remained something of a mystery. To my mind it was perverse to allow the Church to investigate itself. Along with many others, I rejected the idea of this investigation, and in time it was abandoned. The commissions established in other countries were subsequently discredited. In the US the first chair of the national board established by the US bishops, former Oklahoma Governor Frank Keating – who had also served as an FBI agent and federal prosecutor – quit in protest at what he saw as a continuing failure by the hierarchy to deal properly with the scandals.

'I have seen an underside that I never knew existed,' Keating said. 'I have not had my faith questioned, but I certainly have concluded that a number of serious officials in my faith have very clay feet. That is disappointing and educational, but it is a fact. To act like La Cosa Nostra and hide and suppress, I think is very unhealthy. Eventually it will all come out. To resist grand jury subpoenas, to suppress the names of offending clerics, to deny, to obfuscate, to explain away; that is the model of a criminal organisation, not my Church.'

Cardinal Roger Mahoney of Los Angeles was outraged at Keating's comments and demanded an apology. Keating resigned, but insisted that his words were 'deadly accurate', and said, 'I make no apology.'

In Australia, the Catholic Church had appointed Bishop Geoffrey Robinson to head a body to deal with the scandals there back in 1994, long before the scandals emerged in the US and Ireland. Bishop Robinson turned out to be a principled and determined man who worked hard to establish and enforce high standards in child protection in the Australian Church. He succeeded in many ways but the Vatican was often less than supportive of his efforts.

He would later reveal that he had been strongly reprimanded after he told an abuse victim he was unhappy with Rome's response. The comment, a response to a question from the victim, was made at a public meeting at which the media were present. He was sent an official letter expressing the 'ongoing concern of the Congregation for Bishops' and that his publicly stated opinion was 'seriously critical of the magisterial teaching and discipline of the church'.

Two months later he received another letter, informing him that his case had been sent on to the Congregation for the Doctrine of the Faith, a signal of deep suspicion and disapproval on the part of the Vatican.

However Bishop Robinson only became more challenging of the Vatican. In 2007 he released a book, *Confronting Power and Sex in the Catholic Church*, calling for new approaches and greater openness from the Church.

In a speech delivered at the launch of the book he had challenging questions for the Pope.

'Where is the papal statement addressed directly to victims with the word "sorry" proclaimed clearly? Where is the papal promise to investigate every possible source of abuse and ruthlessly to eradicate it?' he asked.

'Where is the request to those institutes especially set up to treat offending priests to present their findings on the causes? Where is the request to the bishops to coordinate the studies in their territory and report to Rome?

'Where is the document placing everything on the table for discussion, including such things as obligatory celibacy and the selection and training of candidates? With power go responsibilities. The Pope has many times claimed the power and must accept the corresponding responsibilities,' he continued.

Thankfully back in Ireland the Government agreed to put in place a State investigation into the handling – by both the Catholic Church and State agencies such as the police and child protection services – of complaints, allegations and suspicions of child sexual abuse perpetrated by priests of the Diocese of Ferns. A former Irish supreme court judge, Mr Justice Frank Murphy, would head the investigation, called The Ferns Inquiry. Having negotiated the terms of reference for the inquiry with the Departments of Health and Justice, I was confident that it had the resources, authority and, most importantly, the determination to do a good job. If we could focus on Ferns where we already knew so much, then we had a very good chance of uncovering and exposing the wider failure of the Catholic Church in other dioceses and at all levels up to and including the Vatican.

At the same time I was talking to the Government about calls for me to open a One in Four branch in Ireland. The response was positive and it was made clear to me that funding would be available to establish an Irish version of the organisation based in Dublin.

My work meant I would continue to have a very public role, and I was aware I would continue to live in the public eye for a while. I knew this was both a useful tool and also a potential danger. In taking on very powerful forces in Irish society I had to be prepared for the fight to get dirty, and to find my own life closely scrutinised.

Before finally making the decision to move back I needed to know that my personal life could not be used publicly against me. Given some of those comments made by callers to South-East Radio a few months earlier, I wanted to deal with the issue of my sexuality myself, and on my own terms.

Carrie Crowley, the presenter of *Snapshots*, an Irish radio programme similar to the BBC's *Desert Island Discs*, asked me to appear on her show broadcast on RTE Radio 1. Her guests choose their favourite music and discuss their lives and loves. I agreed to do the show, deciding it was a perfect way to out myself publicly, in a matter of fact way and without any sensation. I didn't think my sexuality was a big deal, so the opportunity to reveal it in an honest, open way suited me.

I talked about my relationship with Paul, about meeting him and how valuable and life-affirming our relationship was for me. It was a really good experience, and most importantly the public response was entirely positive. Once again the truth, put simply and boldly, dealt with the possible negative spin others might have created. I got some really supportive emails after the show, all from ordinary people, many of them older married couples expressing their support and delight in hearing me talk about my relationship with Paul. It was a lovely response, and helped us make up our minds about whether to move home.

We decided to go for it. Paul and I put our home in London on the market and prepared to return to Ireland. For a while we commuted back and forth, sleeping for a few months on the floor of a friend's converted attic and later moving to an apartment rented on a short-term let. It was all very unsettled and I missed having a home to go to at the end of a long day. I was eager to get on with it and make the move permanent.

In November I was named one of the People of the Year. The awards are presented in Ireland each year to people who have made a particular contribution to Irish society. It was a real honour.

I received a call from the organisers earlier in October to ask if I would accept the award. I decided I would, in the name of all those who had been abused and as a powerful statement rejecting the idea that anyone who had been abused as a child should feel shame because of it.

An hour or so after the call I sat in Bewley's coffee shop on Westmoreland Street in Dublin. Twenty years earlier I'd walked up and down that same street, homeless and lost. I was the same person back then, but people had looked away, avoided me unless they wanted to use me. I was invisible and alone. Now I was one of the People of the Year!

We so easily dismiss people living on the margins. If we see someone in a doorway, huddled against the cold, or hanging around a street corner in such desperate straits that they would allow themselves to be exploited in order to survive, we ignore them. They become less than human; they become their situation and we do not afford them their dignity as human beings.

The citation for the award read:

> *Ernest Hemingway described courage as 'grace under pressure'. Colm O'Gorman founded the organisation 'One in Four' to highlight sexual abuse and its devastating consequences for victims. He has spoken frankly, fearlessly and without rancour in describing the extent of the scandal. For his courage in telling of his own experiences, which has helped others who have suffered sexual abuse to speak out, Colm clearly deserves this award. Mr O'Gorman, who was abused by Fr Sean Fortune, was honest and forthcoming, in a way that the Church authorities were not.*

I received the award from Tánaiste Mary Harney, the deputy Irish prime minister, at a big award ceremony in Dublin. My family was there with me: Paul, Barbara, my brother Eamon and his wife Jean. Sarah was there too, back in Ireland to film an update on *Suing the Pope* for the BBC. It was a great night.

There is usually a Catholic Church representative at such events in Ireland. That night the bishop in attendance was Eamonn Walsh, the newly-appointed Apostolic Administrator of the Diocese of Ferns, the man sent into the diocese by the Vatican to sort out the scandal.

Other awards followed. One that stood out for me was when I received the first ever James Larkin Justice Award from the Irish Labour Party in 2003. James Larkin was one of the founders of the Irish Labour Party and a leading trade unionist and social activist. He had a huge impact on Irish society, championing workers' rights, condemning poverty and injustice and calling for the oppressed to stand up for themselves.

To receive an award named after him is an enormous honour. I was presented with the award at the Labour Party Conference. In my speech to delegates I asked them to consider the need to respond to those who struggled to survive the impact of child sexual abuse.

> 'There are times when it's hard to receive such encouragement and support. I think: "Where were you when I was struggling, when I couldn't cope and couldn't speak?" I sit with others who cannot speak, who cannot cope, who cannot be what we value in this society. Who are not "functional" or articulate, who can only speak of their agony by turning it inwards, by harming themselves through self-hatred, drugs, alcohol or by slashing their bodies in an attempt to express their pain.
>
> 'I am the acceptable face of sexual abuse and that is not ok. Now that I have a home people invite me to theirs, now that I can feed myself people buy me dinner. It's good, it's great and I appreciate it ... but it's strange. It's extraordinary to find myself walking the same streets as I did at seventeen when I was homeless and have people look at me, before they looked away.'

Paul and I finally moved back on St Patrick's Day, 17 March 2003, taking the ferry from Holyhead to Dun Laoghaire with our dog and two cats, and all our worldly goods due to follow on a few days later in a removal van. It was a really big step, and we didn't have the time or space to plan our leaving properly. We didn't get time to have a party, or to say a proper goodbye to our friends, colleagues and a life built there over the years, and I regret that still. London had been so good for me in so many ways, and while I love living back in Ireland, I miss our life there too.

As I sat on the ferry that day and watched the waves fall and rise I remembered all the ferry trips taken over the years as I headed back to constant meetings with lawyers, or the trip back for the trial in 1999. I thought back to that lonely St Patrick's Day in 1983, when I was homeless on the streets of Dublin. It seemed like a lifetime ago, and yet in some ways I felt closer and more connected to that seventeen-year-old boy than I could have imagined. I was going home, but not only to a physical place, I was going home to myself.

# 22

# Resolutions

Moving back to Ireland was indeed a huge step. A year earlier I would never have predicted it, but now I knew it was the right move. Paul was fantastic, taking it all in his stride. He'd just completed his first year of a degree at the University of London, but transferred to Trinity College Dublin. He also worked hard with me to help establish the office in Dublin. It was busy and challenging but also an incredibly fulfilling time.

Property prices had rocketed in Ireland in the years since I left and we struggled to find any house we wanted to buy close to Dublin. We began to look farther afield, determined to find a home that was at least as good as the one we'd left behind in London. Eventually we settled on an area just beyond Gorey, a town in north County Wexford. So not only did we move home to Ireland, but I also returned to my home county. I was a little conflicted about moving there since it was also Sean Fortune's hometown.

In Alison O'Connor's book about Fortune there is a passage about him as a child, which describes the time he was sent to town to buy a bag of sugar. When he got to the shop it was closed and he was afraid to go home without the sugar. He was discovered later that evening in a dark shop doorway, scared and anxious.

That story troubled me whenever I drove through the main street in Gorey on my way home to Wexford. I always imagined him as that frightened boy. It forced me to see him as fully human, rather than solely as the predator he would later become. He was once a boy who felt fear and anxiety, just like me. I didn't want to empathise with him in any way, but I couldn't avoid it. I had to acknowledge his humanity. It's not easy to just hate someone when you have to acknowledge that. It's not so simple anymore.

I was worried that moving back to Gorey might be too much. Fortune was buried there and I would have to drive past that graveyard several times a week. I was concerned that that kind of proximity, those constant reminders, might be difficult.

We'd found a house we loved, but hadn't been able to secure it. In the end we decided to rent a house in Gorey for a while and see how it all worked out. It's a beautiful area, right on the coast with several great beaches and country walks, but close enough to the city to commute. It was a huge change from where we'd lived in London. The first morning we got up to commute the fifty miles to work, the entire area was blanketed in a thick fog. I could hardly see ten feet in front of me as I drove, and got lost trying to find the main road to Dublin. I hoped it wasn't an indication of things to come.

One in Four was now well established as one of the leading sexual abuse support organisations in Ireland. Setting up the service was very exciting and we all had a great sense of being part of something new and much bigger than ourselves. The staff were a tremendous team of deeply committed individuals, full of energy, idealism, courage and integrity. The charity was supporting hundreds of people every year, providing advocacy and therapy to women and men who had experienced sexual abuse in any context, whether in their families, schools, churches or communities. We campaigned for improved responses to the needs of victims, their families and communities. Crucially, we also campaigned for treatment for offenders, recognising that only by providing such treatment could we hope to effectively prevent future abuse.

I was by now a regular contributor to the public debate on TV, radio and in the newspapers. I also learned that if you wanted to achieve change it was necessary to do more than just demand it; it was essential to offer solutions and work constructively to make change happen. With the assistance and support of my colleagues at One in Four I instigated the development of better policy and legislation in the area of child protection, meeting regularly with Government departments and ministers as well as with opposition politicians.

By February 2003 it seemed clear that the Church wanted to finally settle my case. There was little sense in their continued defence of a case largely proved in the public arena. They may also have hoped that if my personal case was settled, I might stop my public campaign to reveal the overall extent of clerical child sexual abuse in Ireland. I was very eager to see the case settled, but it was now much bigger than me. I wanted it settled so I could focus exclusively on the wider issues.

It had been extraordinary to see the lengths the Church would go to in its efforts to defend itself against cases like mine. At times the strident legalistic approach taken by the Church proved very traumatic for victims of abuse, and it appeared to me that some of the approaches adopted by their lawyers were designed to intimidate.

For instance, those taking cases would often be asked to provide details of every address they'd ever lived at, every job they'd held, the jobs held by other family members, details about their parents' backgrounds and many other personal questions. It seemed clear that the Church intended to delve into every detail of one's life. By contrast, claimants were forced to go to extraordinary measures to get information to support their case. They had to fight to secure court orders to force the release of documents or information vital to their cases, a very time consuming and potentially costly process, and be willing as in my case, to lay out the whole sorry story in public.

Letters were routinely issued, denying any responsibility in law for acts of abuse by priests and threatening to recover the costs involved if the case was not withdrawn.

One letter I received at this time was particularly intrusive. It included the question of whether I had ever received payment in exchange for sexual encounters with men. I was furious. What was the relevance of such a question, whatever the answer? What did it have to do with the fact that the Catholic Church had ordained a known child abuser and allowed him to rape and abuse me for a period of two and a half years?

Apart from everything else, the Church already knew the answers to most of the questions they asked in the letter. I'd already been subjected to a detailed psychiatric examination undertaken by an expert appointed by them.

In those consultations I'd been very forthright and open about my past, detailing everything that had happened to me up to and beyond the abuse by Fortune.

I was really upset by that letter. Despite how well I was and how far I had come, it really knocked me back. I felt accused and belittled by its tone and the nature of the questions.

I remembered the words of Bishop Colm O'Reilly when he appeared with me on the 'Primetime' programme on the same night *Suing the Pope* was broadcast: 'I long, just as much as anybody else obviously, for the day to come when both for the Church and for the people who have been victims that a point is reached where reconciliation and healing is possible for everybody.'

How could healing be possible when the Church, through its lawyers, behaved in this way? How could they preach a desire for healing and then be so aggressively legalistic in their dealings with victims under cover of the law? How could they seriously work for reconciliation at the same time as they beat people up with this kind of vicious behaviour?

Following Brendan Comiskey's resignation as Bishop of Ferns, the Vatican took direct control of the diocese when it appointed its Apostolic Administrator, Bishop Eamonn Walsh. I'd met the bishop on a few occasions since his appointment. He professed his desire to deal with the entire issue of child sexual abuse in an open and compassionate way, but the letter from his lawyers seemed very much at odds with that desire.

I decided I would answer every single question in the letter as honestly as I could, then sent it back via my own lawyer. I made contact with Bishop Walsh and called him to explain how distressed and angry I was at the approach he'd adopted via his lawyers.

He seemed uncomfortable with the conversation. 'In dealing with this I have tried to keep the legal issues separate,' he told me. 'I keep it all on the long finger, the lawyers decide how to handle the cases and I don't get very involved.'

'Bishop Walsh,' I replied, 'your lawyers act in your name. That letter was written on your behalf by lawyers instructed by you.

'I instruct my legal team, and I am responsible for making decisions based upon the advice they give me. If I send a mad dog into a room and it bites someone, it's not the dog's fault, it's mine. If you instruct your lawyers to act compassionately and deal sensitively with victims of abuse, then they will. If you don't, and it seems that you have not, then they won't. And that is your responsibility and yours alone.'

Finally, the Church told my lawyer they wanted to have settlement talks with me. I agreed. And so I found myself in yet another dark and dull room in a courthouse, this time Dublin's Four Courts building, the home of the Irish High Court and Supreme Court. It was a much more impressive building than the courthouse in Wexford, but that little room was remarkably similar to the one in which I'd been asked to accept reduced charges against Fortune four years earlier.

I met with Pearse and my barristers to explore the kind of settlement I wanted to achieve. With their guidance I agreed to seek a financial settlement of €300,000 and a statement to be read in the High Court, in which the Church accepted responsibility for failing to prevent my abuse in the first place. For me, the statement was much more important than the money. Up until that point, all settlements in similar cases had been on a 'no liability' basis, which meant that the Church paid people off but did not admit either liability or responsibility in law. I was adamant that no settlement would be possible unless the Church admitted responsibility. That's what the case had always been about, and I knew it was vital for other cases and victims. I couldn't let them down.

There was also the issue of the case against the Vatican. By now I knew it was a case I could never have won. The Roman Catholic Church is a unique and complex organisation. It has many manifestations: a religion, an international charity and provider of education and health services, a major global corporation of extraordinary wealth and influence and, of most significance to my case, a sovereign state. In its guise as the Vatican State, it is unique among world religions. The Pope as Head of State has sovereign immunity from legal action in other states, and his representatives, the Papal Nuncios, have diplomatic immunity in the countries where they are based.

I could not, in law, sue them in an Irish court should they choose to claim immunity. My purpose in taking the case was to force them to show their hand. And they did. The Papal Nuncio claimed diplomatic immunity, and his lawyers told me that if I pursued the case they would use that immunity to have it thrown out and then seek full legal costs from me.

In truth I had only continued with the case against the Vatican because I was determined not to allow them to walk away easily. If they chose to use diplomatic immunity, then at least they would be exposed for refusing to answer questions truthfully and evading accountability.

This use of legal technicalities and convoluted structures is by no means restricted to the Irish Church. The Vatican has claimed sovereign and diplomatic immunity against suit in many other countries including the US and Canada.

When Pope Benedict XVI apologised to victims of clerical sexual abuse in Australia in 2008, a Melbourne-based lawyer acting for victims suggested that the Church there still routinely uses legal technicalities to defeat cases taken by victims.

Vivian Waller said an apology was one thing, but justice and compassion were another.

'The Catholic Church routinely takes every technical objection in the book to prevent sexual assault victims suing successfully in the courts,' she said.

'The defences revolve around claims being out of time and a smoke and mirrors approach to identifying the precise legal identity of the church.'

My experience was far from unique.

After I agreed the basis of a possible settlement with my legal team they went to meet with the other side. All this happened in separate rooms and I never actually met the Church's lawyers. Bishop Walsh wasn't there either but was consulted by phone as the lawyers worked to find a deal.

I sat on my own in that grey room for what seemed like an age. There was nothing to do but wait. The room was empty apart from a varnished wooden table and some chairs. I couldn't even call anyone as my mobile phone couldn't get a signal. At one point I perched on the windowsill, holding my phone up to the barred windows trying to get enough of a signal to at least send a text message to Paul and let him know what was happening. It was a strange position to be in, all by myself in a small room after a very public battle that had started more than eight years earlier.

After about half an hour Pearse and my barristers returned. The Church had agreed to the financial settlement; that was the easy part. What was proving difficult was agreeing what form any public statement might take. It was decided that a draft would be prepared and agreed before any settlement was finalised.

I left the court that day with real hope that my personal battle was almost over. But by now I was so used to seeing hope turn to disappointment that I didn't dare get too excited.

My legal team worked away with the Church's lawyers, and it took almost two weeks to finally agree the statement. Then on 1 April 2003, exactly one year from the day of Brendan Comiskey's resignation, I received a fax copy of a suggested text for the statement. It read:

'The matter has been settled on terms that Bishop Eamonn Walsh as Apostolic Administrator of the Diocese of Ferns, admits negligence and agrees to pay Colm O'Gorman compensation and costs.

He acknowledges and sincerely regrets the distress, trauma and hurt caused to Colm O'Gorman by virtue of the acts of sexual abuse perpetrated on him between 1981 and 1983 by the late Fr Sean Fortune.

He further acknowledges the failure of the Bishop at the time to recognise and act on the threat posed by the late Fr Fortune to Colm O'Gorman. Bishop Walsh wishes to apologise unreservedly to Colm O'Gorman for these failures and for the harm which he suffered in consequence.'

I was elated. It was all there. It could finally end.

I agreed to the settlement on those terms, provided the statement would be read in the High Court and put on the record there.

Finally, on 9 April, my barrister Jack Fitzgerald stood in the High Court and read the statement. I was in my office. Pearse and I were in constant phone contact all that morning. He assured me it would happen, but even then I couldn't quite believe it.

I remember the moment I got the call telling me it was done. I was sitting at my desk, trying to concentrate on work and failing miserably. Then my mobile rang and I could see it was Pearse. My hand shook as I answered it, and I almost missed the call because I was so nervous I couldn't press the answer button. I put the phone to my ear, holding my breath.

'Colm, it's Pearse. It's done, it's over,' he said.

I couldn't quite believe it, I couldn't get my head around the idea that this was really it, that it was over and I had won.

'Are you serious? It's really done?'

'Jack read the statement into the court a few minutes ago. There's a lot of media here. I won't stay on the phone. I'm on my way over to you now.'

'OK, I can't believe it though. My God.'

'Congratulations Colm. It's no less than you deserve. See you shortly.'

As I hung up the phone I didn't know whether to laugh or cry. In the end I did both. I sat there for a few minutes on my own, sobbing and laughing. Then it was time to get ready for the media onslaught I knew was to come.

Pearse and I had previously agreed that I would wait at the office and we would make no comment until after the statement was read into the court. We arranged a press conference at One in Four's offices for a few hours later.

That afternoon I walked into a packed room as cameras flashed and whirred. I looked around and saw not only media but many friends and family. Paul was there of course, as was my brother Eamon and all my colleagues. It was a huge moment.

I stood at a podium as Pearse read out the statement from the bishop to the press. Then I spoke.

I read a long, heartfelt statement in which I was finally able to summarise my twenty-two-year journey from the day I was first sexually abused by Fortune to this day, when I achieved a real and significant level of justice. I said that from the very first moment I made my decision to report what I had experienced, I wanted above all to have the burden of responsibility for that abuse taken from me. The day had finally arrived that the boy I was had been vindicated, as those directly responsible for the abuse through their acts of negligence had finally acknowledged that gross failure.

'Today, for the very first time following huge public and media pressure, the Catholic Church has finally acknowledged what many in Irish society had believed for a number of years: that the Church authorities were negligent in how they handled and responded to cases of clerical sexual abuse and that such negligence had led to the abuse of more and more children.'

'What was finally and fully acknowledged by Bishop Eamonn Walsh in his statement this morning is that the failure to act upon the threat posed to me by Fr Sean Fortune was directly responsible for that abuse, that if they had acted earlier I would not have been sexually abused, that such abuse was avoidable and preventable, and that they were negligent.'

I expressed my hope that while for many of the more than one million Irish people sexually abused as children there was little chance of their achieving justice in such a meaningful way, my victory might make it possible for more of them to name their hurt and come forward to seek support and care.

I criticised the Catholic Church's adversarial and legalistic response to victims and pointed out that, had they simply come forward and acknowledged their failures and negligence in a clear and honest way, many victims could have been saved significant further abuse and suffering. I also spoke scathingly of the Papal Nuncio's use of his privileged position as a diplomat to refuse to answer questions relating to what the Vatican knew about the abuse of children perpetrated by one of their priests. I said it spoke volumes about the Vatican's continuing failures to respond effectively and meaningfully to the hurts and concerns of the wider Church, which was tantamount to moral abandonment of its own flock.

I acknowledged and thanked the hundreds of people I didn't even know who had encouraged and supported me, and the media, the journalists, broadcasters, editors and publishers who shone a powerful light into the darkest corners of Irish society, showing courage, foresight and tenacity in revealing the truth of clerical sexual abuse.

And I said how lucky I was to have the support of my family, especially Barbara, who had sat with me as I made my initial statement, and my father: 'My father, Sean, was an inspiration to me. He supported me in ways I could never have imagined. His integrity and powerful, loving heart remain an inspiration to me to this day. They always will ...'

At this point I started to break down as all the emotion of the past few years overcame me. I really wanted to get through it without cracking, but I couldn't. As I spoke of Dad, imagining him there with me, I couldn't hold back the tears. I looked at my brother Eamon standing to my right, and he had tears running down his face too.

Paul was beside him. He looked me in the eye, steadying me, urging me on. I took a breath and kept going. 'Dad died ten months after I made my statement. When he found out he was dying, he told me that he only wanted to live long enough to see this through with me. He died too soon for that, but I know he has been with me. His memory, his love has seen me through this.'

As I got to the end, I steadied myself and dealt with a few questions from the press. I don't remember much about the rest of that press conference; I was so glad to have made it through my statement and I just wanted to get out of the room and be with Paul for a few minutes. It had been a very long and very public journey, and now I wanted a little time and space to myself, away from the cameras, with the people I loved and who had loved and supported me over the years.

I was so relieved it was over. More than anything else I was delighted that I could now move beyond my personal battle for justice and focus fully on the Ferns Inquiry and the work of One in Four. My victory left me more determined than ever to do whatever I could to achieve justice for others.

# 23

# The Full Report

I slept more soundly than I had in years that night, right through until half past twelve the next day, which I'd arranged to take off work. When I did eventually wake up I'd forgotten the drama of the previous day. The sun was streaming in through the curtains and I awoke in a panic, thinking I'd slept in and would be late for work. I grabbed my alarm clock, wondering why it hadn't gone off.

I was just about to jump out of bed when I remembered the events of the day before. I fell back on my pillow with a big grin spreading across my face. It was over, my battle was finally over! I laughed out loud and leapt out of bed, took a shower and headed off for a walk on the beach.

When I got to the beach I sat on a big rock with the sun on my face and breathed deeply, taking in the peace and serenity of it all. I was so used to carrying the heavy load of the legal battle that I didn't realise just how much space it took up inside me. It was an incredible feeling, sitting looking at the sea and feeling an ocean of space and calm inside myself.

I sat there for ages as the waves rose and fell around me. It was now twenty-one years since Fortune had first taken me from my home and abused me. Twenty-one years of baggage that should never have been mine lifted from me and floated away across the sea.

It was a great personal moment. I'd often felt very exposed, but now it felt like I could finally cover myself up and no longer have to comment on deeply private things so very publicly. For many years my ability to finally move beyond my personal experiences had been limited by the ongoing legal battle, but now that was over. From now on I could focus on the Ferns Inquiry and my work with One in Four. It would no longer be such a personal battle.

I was back at work the next day, fired up and eager to get on with it all. There was still enormous press interest in the case and news of my victory made the papers all around the world. I was especially pleased that the admission of negligence was widely reported and hoped it would have an impact on other cases.

In September the Ferns Inquiry placed ads in the national press asking people who might have information relevant to its investigation to make contact with them. One in Four also made a public call for people to come forward, and offered support to anyone who needed it. In all over one hundred witnesses would give evidence to the investigation, many of them speaking on the record for the first time, breaking their long silence.

At the same time we were involved in discussions with the Minister for Justice over the need for other investigations. After *Suing the Pope* was broadcast, RTE carried out a similar investigation into sexual abuse in the Archdiocese of Dublin. That film was equally shocking and caused enormous public outrage. Working with two victims from

Dublin, Andrew Madden and Marie Collins, One in Four sought to ensure a meaningful process of investigation into the Archdiocese.

I continued to meet with the Ferns Inquiry team, along with my colleague Deirdre Fitzpatrick, and made a detailed submission to the investigation, setting out our knowledge of numerous cases and highlighting what we believed to be issues of particular concern, such as the role the diocese had played in appointing as managers of primary schools priests who had abused children.

We also set out clear evidence of the centuries-old historic awareness of child sexual abuse in the Roman Catholic Church. We made sure that Fr Tom Doyle was called to give evidence. I was determined to ensure that the inquiry examined the role of the Vatican in the abuse, and Tom's expert knowledge of child sexual abuse by priests and the institution's cover-up was of crucial importance.

The Catholic Church promised to co-operate with the inquiry. They really had little choice. The terms of reference we secured made it clear that any failure to do so would result in an investigation that would compel co-operation in law. The Church knew that any failure to be seen to co-operate would be publicly devastating.

The Ferns Inquiry lasted two and a half years. It uncovered allegations of child sexual abuse against a total of twenty-seven priests from the Diocese of Ferns, involving more than one hundred victims going back forty years. The scale of the abuse documented in its final report shocked everyone concerned.

I'd seen drafts of the report – particularly the parts relating directly to myself – a few weeks earlier. I was eager to see it published, but last minute legal difficulties suggested it might be delayed.

Only a small number of the priests against whom allegations were made – those who had died, been convicted or already accused in public – could be named. There had been relatively few prosecutions of those accused since most of the complaints had been made to the diocese and the Church hadn't notified the police or child protection services of the allegations. All the others accused were given aliases, as were all the victims who gave evidence.

At first it was planned to publish the report on the Department of Health and Children's website. Then the Government received legal advice that if they did this they could be sued by a former priest named in the report and now living in the US. At the last minute, it was decided that the Minister for Children would launch the report at a press conference and it would be distributed to the media.

I didn't believe it was reasonable or appropriate for the victims who had given evidence to the inquiry to hear the details of the report from the media. So on the day it was launched it was agreed that we would courier copies of the report to all those we had worked with, ensuring they received a complete copy before the media reported on it.

The month or so prior to its publication was fraught. Deirdre and I worked hard, meeting with the inquiry team to press for the inclusion of specific recommendations in the report. It was one thing to identify the scale of the problem and the failures of the past, but the inquiry would have little impact if it didn't ultimately result in better child protection for the future; many changes were needed in Irish child protection law.

The report was finally published on 25 October 2005. It ran to 271 pages and detailed a horrific catalogue of child rape and abuse by Roman Catholic priests dating back to 1966, the year I was born. It was in that year that the diocese was informed that Fr Donal Collins had measured the penises of twenty boys in a dormitory in St Peter's College in Wexford.

Bishop Donal Herlihy refused to acknowledge the seriousness of the crime, seeing it as a 'moral lapse', and Collins was sent to London to do two years 'penance' working in the Diocese of Westminster. Herlihy didn't even bother to inform the Bishop of Westminster of Collins' behaviour. Two years later he was back teaching at St Peter's.

Herlihy's decision to reappoint him to his post as a teacher in a boys' boarding school 'would seem to have been extremely ill-advised as subsequent events were to prove in a comprehensive and tragic fashion,' according to the Ferns Report.

Collins continued to sexually assault boys. He used the pretext of conducting physical examinations to carry out the abuse, telling boys that he needed to check their genitals to ensure they were developing properly. Then he would masturbate them, perform oral sex on them and was alleged to have attempted to rape one boy. He often used alcohol and pornographic films in grooming and abusing his victims.

Bishop Brendan Comiskey appointed Collins as principal of St Peter's in 1988. Two priests claimed to the inquiry that they had expressed reservations to Comiskey about the appointment, but it still went ahead.

In April 1989, within seven months of Collins' appointment, Comiskey received an allegation of sexual abuse. A further allegation was made in May 1989. Collins denied the allegations and remained a priest and principal of the school.

In May 1991, Comiskey received an anonymous letter with a further complaint. Collins denied the extent of the charge made against him but did not dispute that he 'engaged in indiscreet and inappropriate conduct with young boys'. In July 1991, he resigned as principal.

His resignation came after twenty-five years of abusing children, and the Catholic Church had been aware of complaints during all that time.

Later in 1991, Collins attended a course in Florida to seek counselling. He was also attached to a parish there, and Comiskey admitted he didn't inform the bishop of the diocese in Florida of the allegations made against Collins.

The report said that in September 1993, Collins admitted 'the broad truth' of many of the allegations. Comiskey told the inquiry he did not consider reporting this to the police or social services.

In a statement to the police in May 1995, in connection with allegations made against Collins by one particular man, Comiskey said Collins continued to deny any wrongdoing. The report said this was incorrect and that Comiskey knew from 1993, if not 1991, that Collins had admitted the abuse of boys at St Peter's. Comiskey misled the police.

In 1995, Collins was charged with twenty-one counts of indecent assault and gross indecency and one of buggery against four former students at St Peter's. In March 1998, he pleaded guilty to four charges of gross indecency and one of indecent assault. He was sentenced to four years' imprisonment and served one year at the Curragh prison. He was released in 1999.

It was Collins' sentence that left me convinced I should not agree to a 'guilty to lesser charges' plea from Sean Fortune. Collins had abused children for twenty-five years, using alcohol to drug them and his position as principal of St Peter's College to intimidate them. He had tried to rape at least one boy, yet he served just one year in prison.

The Ferns report detailed allegations of serious sexual abuse by Collins on a total of thirty-four boys.

In the case of Fortune, the report detailed allegations of sexual abuse of more than twenty-seven boys. The first incidents were in the 1970s when Fortune was training for the priesthood. Numerous complaints were made to the college authorities and to Herlihy, including repeated complaints of Fortune sexually abusing boy scouts. The bishop and the college appear to have done nothing to stop him. In one case the college principal is reported to have threatened a boy with expulsion if he persisted in saying such things about Fortune.

Many of those who came forward to tell their stories to the Ferns Inquiry said that when they saw *Suing the Pope* on television they realised that what had happened to them had also happened to other people and that this realisation gave them the courage to speak out.

Judy was at primary school when Canon Martin Clancy, her parish priest, abused her. She was sent to the priest's house for sex education classes by the school principal. She told the Ferns Inquiry how Clancy removed her underclothes and physically examined her very painfully. She was twelve years old.

Ciara was another of Clancy's victims. A keen musician, she regularly played in local concerts. At one of these concerts, when she was eleven, Clancy dragged her into a cloakroom and molested her. He continued to abuse her for years, starting to have full sex with her when she was fourteen. Ciara became pregnant and had a daughter at fifteen. Clancy threatened to have her daughter taken from her if she ever revealed him to be the father.

Kate was eight when Clancy abused her at her primary school. The priest would take her out of class to 'give her music lessons' in school or at his own house. This was never questioned by any of her teachers or the school superiors. Clancy raped Kate on a weekly basis until she was twelve. The abuse stopped because the priest was moved to another parish in 1991.

He was moved five months after yet another of his victims wrote to Comiskey, telling him that Clancy had sexually abused her as a twelve-year-old.

Clancy died in 1993. He never faced any criminal charges as a result of the abuse and rape he inflicted on young girls for almost thirty years.

The Ferns Report says that 'the inquiry was shocked at the duration and extent of the abuse allegedly perpetrated by this priest which in some instances appeared to involve the rape of very young girls. He appeared to use his position as Manager of the local national (primary) school to freely access children ...'

The report also found that at various points during this thirty-year period members of the police, teachers, the medical profession and the Church were aware of the rumours and suspicion about Clancy but that no action was ever taken against him.

And so it went on in case after case. Documented in the report's pages are horror stories involving the rape and abuse of over one hundred children, and these reflect only the victims who came forward. Each case is a tragedy, a shattered life and a testimony to lies and evasion at the highest levels of the Holy Roman Apostolic Catholic Church.

We didn't stand a chance; that we would be raped and abused was inevitable. The Catholic Church knowingly sent paedophiles into our churches, our schools, our hospitals, our youth clubs, our communities and even our homes. They sent them with knowledge of the crimes they had committed against other children. And when they abused again they covered it up, denied all knowledge of the abuse, and when they had to, moved them on to new parishes and fresh victims.

They had the authority of two thousand years of dogma behind them, the might of the most powerful religious institution on earth. They had their own laws that were written to ensure they were never in the wrong, laws that made a lie the truth and the truth a lie, laws that silenced and intimidated victims and their families. And if that wasn't enough they had civil lawyers to help them elude responsibility.

For years, bishops, cardinals and even the Pope made statements suggesting that they didn't fully appreciate the scale of the problem of clerical sexual abuse. They told us that they'd failed to recognise the nature and seriousness of the crime, seeing it more as a moral issue, a failing on the part of the individual priest. As the scandals erupted in Ireland, bishops told us that they couldn't speak as one Church, that each was essentially the master of his diocese and reported directly to Rome, with no awareness of what was happening in other dioceses. The Ferns Report exposed those protestations and mealy-mouthed excuses as lies.

The report also revealed that in 1986, the Archbishop of Dublin, Kevin McNamara, had consulted lawyers to discover what legal liability the Archdiocese might have in cases where its priests had sexually abused children. This was eight years before the first case from that diocese became public knowledge.

His lawyers advised the Archbishop that if a priest was returned to ministry after receiving some kind of treatment and went on to abuse again, the Church could face legal and financial liabilities. He was also told that a bishop had a duty in law to withdraw a priest from ministry if an investigation established that there was a basis for a complaint.

So what did the Archbishop do? Did he immediately remove from ministry priests who had been accused? Did he inform the police and social services of all accusations and ensure a proper investigation? Did he put in place a robust child protection policy? Did he inform his brother bishops of what he had discovered and alert them to this legal difficulty and their responsibility in law to remove credibly accused priests?

No, he did none of that.

Instead, on the advice of his lawyers he approached the insurance company Church & General and took out an insurance policy to protect against the cost of any claims

resulting from his priests raping and abusing children.
He did not act to protect children; he acted to protect the
Church's money.

Within two years the insurance company involved had
circulated that same legal advice to all other bishops in
Ireland. By 1990 most of them had taken out the same
policy. Comiskey did it in August 1989, a year after
appointing Collins principal of St Peter's College and only
months after receiving two separate complaints that he
was sexually abusing boys. No matter though, at least the
diocesan money was safe, no matter about its children.

In 1996, Church & General and representatives of
the bishops held discussions to terminate the insurance
cover. Perhaps the insurance company was concerned that
the bishops had not disclosed the extent of the abuse of
children by its priests when taking out cover. Whatever
the reason, in March 1996 the insurance company made a
payment of €4.3 million to be divided among the dioceses,
and the insurance policies were revoked.

Rather than divide the money the bishops decided to place
it in a trust to be administered by the four Archbishops of
Ireland. The trust would fund money to bishops towards
the costs of damages and fund child protection and victim
response programmes. In 2000, Church & General paid
another €6.3 million to the trust; it was now in possession
of more than €10 million. Despite their statements to the
contrary, Irish bishops had been working together on this
issue for a long time. But not to protect children like me –
instead, they were working to protect their money.

The report also made very significant statements about
the role of the Vatican. It set out how early Church law saw

the sexual corruption of young boys as among the gravest of offences, how early Canon Law dealt with the issue and how in 1962 Pope John XXIII issued a new law to deal with cases of priests who solicited sex in the confessional. This document, entitled *Crimens Sollicitationis*, had already been the subject of significant media attention when it was first uncovered in 2003, but the Ferns Inquiry was the first such investigation to study its relevance to the abuse of children by priests.

Mr Justice Francis Murphy and his colleagues on the Ferns Inquiry were clear in finding that the document 'specifically dealt with how priests who abused children were to be handled and imposed a high degree of secrecy on all Church officials involved in such cases'. The supreme Catholic Church penalty – automatic excommunication – would be imposed on any person who broke the oath of secrecy required by the policy. Even witnesses and victims could be excommunicated if they broke the oath.

Some people reject the finding that *Crimens Sollicitationis* deals with child sexual abuse, pointing out that it was issued to deal with solicitation and not child abuse. I asked Tom Doyle to explain this to me when we first heard about the document.

'Whenever the Catholic Church issues a new law, you have to look under the headline. Usually the real purpose for the law can be found in the other issues it attempts to deal with, and not the primary issue as presented. In this case, the primary issue dealt with is solicitation, that is priests asking for sex in the confessional, but the document clearly says that the same approach is to be adopted in the cases of priests abusing kids. It's there.'

I once debated the same issue with a Canon law expert on radio. He kept saying that I didn't understand the document.

'It's not about child abuse, but about solicitation,' he insisted. 'You have simply confused its purpose. It would only apply to cases where a priest solicited sex from a child in the confessional.'

'Well, the document also deals with bestiality. Is that true?'

'Yes, it also deals with that.'

'But then how can it only apply in cases where a priest solicits sex in the confessional? Goats don't go to confession, do they?'

There was no answer to that. The fact is that *Crimens Sollicitationis* deals explicitly with child sexual abuse and is the first document from the Vatican in the past fifty years to set out the response in such cases. Significantly, it does not demand any intervention designed to prevent further abuse or to assist the child who has been abused. It doesn't insist that the civil authorities be informed. It keeps it all in-house, with everyone sworn to secrecy.

The Ferns Report also described how, as early as the 1950s, the Roman Catholic Church was aware that child sexual abuse was not only a moral issue but also a psychological one. From the 1960s Catholic bishops and superiors were trying to tackle some of the more severe cases of priestly sexual misconduct through the use of psychology and psychiatry.

A leading expert in the field, Dr Richard Sipe, himself a former Catholic priest, is quoted in the report: 'By the late 1970s Catholic treatment centres were on the cutting edge of psychiatry and psychology in the use of sophisticated techniques for the treatment of Catholic priests who had acted out sexually with minors. It is reasonable to ask; what care was given to known child victims of priest sexual involvement? What steps were taken to protect Catholic children and their families from the known risk of future abuse?'

As well as highlighting the Vatican policy of sworn secrecy in cases of clerical child sexual abuse, the report also criticised Catholic Church authorities for not alerting all priests to the threat of sexual abuse. Quite rightly the report pointed out that 'when an organisation is aware of a serious problem within its structures with criminal and child protection implications, it has a duty to alert and inform its personnel of this and to ensure that every step is taken to eliminate it as soon as possible.'

It was all there, and I felt entirely vindicated by the report. It was painful for me to read, as I knew it would be for very many people, but I knew that the report wasn't the source of that pain, it just named it. And in naming it, it also offered an opportunity for healing.

# 24

## *Vatican Silence*

The publication of the Ferns Report was welcomed around the world by people working to confront clerical child sexual abuse. In the US, campaigners hailed it as a breakthrough in the battle to hold the Catholic Church to account.

'We at last now have a government coming out on the record against this institution,' said Paul Baier, a director of Bishop Accountability, a non-profit group based in Boston that documents cases of sexual abuse by priests. 'It is showing what a lot of us know, that this is a worldwide problem.'

David Clohessy, director of the US organisation Survivors Network of those Abused by Priests, said that the Ferns Inquiry uncovered greater detail than six American grand jury investigations held to investigate abuse there. 'Tremendous secrecy is still the norm,' he said. 'Any external peek into how it works is very rare and very valuable.'

In Ireland, the report led to calls for a new approach to the relationship between the Irish State and the Roman Catholic Church. The former Minister of State at the

Department of Foreign Affairs, Liz O'Donnell, was one of a number of politicians who highlighted the issue in Dáil Éireann, the Irish parliament:

> 'The mighty Church has fallen from grace because of its failure to protect children. The first response of the State must be to unequivocally state that the special relationship is no more and to take steps to demonstrate that disconnect between State and Church.
>
> 'From now on, with that veil of deference removed, the State can deal with the Church authorities in the same way as it would any other voluntary or State agency that provides services for children and families. This means no longer accepting the good offices of an admittedly remorseful hierarchy, after the event. The track record is such that we cannot accept that the Church will be truthful or capable of self-regulation.'

It was strong stuff in a country where until very recently the Catholic bishops held enormous political and social power. A Government minister once told me that it had been normal practice to run all major policy and legislative proposals past the hierarchy of the Roman Catholic Church, seeking their approval before advancing any plans.

The Irish Government announced that it would accept and act on the recommendations of the report. One of the key recommendations I'd sought was for the introduction of new legislation to ensure that in future any person, no matter how privileged their position, who recklessly placed children at risk of harm would be guilty of a criminal offence.

In the wake of the report, national opinion polls showed that 80 per cent of people believed that bishops should stand trial for failing to protect children. While the law didn't provide a means for this with Comiskey and others, it would at least now be in place for the future.

In 2002 the state of Massachusetts had enacted a similar law. The only case I know of where a bishop was convicted of a crime as a result of his cover up of child abuse was that of French Bishop Pierre Pican who received a suspended jail sentence in 2001.

There had also been strong statements made in Australia about the failure of senior Church leaders. Senator Andrew Murray had condemned Church leaders as complicit in crimes against children.

'There are two types of criminals and two types of crime: those who commit the crime of sexually assaulting children, and their fellow travellers, their accomplices; and those who criminally conspire to conceal those crimes and protect the perpetrators. Some church leaders are rightly accused – but far too few have been charged – with aiding and abetting, being an accessory after the fact, obstructing the administration of justice, compounding a felony and criminal conspiracy,' said Murray.

The acting Bishop of Ferns, Eamonn Walsh, unequivocally accepted the findings of the report. This was especially significant given its criticism of the Vatican and its finding in relation to the 1962 Vatican document swearing all involved in abuse cases to secrecy.

Within days of the publication, Roman Catholic dioceses across Ireland began to publicly reveal hundreds of cases of allegations of sexual abuse involving their clergy. The same bishops who had for years worked to deny and then minimise the scale of the abuse now disclosed that more than three hundred of their priests had been accused of child sexual abuse.

'I am deeply shocked and saddened by the findings of the inquiry into child sexual abuse by priests in the Diocese of Ferns. The revelations make for very uncomfortable reading,' said Archbishop Sean Brady, Catholic Primate of All-Ireland. 'The pages retelling the pain experienced by those who have suffered are especially heartbreaking. I apologise to all those people who have suffered lasting hurt at the hands of abusers in the Church. As priests they should have been protecting and nurturing the talents of these young people. The betrayal of trust is horrendous. Today the Church is ashamed of its past failings regarding child protection.'

He went on to announce new child protection standards and the establishment of a new National Board for Child Protection. 'No one who is a danger to children is permitted to minister in the Church,' he pledged. We would have to wait and see if that would prove true.

The Vatican, however, remained entirely silent. No statement was issued in response to the report, no denial of its findings that the Vatican had failed to act to protect children and had instead instituted a policy of secrecy since 1962.

Six months earlier, Cardinal Joseph Ratzinger had been elected Pope Benedict XVI. The new Pope was reported to have denounced the 'Harry Potter' novels as a corrupting influence on children and had in the past blamed the media for the scandal of clerical sexual abuse. He had nothing to say about the Ferns Report.

In the US, bishops had often sought to create a link between homosexuality and child sexual abuse. After a crisis meeting at the Vatican in 2002, the head of the US Bishops Conference, Bishop Wilton Gregory, clearly expressed that view: 'It is most importantly a struggle, to make sure that the Catholic priesthood is not dominated by homosexual men. Not only is it not dominated by homosexual men, but that the candidates that we receive are healthy in every possible way, psychologically, emotionally, spiritually, intellectually.'

One month after the Ferns Report was published the Vatican issued a new policy on gays and the priesthood. The document declared that men with what it called 'deep-seated' homosexual tendencies could not be ordained. While it did not mention the sex abuse scandals, it was widely believed to be in part a response to the issue. It caused widespread dismay among victim support organisations, many of which believed that the Vatican was once again sidestepping its responsibility for the scandals and scapegoating gay men as the cause of the problem in the first place.

The Ferns Report had researched this issue, having formed an expert group of clinicians with specific experience of working with priests who had sexually abused children. The group was unanimous in its view that homosexuality is not a factor in increasing the risk to children. It would be seen as a factor in increasing the risk to adolescent boys, but no more than a heterosexual priest would be a risk to adolescent girls.

One member of the group, Joseph Sullivan, said, 'It's easy to make the link between someone abusing boys and being homosexual, but would we call someone who sexually abuses 12 and 13 year old girls heterosexual? No, we wouldn't; we'd call them a child abuser.'

I was asked to speak about this at an event organised by Voice of the Faithful, a lay Catholic organisation established to show solidarity with victims of clerical sexual abuse and ensure greater participation of lay people in the power structures of the Church.

'Any church that sees itself as the true church of Christ must surely embrace truth and be open to its own failings. The naming of truth should never be seen as a challenge to the church of Christ. Surely Christians have a duty to respond to hurt with care, compassion, integrity, honesty, courage and love?

'As a man who often reflects on my own relationship with God I find myself questioning where Christ would be in this debate. Would He be seated in Rome telling us these scandals are the fault of the corruption of western society, of an anti-Catholic media, of greedy victims, of homosexuals, of all and any but those who ignored the truth and moved offender after offender to places where any sane and objective person would know there could only be one consequence: more rape and abuse? Or would Christ be here? What or who would Christ clear from the Temple in this third millennium?

'How can it be that a Church hierarchy who comments on the content of a children's film can fail to comment on a report commissioned by this State and authored by a former Supreme Court Judge that found Rome culpable in the rape and abuse of Irish children? How can the highest authority in the Roman Catholic Church see fit to suggest that Harry Potter is a threat to the development of children yet refuse to acknowledge findings by this sovereign State that the institution he heads has permitted the rape and abuse of children?

How can a church that speaks in the name of Christ fail to respond to the hurt of its people, its faithful, who are struggling to understand how this could have happened?'

But the Vatican remained silent. I have no doubt that this silence inflicted further serious damage to the reputation of the Catholic Church in Ireland.

For those of us who spent years fighting to establish the truth and be heard, the Ferns Report was a moment of real vindication. The voices of those who had told us that the abuse was 'all in the past' and that we should 'get on with our lives' finally fell quiet.

The report didn't just make real a past denied, it also revealed the impact of that past today, on the lives of those who had been abused and on their families. In dealing with the past, as difficult and frightening as it was, we had found a way to name it, respond to it and learn from it. In understanding the failures of the past we could work towards a better future.

The Ferns Report ensured that Irish society faced up to the fact that thousands of children had been raped and abused by some of the most powerful members of our society and that many of us turned a blind eye, or refused to believe it was possible in the first place. We could never again say, 'I didn't know.'

The scandal that is clerical sexual abuse has caused enormous hurt to very many people. People like my Dad, my family and me and all other victims and their families.

People like Monica and John Fitzpatrick who lost their son Peter. People like the very many faithful and loyal clergy and lay Roman Catholics who were failed by a Church hierarchy that betrayed the teachings of Christ. People like the families of those who perpetrated the abuse who find themselves shamed by the acts of their loved ones, despite their own innocence. Secrets and lies and the fear of the truth have had many victims.

So what of the future? Can we move on with confidence? Has the time come to consign all this to history? I don't think so.

As long as stories such as mine have something to teach us about what it means to be human we must be open to hearing them again and again. We must learn that the terrible things that happen in the world, the things we humans do to each other, are only possible as long as we choose to tolerate them. We must learn that doing nothing in the face of great wrong is not passive, it is an act of violence – a violent refusal to act when we have the capacity to understand the harm caused and the power to prevent it.

We have created the world we live in and we have the power, individually and collectively, to change it when change is needed. It may not always be easy, but it is possible, even inevitable, if enough of us decide to stand up and demand change, be it ending the cover-up of clerical sexual abuse by the Roman Catholic Church, or closing Guantánamo Bay and ending the use of torture, or outlawing the death penalty, or challenging human rights abuses in China or at home in our own countries. Every one of us can be a powerful force for good, but only if we choose to be.

What would it be like if we were to change? What would that demand of us, and what would it mean for us?

We are so frightened of the darkness in our collective humanity that wc fail to embrace the light that exists in at least equal measure there, the profound beauty in our own humanity that can respond with truth and courage to the things we see and do that are wrong.

We are so frightened of acknowledging the awful things done to others by people close to us, and even by ourselves, that we end up through denial allowing such things to happen. In our silence we collude, in our denial we facilitate and in our softly-spoken words of gossip we fail to take responsibility for what we know.

We can only be enriched if we have the courage and compassion, the humanity and integrity to name injustice wherever we see it, especially when we are party to causing injustice ourselves.

As for me, I am happy. I've learned so much on my journey so far. And for that I am grateful. Life offers so much, especially if we remain open to it. Rediscovering myself made me open up to life once again. I was so frightened for so very long that I forgot how to really live.

And I have learned to forgive. Not to forgive others, but to forgive myself. For years I hated and blamed myself for what happened to me. But not anymore.

Facing the truth of my past has been painful, heartbreaking, at times deeply humiliating, but ultimately liberating. I was so scared to look back, convinced I would see only the terrible things I had done. But it wasn't like that. When I looked and allowed myself to see the past in its totality, I realised that all I did was try to survive and then find a way to live with some integrity. I did my best, and I did survive.

For years I blamed myself for the choices I made, when in fact those choices were not about the things I did, but about my determination to live and find a better way. I am happy with who I am.

And what about those others, the people who hurt me, have I forgiven them? Have I forgiven Sean Fortune? No, I have not. Not because I refuse to or because I feel any bitterness towards him. I have not forgiven him because it is not within my gift to do so. Maybe that's because I've been caught up for so long in a very Catholic notion of forgiveness, seeing it as a kind of absolution, a wiping clean of the slate. I cannot absolve Fortune or anyone else of the harm they did me. I cannot make that OK.

Forgiveness for me is all about truth, acceptance and compassion. I have learned to accept the truth of my past and my own actions for what they were, and to have compassion for myself in the midst of it all. I can only do that for myself. It's a very personal process. I can't know the full truth of another's experiences and actions, and it's not for me to accept or deny their experience. Each person must do that for themselves.

I can, however, have compassion for someone like Fortune. I know that the harm and the terrible things he and others did are not the full truth of who they were or are as human beings. I know that they loved and were loved, that they themselves were once children, as innocent and beautiful as any other. And I feel sadness at their loss of connection with that beauty. They were someone's son, someone's brother. They could have had a different life. And that is a tragedy.

I felt rage when I looked at the full truth of what they did to me. I even fantasised about revenge, how I might inflict terrible harm and pain upon Fortune. I fantasised about tearing the flesh from his bones with my bare hands, about killing him with great violence. But that was only a passing thing, a moment of anger that needed to clear so I could see the greater truth of how I felt and what I believed.

That's why the image of Sean Fortune as a boy, hiding in a shop doorway too frightened to go home without that bag of sugar, was so important to me. It made him human, and when he was fully human, I couldn't just hate him. He wasn't only a beast who raped me. It wasn't that simple anymore.

And that's why I wept for him when he died. Because everything he was died in that moment, the boy he was and the man he might have been. And now all he would ever be was Sean Fortune, the paedophile priest, the monster. No life should be reduced to just that.

And so I wish for him forgiveness. I hope, if he has found an afterlife, that he has been able to face his truth and have compassion for himself, to accept his actions, work to understand them and then finally, to forgive himself.

# Afterword

*Gorey, County Wexford – December 2009*

What will it take for the Vatican and Pope Benedict XVI to acknowlegde the depth of their failure to protect children? How many reports, how many gut-wrenching stories of lives and communities devastated as a result of the cover-up of endemic child sexual abuse by priests, will it take before they finally set aside self-preservation and self-interest and protect children?

Over the years I have worked hard to be objective and reasonable in my work to expose the truth of the cover-up of child abuse by the Roman Catholic Church. I have made every effort to ensure that my challenges to the institutional church were not confused with an attack upon the faith itself or those who practised it. I have hoped that by exposing the true nature of the cover-up, we might force real and meaningful change in how that church deals with child abuse.

But to no avail.

It seems clear that the Roman Catholic Church has consistently placed self-preservation and the protection of its wealth and privilege ahead of the safety and well being of children.

Does that seem a bit extreme even after all you have read in this book? If so, then consider the findings of two further state investigations here in Ireland into child abuse within the Roman Catholic Church whose reports have been published in the past year.

The Ryan Report detailed 'endemic' rape and sexual assaults in Catholic Church-operated child care institutions in Ireland over six decades up until the 1990s. It reported a culture of systemic abuse and 'high levels of ritualised beatings', and the savagery described in its 2600 pages provoked worldwide outrage. The report told how church officials protected paedophiles from arrest amid a 'culture of self-serving secrecy' and when confronted with evidence of sex abuse, Catholic Church authorities responded by transferring offenders to another location, where in many instances they were free to abuse again and again.

In late November 2009 the report of the Commission of Investigation into the Archdiocese of Dublin was finally published, six years after we had successfully secured that investigation. In now familiar language, this latest report of an Irish judicial investigation laid out evidence of the deliberate cover-up of crimes against children.

'The Commission has no doubt that clerical child sexual abuse was covered up by the Archdiocese of Dublin and other church authorities,' it said. 'The structures and rules of the Catholic Church facilitated that cover-up.'

That the Commission made mention of 'other church

authorities' is telling. The structure of the Roman Catholic Church is highly centralised. For years bishops have explained that they have no responsibility for the action of their brother bishops, that national church leaders have no authority over individual bishops and that each bishop is king in his diocese and reports only to Rome.

The Commission did try to engage with the Vatican to uncover the truth of its role in the Archdiocese of Dublin. It wrote to Pope Benedict XVI's former Vatican department, the Congregation for the Doctrine of the Faith (CDF), seeking explanations of church policy as detailed in documents like *Crimen Sollicitationis* and also a letter sent by Pope Benedict XVI to every bishop across the world in May 2001. That letter reminded bishops that the CDF would continue to have exclusive competence in deciding how all cases of clerical sex abuse were to be managed and that bishops must report every case to Rome.

The Commission also wrote to the Papal Nuncio, the Pope's representative in Ireland, about its work. But neither the Vatican nor the Papal Nuncio replied to the Commission's request.

It reminded me of the story I heard from Rick Romley, a former District Attorney in Phoenix, Arizona. I had interviewed Rick when making the film *Sex Crimes and the Vatican* for the BBC in 2006. Rick had secured convictions against eight paedophile priests in that diocese, and most significantly got a written confession from the bishop there that he knowingly hid child sexual abuse by priests from the police.

'The secrecy, the obstruction that I saw during my investigation was unparalleled in my entire career as a DA here in Phoenix, Arizona. It was so difficult to obtain any information from the church', he told me.

'We had information that there was an instruction from the Nuncio . . . to ship all this incriminating type of information to him because under the law we could not subpoena that material because he would have protective status as an ambassador from the Vatican.'

Three priests accused of abuse in Phoenix had fled the US. One, Fr Joseph Henn, was wanted on thirteen molestation charges. At the time I interviewed Rick Romley, Henn was living in Rome and fighting his extradition from the headquarters of his religious order a five minute walk from the Vatican.

Rick decided to write to the Vatican to ask them to ensure that Fr Henn be returned for trial in Phoenix.

'I knew that these priests owed a vow of obedience to the Vatican so I decided to write to Rome to ask them, now that formal charges had been brought, to . . . come back and surrender themselves so that the court system could take the cases as we wanted it to.'

He wrote to the Secretary of State at the Vatican asking that the priests be ordered to return to the US to face the courts. His letter was returned, unopened.

'They didn't even open it, they didn't even acknowledge or give me any type of response, they just refused to accept it.'

Across the world the Vatican continues to use the complexity of its structures, and the privileged position granted it as a State under international law, to avoid accountability for the cover-up of child sexual abuse.

The man who was responsible for the management of child sexual abuse cases at the global level for some twenty years is now Pope. However, Pope Benedict XVI has not acknowledged the findings of cover-up and collusion established in any of the reports from Ireland. Instead he has expressed his 'regret at the actions of some members of the clergy.'

In the aftermath of the report of the Dublin Archdiocese Commission there were many calls for the resignations of bishops. Four have now resigned and there may yet be more to follow. Indeed, a total of six Irish bishops have now resigned from office as a result of the child abuse scandals. But are resignations enough?

Will such resignations lead to better child protection practice in the global Catholic Church? Are the continuing scandals likely to force the Vatican to introduce global mandatory child protection policies?

I spoke recently with someone who has worked in child protection for the Catholic Church at a senior level and I was told that things are improving, especially within English speaking countries. It seems that pockets of better practice are emerging.

But this is only happening in countries where people like me have spoken out and forced change. The cover-ups are the result of church policy; change has not been proactive but forced. In countries where there have not yet been such revelations, little has changed, and, no doubt, children continue to be abused.

Why is this? Why has Pope Benedict XVI not acted to ensure better child protection at the global level?

The answer seems clear enough to me.

The Vatican has worked hard to ensure that it cannot be held accountable for the cover-up of child abuse by priests. It has used sovereign and diplomatic immunity to prevent itself being held to account by victims like me before the civil courts. It has worked to avoid accountability and the enormous financial losses that would be the result of a successful case. If the Vatican was found responsible in just one case anywhere then it would face many thousands of other cases and financial losses likely to run into billions of euros.

So if the Vatican were to acknowledge its central responsibility for child protection by introducing new laws, then it might expose itself to legal action for not having done so in the past.

If this is the case, then it appears that at the highest level, the Roman Catholic Church continues to fail to protect children because it remains more interested in self-preservation and the protection of its wealth than in the protection of children. It must therefore be of enormous concern that this church remains responsible for the welfare and education of many, many millions of children worldwide.

Over the past fifteen years I have done all I can to ensure that other children will not suffer in the way I did. I have been joined in that effort by countless other victims who have spoken out and demanded justice. But it cannot be down to us alone.

It is clear to me that the Roman Catholic Church will not

choose to change. Such change will have to be forced by ordinary people. In the absence of leadership of integrity, then it is up to people, Catholics and non-Catholics alike, to stand for truth and justice.

*Let Justice be Done, Though the Heavens Fall*

*Cicero*

www.colmogorman.com